# LANDSCAPE IN AMERICA

Washington, D.C., 1 January 1978. Photograph by Gregory Conniff.

# Landscape in America

Editing and Sequencing by GEORGE F. THOMPSON
With a Foreword by CHARLES E. LITTLE

Austin    UNIVERSITY OF TEXAS PRESS

LIBRARY OF CONGRESS CATALOGING-IN-PUBLICATION DATA

Landscape in America / editing and sequencing by George F. Thompson.—
1st ed.
     p.    cm.
    Includes index.
    ISBN 0-292-78135-0 (alk. paper).—ISBN 0-292-78136-9 (alk.
paper)
    1. Landscape—United States.  2. United States—Description and
travel.  3. Human geography—United States.  4. Landscape
architecture—United States.  5. Landscape in art.  I. Thompson,
George F.
E169.04.L36    1995
917.3—dc20                94-18049

Requests for permission
to reproduce material
from this work
should be sent to
Permissions,
University of Texas Press,
Box 7819,
Austin, TX 78713-7819.

Design and typography
by George Lenox

*In memory
of Norman Maclean,
who believed in this book
and who loved the land,
its culture, and its beauty
in uncompromising ways*

Dawn breaks through two giant oaks on Rolling Hills Farm in Clarke County, Virginia. Photograph by George F. Thompson, 1988.

# Contents

*My father was very sure about certain things*
*pertaining to the universe. To him, all good things—*
*trout as well as eternal salvation—come by grace*
*and grace comes by art and art*
*does not come easy.*

—NORMAN MACLEAN

**Charles E. Little**

# Foreword

CHARLES E. LITTLE is book review columnist for *Wilderness* magazine and author of a dozen books, among them *Greenways for America* (Johns Hopkins, 1990), *Hope for the Land* (Rutgers, 1992), and *The Dying of the Trees* (Viking, 1995). He lives and works in Placitas, New Mexico.

THERE IS SOME sort of linguistic tendency for words to get broader and broader in meaning as the centuries pass since their coinage. Sometimes this is powerfully annoying. Often a serviceable word, as, for example, *decimate,* which means to destroy a significant part of something, is simply lost. The word derives from the Roman practice of executing every tenth legionnaire as an object lesson to recalcitrant troops. Yet, in describing air attacks on Iraqi military targets in the winter of 1991, a television commentator asserted that the targets had been "nearly decimated" by the U.N.-sanctioned air forces. Surely he did not mean that one in fifteen were hit, as opposed to one in ten. He simply meant "nearly destroyed," but wanted to use a fancier word for it.

On the other hand, the broadening of word meanings can be downright helpful. A case in point is *landscape,* a richly nuanced word that started out as an early seventeenth-century term (originally spelled *landskip*) for a painting or drawing of a countryside scene, as opposed to a picture of the sea, or a person, or a building. As James A. W. Heffernan describes it in *The Re-creation of Landscape,* the word was soon used "to mean a particular tract of land that could be seen from one point of view, *as if* it were a picture; and finally it came to mean the whole of natural scenery."

Now, of course, we must say "landscape *painting*" when we wish to use the word in its original sense. Yet, unlike *decimate,* which has tended to lose its meaning, *landscape* has accumulated meaning, for within it the connotations survive: of artistic expression, of personal perception, of beauty (or sublimity), and even, in some sense, of taste, whether expressed by elites or in vernacular forms.

In Britain, where the term really took hold, these connotations have posed no problems. Perhaps this is because of a greater appreciation of, and education in, cultural topics, or more likely because the English countryside and the paintings of it present no disunities. There is something of a normative landscape in Albion itself even if, as Raymond Williams points out in *The Country and the City,* the green and pleasant land is but a chimera to the underclasses, a landscape unseen by those who labor in the coal pits beneath it or behind the factory walls in Midland dales.

In the United States, we have great difficulties with this word *landscape*. To us, it seems vaguely effete and needful of modifiers—landscape *architect,* landscape *analysis,* landscape *ecology,* landscape *history*—as if the thing itself were somehow inappropriate or incomplete or undemocratic. Accordingly, in our country, the idea of landscape has been lacking not only in terms of a consensus about what we mean by it, but also in the very language, the ideation, we use to apprehend it.

It is true, as many of the distinguished authors in this volume point out, that the United States, unlike England, does not have a normative landscape. Deserts, forests, mountains, volcanoes, swamps, near jungles, savannas, prairies, barrier islands, glaciers, great lakes, and more—all are contained within our continental nation. Perhaps this is the reason we have our difficulty. But maybe it's something else, an intellectual failure that cannot be so easily excused. Indeed, as *Landscape in America* shows, the diversity of landforms and culture should strengthen and enrich the idea of landscape in the United States, not the reverse. And so it is high time that writers and artists, scholars and teachers, and designers and planners create the intellectual framework we need—indeed, the critical apparatus—to apprehend finally what marvelous gifts we have been given from sea to shining sea. When such apprehension is achieved, then, perhaps, we can manage to use the land with love and respect, as conservationist Aldo Leopold so fervently wished.

And that is the great utility of the essays in this book, all of them commissioned over a period of years by George F. Thompson, a gifted editor, writer, and publisher who has done much in his career as a bookman to advance landscape scholarship, art, and literature in North America. That this volume contains contributions by authors whose names will be well known to many is a testament to the reputation he has built. He has gathered for us a truly remarkable symposium to celebrate the idea of landscape in America. And once we understand the idea, then, perhaps, we can protect the land's values, for ourselves and for posterity.

**George F. Thompson**

# A Message to the Reader

GEORGE F. THOMPSON is founder and president of the Center for American Places, a nonprofit organization based in Harrisonburg, Virginia, and Mesilla, New Mexico, that is dedicated to enhancing the public's understanding of geography and place, especially through books. He previously worked as an acquisitions editor for Johns Hopkins University Press, was a founding editorial member of *Landscape Journal* and *The Black Warrior Review,* and has taught at The Colorado College and University of Wisconsin-Madison. He is coauthor of *Beyond the Great Divide* (Rutgers, 1992), coauthor of *Registered Places of New Mexico* (New Mexico Geographical Society, 1995), coeditor of *Ecological Design and Planning* (Johns Hopkins, 1995), and founder and director of the Johns Hopkins series *Creating the North American Landscape.* Books he has developed and brought to publication have won or shared more than twenty major prizes and honors, including the PEN Center U.S.A. West's Literary Award for the best book of nonfiction published in the United States. Born in Colorado and raised in Connecticut, he has lived in the Shenandoah Valley of Virginia since 1983.

BOOKS, perhaps more than any other medium, provide the necessary intellectual and emotional foundation for a new awareness and understanding of the values of *place*. Imagine a world without Aldo Leopold's *A Sand County Almanac,* Joseph Wood Krutch's *A Desert Year,* Barry Lopez's *Arctic Dreams,* or Henry David Thoreau's *Walden*. These are books that have made a difference in how we perceive land and culture, in how we discover and respect the "interconnectedness of the natural and humanly constructed worlds," to borrow Yi-Fu Tuan's phrase.

My life's work involves the study, interpretation, and comprehension of places—urban, rural, and wild—especially by creating and developing books on environmental and geographical topics for publication by leading university and trade publishers. But anyone who studies *place* knows that it is a complex word for which no single definition will suffice. *Place* involves not only the great regions and wonders of our world—Yellowstone, Central Park, Big Bend, Monticello, the Great Lakes, the Pine Barrens, the Indian pueblos—but also our own backyards, city streets, and places of everyday existence. *Place* involves both the physical landscape (landforms, vegetation, rivers, and other elements of the natural world) and the cultural landscape (towns and suburbs, cities and parks, farms and ranches, battlefields and airports, parkways and interstates, and so on), but rarely in public policy or in the design of our own properties and communities does an appreciation for both meet. As individuals, and as a nation, we tend to emphasize nature over culture, or culture over nature, as if one can separate the two in the first place.

As an editor, author, publisher, and occasional teacher, it became apparent to me that the person who is beginning to learn about the land and its culture needs a book that provides a philosophical grounding in the richness and diversity that is the American landscape. It also occurred to me that, no matter how valuable books such as John Conron's *The American Landscape: A Critical Anthology of Prose and Poetry* or Don Meinig's *The Interpretation of Ordinary Landscapes: Geographical Essays* or May Theilgaard Watts's *Reading the Landscape of America* or Hal Borland's *Our Natural World* might be for the student or the general reader, no one text that is strictly oriented to an academic discipline, literary genre, or art form can provide a complete introduction to, or a full appreciation for, what landscape is, means, and represents. So between these two covers is an attempt to present contemporary views on what leading writers, scholars, and artists believe the *idea* of the American landscape to be.

My interest in landscape and in place stems from a multi-disciplinary approach that attempts to make links between geography and history, art and science, words and pictures, a land ethic and environmental design and planning. In the spirit of making such links visible to the student and the general reader, I thought it would be extremely useful to invite an array of distinguished authors who would address the question *What is landscape?* But rather than ask each contributor to espouse, with religious fervor, what their respective art or discipline believes landscape to be (translation: wishing to avoid the literature review), I was interested to learn, on behalf of the book's readership, what landscape means to each contributor, especially as it is revealed in his or her work. Thus, poets were encouraged to use their poems to explain themselves, and historians were supported in their efforts to write about the aspects and periods of American landscape history that they know best.

It is important to understand that *landscape*—as revealed in *place*—is not the province of one, two, or three academic disciplines, but is the concern of at least a score of art forms and academic fields. In this book alone, for example, the following are represented, through education and career: agriculture, anthropology, architecture, art, botany, conservation, dance, ecology, economics, education, environmental psychology, fiction and poetry writing, geography, history, horticulture, landscape architecture, law, literature, music, painting, photography, political science, theater arts, and wildlife management. By my making sure that the book's contributors would represent through their careers and backgrounds a diverse range of interests and approaches to the study and interpretation of landscape, the book becomes, on its own initiative, an aggregate of what the idea of landscape is thought to be in the United States today. To be sure, the book makes no claims of being encyclopedic, but it offers a full appreciation of the diversity of the landscape field and of the ways that *landscape* and *place* can be interpreted, studied, and comprehended.

*Landscape in America* is a creative endeavor, a collaborative project that links artistry with good writing and scholarship, field observation, and imagination. It harkens back to well over a century ago when the great scientific expeditions to the American West included not only scientists, but also artists, photographers, and journalists—in order to get the story right. The sequencing of the essays and the organization of the book are meant to suggest a certain flow in the nature of the responses to *What is landscape?* The book is thus presented in four parts, which are intended to behave like an exhibit in a gallery of fine art in which one moves from one room (and one theme or idea) to the next:

Beginnings—an introduction to interpretations of landscape;
Landscape as historical experience;
Landscape as myth and memory; and
Landscape as artifice and art.

It is not my purpose here to spill the beans before the reader turns to page one by explaining every particular of each section or essay. But please remember that there is a logic to the way the book is organized and the way in which the essays are sequenced. After all, the contributors were not assigned particular subjects, but instead were asked to answer the same question, *What is landscape?*; and, significantly, the organization and sequencing occurred only after the essays arrived on my desk.

As those who have read the advance text for the book have rightly indicated, *Landscape in America* is intended to reach two kinds of readers: "It will prove a wonderful stimulus to the already converted, the already knowledgeable. Here is a back-to-basics refresher course with much new material thrown in"; and "it represents a wonderful book with which to 'break in' the uninitiated." Thus, Part I serves as an introduction for those readers who prefer to become more familiar with some of the basic approaches to landscape study before proceeding to the remaining sections in the book, which represent a careful breakdown into individual points of focus—landscape as history, as literature, and as art. The concluding piece, by Gregory Conniff, is meant to turn the book back on itself, for here the photographer, after reading the entire text, selected passages and quotations from various essays within the book that conveyed for him the proper context for his landscape photographs and the larger thesis that *landscape is a point of view.*

It is my hope that the reader—whether the student who is just coming to landscape studies from whatever art form or academic discipline, or the seasoned scholar, writer, or artist, or the general reader who has a strong, but as yet undefined, interest in the broad subject of landscape, and of place—will appreciate not only the full range of topics presented, but also the many styles of presentation. Some essays contain traditional scholarly devices, such as lengthy notes; other essays present a few notes, as needed, while others require none. Such a range offers the teacher the opportunity to suggest to his or her students the various kinds of presentations that are available for the interpretation of landscape. Just about every form of essay is presented herewith.

There is a real beauty that is inherent in so diverse a subject as landscape—those places where we were born, brought up, educated, and now live, work, and visit. By understanding the interrelatedness of our natural and cultural landscapes—and of the people, creatures, and plants who call those places *home*—perhaps it is possible, despite our past history, to become better stewards of the land and better caretakers of our fellow human beings and compatriot life forms. By appreciating the everyday places of our existence, as well as the spectacular places we often can only imagine from afar with the aid of words and pictures, it is possible for us to comprehend what is at risk when we fail to care for those places properly.

Too often, it seems, decisions are made in government offices, in legal chambers, in business and industry boardrooms, on the campaign trail, and in our own properties and communities that reflect little knowledge of *place* and little realization of the connection between nature and culture. If this book contributes to the public's understanding and awareness of *place*, and of *landscape*, even in a small way, then all of the people who are affiliated with this book will feel that much more enriched. It is as Yi-Fu Tuan once wrote to me:

> *Americans are woefully ignorant of geography*
> *and of place—ignorant, that is, of the natural*
> *and humanly constructed worlds that have nurtured*
> *us, inspired us, and, sad to say, too often frustrated*
> *us. It is hard to imagine concretely how we can know*
> *who we truly are unless we can understand the places*
> *in which we are brought up, educated, and make a living.*
> *And how can we envisage the good life (the humane life)*
> *and plan for the future unless we have some clear idea*
> *as to the sort of places that we wish to exist?*

# PART I

Beginnings

*It is* place, *the relationships among things
in space, that shapes how we see.*

—GREGORY CONNIFF

*Clearly, we can make two observations about
landscape in America—first, the original
source of all geographical knowledge is in
the field and, second, this is going to be
a great country once we get it all paved.*

—COTTON MATHER

# The Spell of the Land

**Denis Wood**

DENIS WOOD was born in 1945 in Cleveland, Ohio. He passed his childhood along the Cuyahoga River, and his youth in Cleveland Heights. He received a B.A. in English from Western Reserve University, and completed an M.A. and a Ph.D. in geography at Clark University. He taught in an alternative high school in Worcester, Massachusetts, until being invited to apply for the position he currently holds, in which as a professor of design he teaches environmental psychology and landscape history at North Carolina State University in Raleigh. Professor Wood has published extensively on a variety of topics that include cartography, children's behavior, and environmental psychology, but his primary concern is meaning in the environment at any scale. His books include *World Geography Today* (Holt, Rinehart, and Winston, 1976; 1980), with Saul Israel and Douglas Johnson, *The Power of Maps* (Guilford, 1992), and *Home Rules* (Johns Hopkins, 1994), with Robert J. Beck. He also curated *The Power of Maps* show at the Cooper-Hewitt Museum in New York City and the Smithsonian Institution in Washington, D.C.

THE LANDSCAPE comes at us from every direction. It comes at us in *every way*. It rushes at our eyes, hurtling toward the retina . . . at the speed of light. It batters at our ears, rattling down our ear canal . . . at the speed of sound. Inhale, and within a quarter of a second the landscape is at our olfactory bulb. Sometimes we have the feeling that the landscape is . . . *out there*, but it is not; it is in our eyes and ears, up our nose and down our throat. It rubs our feet and caresses our cheeks. When things are just right, it plays with our hair, tickles the back of our neck, sends shivers running up and down our spine. It is not out there anywhere; it is right here, in our face.

Unless it's just a word. If *landscape* is just a word—just an idea—then it's some*where* else, on someone else's tongue, maybe, but not necessarily on ours. If it's just an idea, it's some*thing* else, not a thing with characteristics of its own, but . . . a notion, a concept, an intention maybe, maybe no more than a vague supposition, something, at any rate, one can toss around without worrying about breaking, a bunch of lines on a sheet of paper one can move around at will, and see (!) the paper can be crumpled up and nothing's the worse—or the better—for it. But maybe this one doesn't get thrown away, but instead is sent out to direct the behavior of a bulldozer. And suddenly it's no longer just an idea, it's the noise of crashing trees and subsoil slipping downslope into a creek and, when we walk across what used to be a forest floor, the red muck sticks to our boots and we don't come back for years. Or we drive across it but at sixty miles an hour, and in what is now a divided highway we fail to recognize the shivering grove thick with the must of rotting wood and quick with bird song where the loosestrife and sorrel and chokeberry grew. It is easy to miss this. It is easy to relegate to abstractions the suffering and death this landscape's transformation meant when we see it from the inside of an air-conditioned car with *All Things Considered* or *Morning Edition* on the radio. What birds?

What branches? What woods? It was never anything but fine lines on white paper in the first place.

But sooner or later we have to stop the car and get out: instantly the landscape is in our face again. The concrete is hard beneath our feet and the noise of the traffic hurts our ears. The fumes from the gas pumps send sharp signals to our brain. And what's this? Something in our eye? A piece of highway grit to scratch our cornea? The regret is instantaneous. With our hand on the nozzle we wonder, How did it come to this?

I can hear individual insects this late in the year, and pick out the rattle of individual leaves where the dying kudzu clatters in the breeze. I want to say it is quiet here—simply because I can hear no cars—or worse, the poisonous whine of power saw and motorbike—but, of course, it is not quiet, not if what I want to mean by that is silent. In the scrubby second-growth woods across the pond a pair of crows fuss at each other, the muted stridor of a cricket shivers from the silvery grasses, at intervals I hear the *ribbet-ribbet* of a frog and the echoing cry of a bird on the wing. Fall is more apparent here than in the city, and though the slope of the other side of the valley is still more green than anything else, it is a wayworn green tattered with russets and rusts and coppers and here and there a handful of the palest gold. The sky is a dusty blue, softening to chalk along the southern horizon, and the thin, high wisps of cirrus are more down than feather. The sun is warm but not hot. A fly has found me. On the wing of its buzzing drone come snatches of music from the radio of a fisherman somewhere out of sight . . .

I wake up with a start, my forehead clammy with a drying sweat. The sun has slipped west and the shadows have lengthened. A landscape of hues is modulating into one of shades. My eyes follow the track that brought me here around the knee of this thigh of land. Is it the wind in the weeds that lulled me to sleep, that even now sings to reclaim me? Or is it another spell the land has laid on me? Sun besotted . . . it is hard to say.

Three cyclists slip by me, bright in their lycra on their shiny new machines. This wakes me up! I am not alone out here with the birds and the bees, the flowers and the trees. In fact, I'm a little dubious about those flowers. Picking my way in their direction I soon enough make out what they're about—surveyors' flags, marching like dutiful teenagers to a drillmaster's beat, a long straight line of them, down-slope and up, the only thing in view wholly unresponsive to the curves carved by wind and rain. They are not hard to follow. The surveyors have hacked their way through copse and covert, pounding their stakes into the ground every fifty or sixty feet, down and up gully, into and through patches of bramble, out and across an ancient field. There, at the end of a red clay scar squats the great yellow dozer like the bully in a schoolyard. Quiescent this weekend afternoon it nonetheless stews in its reek of gasoline and oil. I don't need to ask what it's doing here—its path is clear enough. Others have preceded me along this walk and the spell the land has laid on them is other than the one it's laid on me.

This is the puzzle about the spell of the land, the way looking out, as at this moment I am, from a height of land—taking in glades green-gold in the westering sun that invests with shadows the wood-clad slopes and coaxes powerful volumes from a landscape flatter beneath a higher sun—*one* can be bewitched by the incantation of light and land, but *another* animated to a vision of homes and shopping malls, speculative office spaces and profit centers. Or, in this case . . . university campuses, for this place whose charms I cannot help but sing (so strong is the spell) is the hundreds of acres of woods, old fields, dusty lanes, and water—calm now and dark at day's ending—on which (so strong is the spell) a state university is raising its Centennial Campus.

To spin a spell, the land must speak. And indeed we talk as though it could. "This piece of land just cries out to be a residential subdivision," one says, as another might say, "It just wants to be left alone." I am writing this with my back against a great old pine. I stand and put my arms around it. Only if another comes with me and we hold hands can we embrace the tree. I wonder what *it* wants to be? A kitchen cabinet? Woodchips for a suburban yard? The "Arts and Leisure" section of the Sunday paper? Or would it like to be left alone? Up close the bark is a skin of layered plates, as topographically varied as the land it springs from, seamed and cracked and drilled by insects, a shifting skein of grays, of mouse and mole, of lead and charcoal, of wet slate and dried dill seed, of cook-smoke curling in the air . . . With my mouth close to the bark I ask the tree, "What *do* you want to be?" My words are lost in the litter of leaf and needle, twig and bough. I am startled to notice how noisy the insects have gotten. From a nearby tree comes a bustle of wings flapping into flight. Suddenly it's chilly. Again I ask the tree, "What *do* you want to be?" Straining to catch its answer I hear only the sound of a frog breaking the surface of the pond. On the farther side, I watch a crow settle on a withered branch.

The land does not speak. Like an autistic child it cannot *say* what it wants. It can only be. But if it cannot speak, then it can *cast* no spell, it can *recite* no incantation. The bewitchment I experience—mouth agape, empty-headed in the presence of this singular moment—is something *I* create, is something *I* construct, is a consequence of *my* way of looking, of *my* way of hearing, of *my* way of reading, even as that of the university is a consequence of *its* way of seeing. That there are at least two responses to the being of this land here in Raleigh in the latter part of the twentieth century is evident from no more than the fact that, where I stand in this roseate dusk, looking back across the valley of Walnut Creek at a fringe of birches burnished to an improbable bronze by a final finger of sunlight, is, on the university plans, the apron of the vast parking lot required by the huge number of cars it will take to serve the enormous campus to be constructed here: on the one hand, a vision of light on the land; on the other, a vision of concrete.

Two constructions of reality, two construals, two readings. But this is not, of course, how they are present in us. I do not feel, in what seems to me to be the crying of the land for surcease, *any* role of my own. It seems to me that the land *really* does cry, that these hills, these grasses, that animal which in the dusk I can only hear scuttling off, have demanded that I recognize in them an existence not utterly remote from my own, that I acknowledge in their individual and collective being the claims I expect others to recognize in me. The land cannot speak—in fact, the very word bespeaks no more than a construct, an abstraction of language, not a thing in the world—but it takes no effort of imagination to ascribe to the land precisely as we ascribe to the collective voice of people, a voice that is the collective voice of everything that lives here.

We have just held an election. In it each individual who voted raised an individual voice, but what was heard at day's end was none of these, but all of them taken together. We do this because we do not live as individuals, but as a community in which the life of any is predicated on the life of all. In the complicated, deeply interwoven, thickly matted world of the present this is *evidently* not a poetic conceit. We literally subsist as nodes in a network through which flows, in a kind of human-made "ecosystem," everything we eat and drink, wear and use. Any break in the web is felt everywhere. It is a whole, disaggregatable only in theory. As is the land. What tree, given the possibility of pleading for its life, would plead for its alone? It lives in an ecological reciprocity with other trees of its own species, with trees of other species, with insects and birds, fungi and moss, fire and wind. *This* is its life, as our life is one of ecological reciprocity with other humans, if as well with plants and animals. It is this whole network of life that we call *the land,* this entire web that is responsible for the land's characteristic forms and colors, scales and dimensions, those fugitive *consequential* aspects whose whole is what moves us. The topography stripped bare to the rock is not the land. The land is a composite of those strong forms as they have come into being through the agency of wind and water, sparrow and squirrel, beech and birch. And people. And it is this whole which, when it is acknowledged to be as alive as I am, seems to reach out to me, to lay on me a claim that I may recognize as a love of the land, or as a spell the land has laid on me.

But if the spell I feel is a consequence of the recognition of the land as a *subject,* then from where comes the spell that is experienced by the developer? I have never looked out over the land and where I have seen one thing envisioned another, so I cannot speak to the nature of the experience of those who do so. I have been with them, however, in the grips of such visions, and in their eager, enthusiastic voices I have heard the symptoms of a spell, as though they, too, had an experience in which the land outside themselves seemed to provoke the vision, as though it really did cry out, "Build me! Pave me! Raise me to my best and highest use!" At any rate, I must provisionally give them the benefit of this doubt—that, when they claim to *see* these things latent in the land, they are not lying. But in what conception of the land could such a view be founded? Certainly it must be one which recognizes the land as an *object,* that appreciates the land as a thing void of subjectivity. We understand this relationship only too clearly in the human domain. For example, one man can say of a woman that evidently she wants to be taken home . . . if not had right there on the pool table. It is unnecessary to read the transcriptions of rape trials to know this. It is sufficient to listen to the bragging at the bar or the loose talk of teenage boys. But another can ask, "How can you tell?" "She is acting in a provocative fashion," the first says. "Look at the way she sits with her legs exposed, she's just . . . asking for it!" The double entendre in that final phrase is seldom noted, but isn't this exactly what the developer asserts of the land, that it, too, is *asking for it,* that it, too, *wants* to be raised to its highest and best use?

Needs to be developed . . . needs to be laid, what's the difference? There isn't any. The victim in the rape is never allowed to speak (she has no subjectivity). Her objectifier reads her and constructs for her a social role . . . without her participation. But this is what happens in land development, only here we do not acknowledge that the land even has a voice. There is nothing metaphoric about . . . *the rape of the land.*

It has to be *rape*. I cannot see how it could be otherwise. I have come back again a week later. Again I top the ridge and look out across the valley of Walnut Creek. The leaves turned late this year, but today they are clots of color scrubbed across a dusty sky. October's moon has bloomed and faded, yet in the daytime the warmth of summer lingers on. I follow the track along the ridge, look out across the former fields toward the town of Garner. Water tanks punctuate the line of the horizon and, if your eyes are good, so do the radio towers, more evident at night to mine that are no longer what they were. The grasses and silvered goldenrod are tall enough to hide this view in places, and where the track plunges through them it has another magic. Among the graying skeletons, the purple fuchsia of the pokeberry does its awkward scarecrow dance. On the stalks of summer, Queen Anne's lace sports weathered stars that could be fossils of the aerial trails traced out by fireworks. Here a vine of honeysuckle still holds its bloom, though when I suck for sugar at its tip I find it's fled. The smell is close and husky—sweet—yet sour with the scent of fermentation. Around a bend, and the view opens up again, as the dusty track sinks to the level of the dam before the pond. Today the crows are having an aerial battle—or is it play? A hawk soars on an updraft. Above it the passage of two planes has sketched in the soft azure an evanescent X. Even in this dying time the land is lovely and it is hard for me to imagine that any who took the time to know it wouldn't love it, too. The leathery red-pumpkin yellow of a young maple with the sun on its leaves stops me in my tracks. The sunny side of an oak leaf is livid, yet the underside is green. Rubbing my finger across its surface I reflect on the fact that I know many of those who developed the Centennial Campus master plan. Some were once students of mine. I have to believe they walked these ridges and roads, sketched these views and vistas. They are sensitive people, attuned to the spirit of place that has moved me, experts at catching it on film and paper. How could they think to plot along the shore of the lake where now I walk in the luminescent shade of a grove of pines a hotel and convention center, unless they had resolutely refused to acknowledge the subjectivity of this land, had stripped it of its coat of root and branch, sod and bird song, reduced it to an object, a thing— though really there is no word in our language for this object solely of our will—refused, finally, the gifts of light and life, must and pungence?

What are the costs of this refusal? There are two of them. The land itself is scorched. Before the bulldozer wildlife flees as from a forest fire. Trees are trashed. That reciprocity of life we call the soil is scraped to a dump. What is the difference between

Sherman's March and that of the developers? But if the land is scorched, so is the subject that scorches it. Is this not what we have been finally forced to acknowledge: that it is not the slave alone who is subverted from his or her humanity; that it is not alone the black whose personhood is perverted by racism; that it is not alone the victim of abuse who is dehumanized; the raped who is raped; but as well the slaveholder, the racist, the abuser, the rapist? And why? Because a *subject* is not simply the locus of a feeling sentience, but the ability to recognize and respond to other subjects. Only to the extent that we do so can our own claims to subjectivity be real. There is here for me no question of philosophy, or even psychology. The reciprocity on which I want to insist is not ethical. It is *ecological*. We are *not* alone, we do not live alone, we do not live as individuals, but as a community; that is, as a network of mutually cognizant subjectivities, a network that simply has to include—because we cannot live *at all* without them—the plants and animals in whose collective reciprocal being we recognize the land.

To objectify any part of the world is therefore to diminish one's own subjectivity, to reduce the extent to which one can be characterized as a subject, that is, as a being capable of feeling thought or thoughtful feeling. One who objectifies is thereby rendered an object. One who brutalizes is thereby brutalized . . . coarsened, hardened, exactly as the flexible, complex, reciprocally living system we call the soil is brutalized, coarsened, and hardened by the blade of the yellow dozer. The land is scorched. The soul is scorched.

I speak generally, almost hypothetically. But we have scorched the land and scorched ourselves already. This is not some parlous future, or a fate reserved to a heinous few. We are already as brutal, coarsened, and hard as the world we have made of concrete and steel, oil and coal. *Poisonous whine* I wrote a few pages back, and I'll bet the phrase was taken metaphorically. But I also meant it for the literal truth it happens to be. The carbon monoxide and heavy metals these stupid, needless machines create are physically toxic. Lock yourself with either of them in a closed space for a few minutes and you *will* die. The carbon dioxides and nitrous oxides are subtler in their effects—slower acting—but in the long run just as deadly. Why rehearse the chilling catalogue? It is a litany that loses force with repetition as we are daily chanted into a black despair. Awareness of these poisons is commonplace today when there is no place on the hundreds of acres of this former farm to escape the stench and stutter of the internal combustion engine. But it is not our lungs alone that scar, but our eyes and ears, our nose and mouth; and indeed the metaphoric quality of poisonous whine pointed toward death not by asphyxiation but by racket, by stink, and by incandescent light.

I have walked these paths at night for years, mourning as little by little the darkness shriveled before the lamp, as the refulgence of the star-struck sky dwindled in the glare of the incandescent bulb. I have watched as I-40 slit its way across the farm, seen how the valley, dark once after dusk but for the fugitive glow of Garner, became illuminated by its flickering but continuous candescent ribbon. No longer do the radio towers semaphore their presence by winking a lazy red, but by blinking a phosphorescent white. The scale of time has changed: from rare, to regular, to all the time. The lights around the farm down Avent Ferry, Trailwood, and across I-40 on Saturn and Sierra, have grown more numerous and they are brighter now as well. There is no longer much dark here, and even on this night—sharp and clean in the wake of a hard cold front—it is hard to make out more than Orion and the Dipper, the red eye of Taurus, the bright collar of the Dog. What is the difference between the loss of a species and that of a star? Our world is equally impoverished. But to lose the star field that sprouts like weeds on a dome of night that reaches down to rake the Piedmont and strike the hills until everything rings like the inside of a bell . . . is to lose the universe. It is a loss that coarsens us. What can the world be without the stars? What will the earth be without the sky? What will the day be without the night? We have lost the night. We are losing the sky. Without the stars, can we save the world?

Its *music* is already muffled. It is not too bad today. The wind in the trees is a shifting pleasure and the intermittent warble, click, twitter, and trill are sharp delights. But all around is the steady 50-cycle thrumming of the traffic that batters its way around the Beltline, the irregular but frequent roar of the jet, the thrumping of the helicopter, the rare—and comparatively pleasant—hum of the single-engine plane. Here comes one now. The pitch drops as it approaches. Despite the distance I can *feel* the pounding as if against the insides of my eyeballs. Why knock the kids' boom boxes and bass-drunk pickup trucks? Their parents jetting from here to there have wreaked more havoc, and the land is deafened with their dimming. Once, the sounds each animal made crafted a special place in the acoustical ecology of the land, each sound slotted uniquely into its own aural niche. Our own human voice seems to have been shaped by the acoustical openings available to us in the "soundscape" of the African savannas. To fill these niches up, to drown them in our own sound making—as the water backed up behind a dam drowns the land it covers—is to abuse—aurally—the fox and the opossum, the junco and the quail. To lose most of the music we grew up with as a species—the bird song and animal chatter, the pattering of leaves sifting through the fingers of the trees, the lisping, gurgling, hissing, burbling of the water slipping through the land—is to deaden ourselves. When we slip off to the beach or into the woods, it is not silence that we seek but *sounds,* those to which our hearts learned to beat and our nerves to tingle.

It is dark now and raining. I slouch through an old field below Lake Raleigh, down along the floodplain of Walnut Creek. Once my eyes adjust, though, it is not so dark, for the light of the city—buzzing with its 60-cycle electric hum—is reflected from the clouds. The damp earth and wet grasses exude a mingled smell. I lay myself flat on the ground, heedless of the wet, and plunge my nose into leaf-trash and grass-mold. It takes a second to clear my nose of the stench of cars, but soon it comes, a penetrating sense of black earth and new-mown hay, of springtime and meltwater, of animal stalls and rot, sour mash and onions, a sharp tone of underarm, roots, grubs, and the undersides of rocks. The grasses may be dying but the earth is alive, pungent with dusky odors. Then I stand up. Even in the rain, the cars are there, at my nose, like an awful accident.

There are people who will not understand what I'm talking about, who will insist that I am going on about this scrubby, one-time farm as though it were Hetch Hetchy or Roanoke Island or the Joyce Kilmer Forest, but I have no illusions about this place that has me in its spell. I have walked here when it was a working farm, amazed to find—just a fifteen-minute walk from my home in downtown Raleigh—cows in pastures, hay in fields, corn and soybeans, nothing "urban" between me and Harnett County except a few lightly traveled roads, Ten-Ten and Holly Springs, Sunset and Penny. Twenty years ago no power lines slashed it like an incision opened with an axe, and there was no I-40 with its swamp of traffic. But there were tractors and farm workers and cattle with wet noses rubbing up against the fence-posts that a three-year-old could touch in fear and wonder. And this farm was cut itself from another, from older Boylan land worked by old man Boylan's slaves, and that was cut from another, and before them came the Tuscarora with their gardens of corn and squash and beans, and others before them for ten thousand years hunting and fishing and harvesting the nuts and the barks, the roots and the berries. This is not a wilderness, if indeed there can be said to be so much as one square mile of the earth that people have not visited and disturbed and made their own.

Let me acknowledge that I have no interest in an unhumanized landscape: I am a human. If it is no more than a path, suddenly it is home. People who exclaim at the sight of wilderness are as often as not looking at a postcard from the window of a train or at a travel poster through the windshield of a car. If they had to spend the night there, the beautiful would become sublime, soon enough grow scary and turn ugly. I have no grief against people, but against the insistence that there is no limit to our dominion even when, as now, the land we would work again is tired and all but gone. It is the failure of subjectivity that rouses my concern, that stirs my protective instincts, for my sake as well as the land's, here in Raleigh and elsewhere throughout the United States.

Kelly and I have come to find the beavers. It is another balmy autumn day, the blue almost enameled since the wispy cirrus has blown away, the day warm as the night was cold. Effortlessly the hawk gyres now. What does it make of us on our bikes, of the big yellow machines on the red clay that it can see if we cannot? Perhaps it doesn't even see us, knows only that there's less to eat this year than last, and less last year than the year before. It is after school, so after work and above on the slope where the work of converting land to Centennial Campus staggers forward, scraper and dozer are finally still. It's pretty quiet here in the dappled broken light through which falling leaves pirouette and plummet, drift and sail. The afternoon is as golden as Kelly's hair—a kid from the neighborhood with a yen for the wild—and is made more golden by the drooping sun that irradiates the dust scruffed up by life in the fall of the year. There's nothing quiet about us, though, as we blunder through the briars and kudzu thickets. This morning I *had* managed to see a beaver—just for a second before it saw me—but I had sat on the bank for a couple of hours not even writing and we will not see another this afternoon. But still the dams are wonderful, terracing the stream into a staircase of convoluted pools. We cross on one, solid as the Grand Coulee. Kelly is delighted by a quality of the water, the way it forms a shallow sheet stretched out *before* but not *below* us.

"You always have to look down at water, but this was, like, right there *at you,* and so calm and still and glassy with that fence sitting in it," was how he later put it. Rusting and broken, the barbed wire fence ran off the hill and into the water, as irrelevant now as all the rest of the remnants of the farm. "A nice place to go exploring," is how Kelly put it, "nice and quiet, no cars going by *vroom vroom*," as they do past his house, twelve thousand a day. He would have liked to see a rabbit or a fox. He saw one once, "doing a dance"—which he mimicked in a Kevin Costner sort of way—"over on Old Stage Road." As we worked our way from beaver dam to beaver dam, down to the water's edge and back—for the way was tangled along the stream—the light grew more and more golden. Something huddled off through the bewilderment of kudzu vines. There were tracks on the muddy banks. There was a strong scent of oak. Time had another scale now. Near the valley's end, below a steep bank, we found the beaver lodge, high and snug. It ought to be a cold winter. "What's that up over there?" Kelly wondered about the land above the slope. "Part of the campus they're building," I told him. "Will the beavers stay?" he asked.

We sat on the bank a while and watched the shadows slide up the eastern slope as the sun slid down in the west. The air danced. The sounds of the Belltower chiming five o'clock drifted down with the leaves. How did John Cage put it? *"But one must see that man and nature, not separate, are in this world together. That nothing was lost when everything was given away."*

IN IOWA

*One eye steaming*
*in a cold wind of cows*
*thin windows, animal-*
*thighed men with daughters*
*that crouch the fields like rabbits.*
*Snow mounts the measuring*
*side of the white church*
*shuttered at the crossroad.*
*Flat, there are no wrinkles*
*to read, to bring the horizon*
*near. Nothing*
*under the noncommittal sky*
*but a staunch fence straight*
*to the yellow-lit kitchen*
*and prayer hushed with gravy.*

—KENNETH LASH

This poem first appeared in
*Ploughshares,* Volume 6, Number 4
(spring 1981), page 43.

# Notes on Living with Landscape

Kenneth Lash

KENNETH LASH was born in 1918 in New Britain, Connecticut, was raised in Connecticut, and became a firm believer in the Maine coast. He received a B.A. from Yale University (Phi Beta Kappa), and completed an M.A. at the University of New Mexico. He also studied at the Université de Lillé on a Fulbright Scholarship and was awarded a Rockefeller Traveling Grant in the Arts to Latin America. He taught English at the University of New Mexico from 1946 to 1955, served as the head of the humanities department at the San Francisco Art Institute from 1955 to 1970, and from 1970 to 1983 taught at the University of Northern Iowa, first as head of the arts department and later as director of the humanities program. He served as editor of *The New Mexico Quarterly* from 1951 to 1955, was a contributing editor to *The North American Review* and a contributor to *The New Yorker*, served as a consultant on the Arts Task Force of the President's Commission on Mental Health in 1977 and 1978, and was the author of the book *A Lot for the Money: Stories, Poems, Essays* (The North American Review, 1982). Mr. Lash moved to Cape Cod in 1983, searching for a peaceful place to write and think. "All else happens around that. And will now, to the end." He died in Boston in 1985.

1. For the purposes of this essay, "landscape" is nature seen at a certain distance.

I HAVE a seventy-seven-year-old friend who recently found that she has cancer. Looking out the window of her summer place on a Maine island, down the green lawn like a path between dark pine woods to the open water, a few clouds drifting by, small islands floating in the distance, she said to me without turning her gaze, really talking to herself, "I wouldn't mind dying if it weren't for all this beauty." There was nothing of "my" in it. Only regret at having to break away from the visual world she had never taken for granted. She wouldn't call her attitude religious, but I would. Just as I believe the universal concept of religion not only owes its origin but its essential shape to landscape.[1] I doubt that my friend is consciously aware of the psychological role that landscape has played in the forming of her. I often noted, for example, the number of aggressively boring guests she invited along with their opposites. It wasn't that she was playing games or being "kind"; she simply treats people alike regardless of face, need, or choler. They exist for her as rocks, water, and flowers exist, as weather exists. Knowing about them is interesting but somehow unimportant; living among them is what counts.

I think you'll find something of her in many people for whom landscape is of clearly recognized importance. And little of her in those impoverished ones for whom it is not.

We think, in our limited way, that we live almost exclusively among people, as if our feet never touched an earth. (In many drawings by disturbed people, the feet of human figures either don't exist or don't touch the ground.) We pick and choose our friends, orchestrate people and our relations with them into a kind of landscape of our life. And complain because the landscape keeps changing. Friends fall away, are crowded out, grow too fast or too slow. Acquaintances come and go like wildflowers . . . or crabgrass. Yet we expect that life should be neat, tamed, unnatural. As if it were somehow a central task of life to remove itself from nature. Science may yet prove to be the anti-Christ.

Conversely, the more we have removed ourself from nature the more we have come to see ourselves as the greater part of it. In this distorting mirror, as in Italian Renaissance painting, nature is backdrop against which to set "man," who is no longer a form of nature but the very point of it. Perspective is discovered. Landscape begins its retreat to scenery.

I don't "know" that all of design exists in nature, but evidence keeps presenting itself. The computer is only the latest. I used to think abstract art was *sui generis,* an intellectual and/or emotional construct, until I saw microphotographs of a cross-section of iron bar. Aerial photography showed me origins of crazy-quilt patterns. Leaf and tree study projected those principles of branching and layering that are reproduced in everything from telephone poles to the bins in hardware stores. Which is to suggest that many "man-made" things may be landscapes in a way not seriously removed from nature. Certainly many painters have seen it so.

Since nature encompasses everything, it can be said that our distinctions of beauty and ugliness are no more than constructs. But only a philosopher would say so. Poets and what it now occurs to me to call industrial poets—psychologists—know better. They know that extremes of environment create physical effect. Sections of many countries are close to intolerable in their arid brutality. There are places "dank and foul" everywhere. To see them is to suffer a lessening of spirit, even a fear. Fear of what? What can a landscape do? Rise up and smite? Yes, because we fear we could not withstand being in it for any length of time, which means its mere existence threatens ours. Just as visual pollution—the combat zones and merchandise zones and ghettoized zones and franchised zones—pulls at the spirit and weighs on it, causing physiological stress and distress. It is difficult to imagine what we think of as the fully human being existing in such circumstance.

You can't go home again, it's said. Neither can you ever leave. The landscape of your childhood is ineradicable. For better or worse it is apt to be the landscape against which all subsequent ones are measured. And if in some remote place you turn a corner and are confronted with an approximation of that original landscape, the reflexive gasp is as physical as that caused by a blow to the chest. It is your "double" that you have run into.

The Japanese miniaturized garden says almost all there is to say about the potency of the *idea* of landscape. Like all "idea," it is not dependent upon physical extent. Nor ultimately upon any physical realization whatsoever. The *bonsai* in its container of dirt and mossy stone is perhaps the transitional step between the physical and nonphysical realization of landscape.

Oriental painting (traditional) is a form of handwriting. This becomes clear in the unrolling of a scroll. Written Chinese (and thus Japanese) is holographic. The characters are shorthand pictorial representations of the meaning. The painting seems simply an expanded account, in signs, of what is being "said," but always with that contemplative economy, that highly evolved sense of the limits of language. Or so it may seem. It may also seem to be nature reduced to thought, symbol, a perfect container of recognition. Unnatural. An icon.

Most gardens are failures, mere assemblages of prettiness neatly spaced. In short, decor. The *act* of gardening is never a failure, there's a giving and a respecting that bounce back. The best garden is an assembling of varied forces, with an eye to what may result coupled with hope for the unexpected.

Art can be dangerous to seeing. It begins by opening one's eyes; it often ends by closing them, by presenting a scene so powerfully and perfectly that afterwards all related scenes are "seen" in that same way. It may even preteach us to see a thing before we have in fact seen it. It may become a technique of seeing, and to that extent lifeless. Or preemptive, a stealing. I've felt robbed by coming upon something for the first time and "recognizing" it from some book or painting or—worse yet—film. At first there's the pleasure of the connecting, those circuits lighting up. But then you're faced with the problem of seeing it for yourself, and it is not so easy to duck under the lines left by a painter like Cézanne or a writer like Naipaul. The problem is that fullest transactions with nature have to be fresh. That's why though in general our experience of what we call landscape comes at a distance, with the necessary abstraction of distance, we must find in it the particular. Otherwise we're back in books and postcards. Nothing has happened. Landscape isn't real just because you see it. Something has to happen. Between you. And it can't if you're stopped up with ideas, preconceptions, habits, purposes. Simone Weil, speaking of the experience of literature, said that before you can really read a book, you must empty your mind. I would only add that you must not on the first reading take notes. Or underline. Or in any way be set to "make use of."

Monet was a brilliant fellow, to both plant and paint his garden. What a life his fingers had.

All we know of enduring peace in this life lies in natural land-scape. It is the only school for studying the complexities of harmony. The world is full of landscapes that are open-air museums; people flock to them to see, to be inside, to feel that odd mixture of calm and awe brushed with sadness that characterizes our experience of beauty.

Joyce Kilmer. Did anyone take so good a thought and express it so soppily? It's enough to put one off trees entirely. Landscape of all kinds takes terrible abuse from the sentimentalists, the pathetic fallacy fellowship. And from sunset exclaimers, who gobble down the spectacular like French fries. When possible, take outings into nature alone. With someone, the damnable urge to talk takes over, and receptivity drowns in static.

Nature presents us with the paradox of an order composed of disorder, of constant change occurring in stillness. Oh, there are those whippings and sawings that the presumed nature films of TV love so well (along with those constant photos of everything chewing everything else) . . . but an essential quality of nature is stillness, that sometimes frightening sense of a vast, unmoving presence outside of human time. It will close over us if we force the issue. A certain kind of noise in the universe will cease.

Trees exist outside of argument.

In landscape it is horizontal space that determines extent. Ocean, desert. Mountains are marvelous, but claustrophobic unless you're on top of them for some reason. Space without forms is also claustrophobic; the "wide and empty sea," the open desert. Form is necessary to define space. Too much form (New York City) destroys it. As in many gardens, overpopulated, overbuilt, jailed in geometry.

One of the nervous-making ingredients of contemporary urban/suburban life is the substitution of clock time for real time. Real time measures itself in rhythms, in "natural" changings. Decrease or cover over these changings by urban artifice and the human body adapts but pays a price, learns to tolerate certain deficiencies, to live less and less synchronized with nature. The logical—and ironic—conclusion is the domed city, the artificial cave. Among the very few major cities in the world that at least partially escape this fundamental urban blight is San Francisco, which does so by virtue of site. It is a city situated within a marvelous landscape, and open to the viewing of it on all sides. The hills, of course. The surrounding water and splendid light, all in a proportion that begins to define "perfection of prospect." The landscape of San Francisco enters even the dullest eye, and owing to blessings of fog and uncertain weather it is so changeful and moving that one does not get used to it, fall asleep as in Southern California. So each day has a visual force and eventfulness that affect one's sense of time, giving it a natural reality and thickening the context of a day.

Little more need be said about the psychological effect of landscape and climate on national character than is inherent in the contrast between the films of Fellini and Bergman. National and local character are often in direct conformity with landscape; that is, with the way life feels to those who live in it . . . and who put together their religions in necessary accord with it.

I "learned" landscape on the Maine coast. There were some things more or less noticed in my Connecticut childhood (winter, especially; it's hard not to notice winter in New England), but most was dulled by familiarity. Luckily I had seen no pictures, read no books, heard no talk of the Maine coast before I went. I was just, one day, there. And have been there every summer since because I cannot imagine otherwise. It is fresh each time, and each day of each time. Here's an attempt I made, looking back, to speak about that first encounter with the landscape of a Maine island: [2]

### ISLANDS

2. EDITOR'S NOTE: Mr. Lash revised "Islands" for this essay. The previous version was originally published in *The North American Review*, Volume 258, Number 1 (spring 1973), pages 81–84. I was unable to confirm Mr. Lash's preferences for line breaks and word position prior to his death. Therefore, the line breaks and position of the first word in each paragraph are reprinted here exactly as they first appeared in *NAR*. One typographical error in the original *NAR* text was corrected by Mr. Lash. "Late" replaces "later" in the sentence, "Not/hearing its horn rounding into the island in late/afternoon, was the final stillness." "Gonta" is spelled correctly.

*There are, you know, islands off the coast of Maine.*
*With on them rocks and farms and Indian blood.*
*Small bodies of land entirely surrounded by lobster.*
*So went the talk, and I. Took myself the house for rent*
*sight, as they say, unseen. That being absolutely the*
*point of it.*
　　　*Diagonally along the bedroom wall a*
*slope of glacial rock; out the window postcards of*
*Norwegian fjords. In back a brown meadow, a well*
*with leaves and waterbugs, one apple tree, twisted.*
*The usual rutted road back into the woods. Springs,*
*runnels, rivulets. In front, the sea. Sun glinting off*
*rock and water, smoking in the giant tops of firs.*
*Mosquitoes. Spooks. The ground spongy. Old shards*
*of granite and buoy. At night the Northern Lights,*
*rattling in the sky without a sound.*

*Mussels, blackberries, crabapples, clams. Mussels grew in thick bunches along a low wall of rocks strung in the water across the neck of an inlet near the farmhouse. Remains of an attempt at a lobster pond. According to Henry the guy bought live lobsters from the lobstermen, dropped them behind the wall into his natural pound, and sat down to await the bounty of nature in Her increase. Fair enough. More than fair, thought the lobstermen. So next spring they set their pots in the sea just outside the inlet. Knowing damn well that no wall of rocks made like a Vermont fence is gonta hold no lobster worth his size, who comes equipped about like a hardware store. So for a couple of years while it lasted, they sold the man his own lobsters, and made good mileage of them. The man himself, who must have come to misdoubt the fertilities of his lobsters, perhaps took comfort in the fact that they were certainly each year growing larger. By the time I got there the wall was visible only at low tide.*

*Many things of the island were accessible only at low tide.*

*There's a temptation to let that go. I think I will. Many things of that island were inaccessible to me at low tide. As for instance a great pond not a quarter-mile sideways from the farmhouse. I never saw it. The only way to see it was to fall in. Thick brush, under and over, went right out into it. Or so I hear. As I heard more than saw old ruins, abandoned logging camps, quarries, houses, fields, people—Scandinavians who long ago came here to the island to work in the granite quarries and never returned. Nor, as with earlier Norse, quite reached America. As a result their eyes didn't focus, or had gone brownish. Blue pupils afloat in vanilla extract. Down in the cellar towheaded kids playing whatever they wanted to play. Or out at the old quarry, swimming in the bottomless pool that was warm enough if you stayed on the surface.*

*There was an old Italian, named of course Tony, who supposedly had a terrible temper, so that no one spoke to him and children were afraid. This bogeyman lived alone in a small house at the edge of the village, across from the docks. Within yards of him were a sardine cannery, stink, fish-heads, screaming gulls, oil and gas, a dump, fog, salt. And in the middle of it, there was Tony in his garden, growing vegetables two feet long or two pounds round. As if, for Christ's sake, it were a slope in sunny Italy.*

*Islands of America. Good God. When in later years Germanesque psychologists began invading the place it felt like the beginning of the end in a Greek play. As if they had been summoned. Dark Furies. But modern ones. They responded to the call by bringing their patients with them.*

*Further confrontations of love. In its fiercest and most inarticulate form. Walking around smiling at snakes. Calling the fishermen sailors. (Do not send to sea for whom the bell tolls.) Looking sometimes under the light of pines like surprised lemmings. Not questioning the leap no, only the landing. If you could call it that on a piece of deliquescent stone dead-center in a horizon. Children and houses less made than extruded, like coral. Still-ness. In the sky, stars echoing it. Underneath, the unpossessed. Away horizontally from the land, verti-cally from the sea, living with their own mistakes. What would you expect if not ghosts? Stillness. Island love with its hatreds. The final enemy not history but memory. Felt history. What's in the mere knowing?—where few live, all are scholars. So after the love and hate stormed off, fogged off, boned and salted, only the ineffable remained in those eyes. Or came like a sudden film over yours. As for example when fog or storm were so heavy that the island boat couldn't try those 12 miles to mainland for groceries and mail. Worse yet if it went but couldn't return. Not hearing its horn rounding into the island in late afternoon, was the final stillness. After that one could*

*only wait. Be content to wait? I suppose so. Yes, that
was the surprise at the bottom. Lord knows sun or
storm, drunk or sober, there was an air of choice about
that place. Saturday night or Sunday morning. Ineffable. Yes. Solitary. Standing scared under Northern
Lights. Great flapwings of them in the night sky. Eyes
ridged and sea-rilled trying to open wide enough
to encompass the doings in that sky. The sound of the
sea incessant, but now truly loud, for once really a
roar. The lion gone ridiculous at the gates. While in
half the sky those Lights flap, without a sound.*

   *During the winter whenever I got a letter
from the island there'd be a message from the post-
master written on the back of the envelope. Hi there.
Orville.*

   *There. The word changes. Places drop
their names like masks. Here, and there.*

       *Never
mind the ocean, that's for visitors. The desert would
do as well. But the farmhouse, the trees, the rocks. The
buzz and ferment of that surrounded ground. The
incredible busyness of that solitude.*


Let me add one thing: About nature in the rawest, about living
in that landscape, I know nothing. Nothing at all. Few of us even
dream about it any more.

# Reading the Landscape

**John Fraser Hart**

*We have to learn to read the landscape*
*instead of merely learning to see it.*

—JOHN BRINCKERHOFF JACKSON

JOHN FRASER HART was born in 1924 in Staunton, Virginia, and was raised in Virginia and Atlanta. He attended Hampden-Sydney College and the University of Georgia Extension Division in Atlanta, received an A.B. in classical languages from Emory University, studied geography at the University of Georgia, and completed a Ph.D. in geography at Northwestern University. His honors include a Citation for Meritorious Contributions to the Field of Geography from the Association of American Geographers in 1969, an Award for the Teaching of Geography, College Level, from the National Council for Geographic Education in 1971, editorship of the *Annals* of the Association of American Geographers from 1970 to 1975, president of the Association of American Geographers from 1980 to 1981, and a John Simon Guggenheim Memorial Foundation Fellowship in 1982. In 1984 Professor Hart received a grant from the Commonwealth Fund Frontiers of Science Book Program for the preparation of *The Land That Feeds Us* (Norton, 1991), a book that won the 1992 J. B. Jackson Prize of the Association of American Geographers. His other books include *The Southeastern United States* (Van Nostrand, 1967), *The Look of the Land* (Prentice-Hall, 1975), and *Our Changing Cities,* editor (Johns Hopkins, 1991). He is professor of geography at the University of Minnesota.

QUEEN ELIZABETH I of England once said that she was "mere English." I cheerfully admit that I am content to be a mere geographer, and I wish to claim no more. I am a geographer because I am fascinated by the complex diversity of the earth we inhabit. In simple terms, I might define geography as curiosity about places. Geographers have both the privilege and the duty of trying to understand and explain the distinctive character of places. The inevitable starting point for geography is the visible landscape, because it is the most obvious feature of any place, although of course we transcend it almost immediately in our search for explanations.

I am quite content with the simple vernacular definition of landscape as "the things we see," and I am saddened by the way the meaning of the word has been transmogrified. Some people have endowed the concept of landscape with magical, mystical, or symbolic significance, or have loaded it with metaphysical connotation. In some quarters the word even has been turned into a talisman, as though it were expected to bring good luck to anyone who uttered it.

Many users have merely purloined part of the word. They have assumed, quite incorrectly, in my opinion, that the suffix *-scape* in landscape is somehow related to the suffix *-scope* (as in microscope and telescope), and they have committed such awkward neologisms as cityscape, farmscape, roadscape, seascape, wildscape, windowscape, and the like(scape).

Some users have treated a single facet of the landscape as though it were the whole. Geomorphologists, for example, have written about "landscape evolution" when they were concerned only with rocks and the features of the land surface. Some botanists and ecologists have used the word when they were interested primarily in plants and vegetation. The landscape of the architect seems to consist mainly of buildings, and often only of those buildings that are "polite."

Some people have used the word metaphorically, with results that can be confusing. The "economic landscape" apparently is no more than a flat, uniform surface on which only markets matter, such as Merrill Lynch's "landscape of investment," but what is a "political landscape," or a "demographic landscape," or the "landscape of shirt features" advertised in the Lands' End catalog, or the "landscape of TV" the Associated Press natters about? The mind boggles at the very thought of a "soil landscape," which presumably would be of interest only to another earthworm.

Confusion over the use of the term has been especially acute in geography, because the German word *Landschaft* can mean either "landscape" or "region," and some geographers have tried to have it both ways. At one time, in fact, some geographers argued that their discipline should be restricted to the study of landscapes, although it is still unclear whether they were talking about what one sees, or about regions, or about both, or perhaps about something else altogether. One suspects they had not thought the matter through very carefully themselves, and the debate became terribly bogged down in mysticism and confusion.

The experience should have made geographers especially gun-shy about the use of the word "landscape," but nevertheless they have bandied it about in ways that surely would run afoul of any truth-in-advertising laws. Unfortunately the word has been mauled so many times by so many users in so many disciplines and art forms that it may well have lost much of its usefulness. Certainly it has no generally accepted technical definition, and each person who talks or writes about landscape has a very real obligation to explain precisely what he or she means when using the word.

I have already said I am content with the simple vernacular definition of landscape as "the things we see." Our perceptions may differ, but I doubt they differ all that much. You and I both see the same thing when we look at a skyscraper, or an elm tree, or the rear end of a bull. Our skills at reading what we see may differ, to be sure, and what we see may well say different things to us. One person, for example, might see picturesque rocky cliffs, whereas another might see the Niagara dolomite outcropping in a cuestaform escarpment, and both would be right. But a few of the Deep Thinkers like to inform us that what we see is not what we see at all, and that reality is not really real. Hogwash.

We need to learn to read the landscape, not just to see and react to it, but what we see is real, and no conceivable amount of sophistry can protect the Deep Thinkers from the reality of getting spattered, not inappropriately, if they get too close to the rear end of that bull.

We need to get out and look and see things for ourselves, because the primary source for studies of the landscape, oddly enough, is the landscape itself. I do not know how one learns to become a careful observer, so I am unable to teach the skill, but I know it is essential.

We also need to learn to think analytically about what we have seen, and to identify the features of the landscape in terms that make sense to, and can be used by, others. Too many studies of landscape have to be taken on faith, because their authors cannot explain the criteria they used to identify the features they have described.

We need to learn to talk to and listen to and learn from the plain ordinary people who are the creators, the inhabitants, and the custodians of the landscape. We must know enough to ask reasonably intelligent questions, and, of even greater importance, to listen carefully to what they tell us. An old adage says that one is not going to learn very much while one's mouth is open.

Good fieldwork requires an open-ended kind of approach. In order to glean the occasional gem, one has to be willing to take the time to relax, to chew the fat and shoot the bull, to listen patiently to a lot of things in which one is not interested. In my time I have listened to far more homilies on politics and religion than I have really needed, but I have also learned a lot because I have been able to hear them out attentively, and then turn the conversation to subjects that interest me more.

We can discover the aspirations and the needs and the values of ordinary people only by listening to them, because they rarely, reluctantly, and with painful effort put pen to paper. One can have little confidence in the work of secondhanders who seldom can be bothered to glance out of their windows, whose experience has been limited to the dusty stacks of the library, and who are hostage to the observations and ideas of others because they rely entirely on the printed page.

The printed page undeniably is important. It enables us to visit unfamiliar landscapes vicariously, and to learn how others have seen and interpreted landscapes with which we are unfamiliar, but far too many of us are far too willing to let others think for us. We must learn to believe what we see and to have confidence in our own observations, especially when they fly in the face of conventional wisdom and generally accepted theory. Most of us are intellectual cowards, and it is far easier to defer to authority than to risk sticking our necks out. We must develop the courage

The recently installed Potomac Gas substation serves a new subdivision, Copperfield, a half-mile away in Jefferson, Maryland; the power lines are courtesy of Potomac and Edison. The view is from U.S. 340 looking southwest toward South Mountain near Harper's Ferry. Photographs by George F. Thompson, 1989.

to believe the evidence of our senses, and to let the facts speak for themselves, instead of trying to force our observations into some procrustean model of theory or conventional wisdom.

The observer of landscape should try to see everything, but most landscapes and their histories are so complex and so variegated that they are virtually incomprehensible without careful analysis, and the person who tries to look at everything may wind up seeing nothing at all. We must be selective. At any given time we must concentrate on a few carefully chosen features, or types of features, and we must never allow ourselves to forget that the features on which we concentrate are related in various ways, some close and some not so close, to all the other features of the landscape. From time to time we must also consciously change our focus and concentrate on another set of features, in order to develop a feeling for the complete landscape. With time and experience we should be able to develop a sixth sense that will alert us to interesting aspects of features other than those on which we are concentrating at the moment.

It is logical, convenient, and defensible to group the features of the landscape into three broad categories—animal, vegetable, and mineral—to facilitate their analysis. The three principal components of any landscape are:

(1)   the landforms, or the features of the land surface;
(2)   the vegetation, or the plants that cover the surface; and
(3)   the structures that have been added by people.

The human structures may be further subdivided into four categories:

(3a)   systems of land division;
(3b)   structures associated with the economy;
(3c)   house types; and
(3d)   agglomerations of houses into villages, towns, and cities, with all of their associated features.

In most parts of the world the aspect of the landscape that makes the most compelling first impression is the form of the land surface, whether mountains, hills, plains, or plateaus. The observer of landscape must have a good command of the basic principles of geomorphology in order to comprehend the character and origin of the major and minor forms of the earth's surface. In addition to their role as features of the landscape, the landforms of an area usually are closely related to the kinds of plants that grow in the area and to the ways in which people can use the land.

The second principal component of the landscape is the plants that cloak the surface of the earth. The observer of landscape should be familiar with such concepts as natural vegetation, contact vegetation, climax vegetation, potential vegetation, and the problems inherent in each concept, but he or she is primarily interested in the real vegetation, which can be defined as the plants that are there now.

The cover of trees, shrubs, grasses, and other plants is also an essential intermediary between the mineral and animal worlds. It is trite, but true, to say that animals (including the human variety) cannot eat rocks, and they would perish if they did not have

The Mayakka River, in Sarasota and Manatee counties in Florida, is a special place in which to see beautiful palmetto palm forests and a rich array of waterfowl and wildlife, including good-sized alligators. Photograph by George F. Thompson, 1993.

plants to convert the minerals of the earth's crust into food they can use. Animals are mobile, and they are free to wander, but plants are sedentary, and they are firmly rooted in the soil. Animals cannot live or roam too far from the places where the plants they need are available, or where they can be grown.

All plants need heat, light, and water. The proper amounts vary from species to species. The requirements of the more important plant species provide the basis for most classifications of climate, and the map of climatic regions looks very much like the map of vegetation zones. Within each climatic region, however, the vegetation varies in response to differences in elevation, slope, exposure, drainage, soil, and other environmental factors.

The plants that grow naturally in an area probably are the best single indicator of its environmental potential, and pioneers in the United States used vegetation as a guide to tell them which land to settle and which land to avoid. Their knowledge is embedded in folk sayings such as "Maple land is good land, but pine land is poor land," and even today the observer of landscape should know how to read the vegetation, because it carries a clear message about the nature of the environment in which it grows.

The vegetation also tells the tale of how people have used and abused the land. For example, most of the eastern United States was wooded when white settlers first saw it, but they cut down the trees and cleared the land so they could grow crops on it. Much of the land still remains in cultivation, but some was cleared unwisely, and those who once farmed it have allowed Old Mother Nature to foreclose her mortgage on it. They may be reluctant to admit they are no longer using the land effectively, but broomsedge, blackberry bushes, persimmon sprouts, cedar saplings, old field pines, and other plants send a clear signal that the land is no longer used for agriculture. The observer of landscape should be able to recognize the plants that invade and colonize unused agricultural land.

We should also be able to identify the principal cultivated crops, and should understand why they are grown and how they are used. A generation ago, for instance, a traveler in the Corn Belt of the American Middle West might have expected to see small, well-fenced fields of corn, oats, and alfalfa, which were grown in a regular rotation to provide feed for cattle and hogs. Today, however, the Middle West seems to have been turned into one vast field of corn and soybeans, both of which are sold for cash instead of being fed to livestock. Fences have been removed, fields have been enlarged, farmsteads have been transformed, and the entire rural landscape has been changed in response to changes in agricultural technology and economy.

The fences, fields, farmsteads, and other structures added by people are the third principal component of the landscape. Every human structure serves some human need, and the form of the structure fairly faithfully reflects its function, or the need it was originally designed to serve. Form and function are more intimately related in some types of structures than in others. They are most closely related in simple, ordinary, workaday structures, such as barns, sheds, garages, and privies, that are necessary for daily living; they are most widely divorced in expensive, pretentious, ornamental, showplace structures, such as houses, and that is why the study of house types is so extraordinarily complex, difficult, and usually unsatisfactory.

I prefer to invoke function to explain as much of the built landscape as possible, but, of course, the form and appearance of the human structures in any area may also be influenced by many other considerations, including the nature of the physical environment, the level of economic prosperity, the technical competence of the builders, the date of construction, the cultural baggage of the people, aesthetic and symbolic motives, and the personal whims and idiosyncrasies of the owner.

Ordinary vernacular structures normally are built of whatever material comes most readily to hand, and as a consequence they often reflect the natural physical environment, which provides the stuff that people have to work with. Take fences, for example. In the eastern United States, which was a wooded area, most of the early settlers put up zigzag fences of rails split from trees they had cleared from the land, but stone walls were more common in the stony, glaciated areas of New England and in areas where the limestone bedrock formed natural flagstones. On the sandy soils of the cutover lands of northern Michigan, Minnesota, and Wisconsin, farmers uprooted the tree stumps left by lumbermen and tipped them on their sides to make picturesque stump fences.

The treeless prairies of the continental interior were not as much of a deterrent to settlement as some people have supposed, but settlers who had come from wooded areas did have to scratch around a bit to find substitutes for wood for fuel, for building materials, and for fencing. They experimented with live hedgerows before the invention of barbed wire facilitated the expansion of settlement westward across the grasslands.

The availability of barbed wire, which was made in distant factories and had to be shipped to the grasslands at no small expense, suggests how the level of economic prosperity in an area can influence the form and appearance of its human structures. Building materials for ordinary structures are not normally transported any great distance, but a prosperous area can afford to ship in materials that a less prosperous area could not afford. Steady improvements in the technology of transport also have enabled many areas to import building materials from ever greater distances, and in the United States today few distinctive building materials are derived directly from the resources of the local physical environment.

The technical competence of the people who built them can also influence the form and appearance of human structures. Barn roofs illustrate the importance of technical skill. Almost any good

Casa Grande (Big House) was built by the Hohokam in circa 1300–
1320 in the Gila River valley, southeast of present-day Phoenix, near
Coolidge, Arizona. The remarkable group of buildings was "discovered" in
1694 by Father Eusebio Francisco Kino, a Jesuit missionary, who described it
as "a four-story building as large as a castle and equal to the finest church
in the lands of Sonora." The building material is caliche, a hard local subsoil
that today erodes easily; to protect the ruins from rain, the National Park
Service erected a steel canopy. The upper floors, long gone, were made
of logs, presumably floated down the Gila from the San Francisco and
Mogollan mountains in southwestern New Mexico. Casa Grande was
abandoned in about 1450; it was set aside by the nation in 1889 and became
a national monument in 1918. Photographs by George F. Thompson, 1988.

carpenter can put up a straight (gable) roof, △⟍ , but straight roofs may be inefficient, because the loft space under the eaves is cramped, and it requires much bending, stooping, and head-bumping. Gambrel roofs, ⟋⟍ , with gentle upper sections and steep lower sections, permit easier access to the space under the eaves, but building them demands greater skill, and arched (gothic) roofs, ⟋⟍ , which are even more efficient, are also the most difficult to build. It appears that most barns in the Middle West in the nineteenth century had straight roofs, but gambrel roofs gradually became more common as carpenters learned how to build them, and many barns built since the Depression have had arched roofs whose principal structural members have been bought prefabricated at the local lumber yard.

The date of construction, therefore, may affect the form and appearance of a building, both because improvements in technology over the years have given builders greater leeway and because the style of a building may reflect the changing fads and fancies of current fashion. House types are a good illustration. In the American colonies before the Revolutionary War, buildings were patterned after models in the home country, and the austere elegance of the formal Georgian style was high fashion. After the Revolution the young republic turned for its model to ancient Greece, the cradle of democracy, and the white pillars and porticoes of Greek temples were copied in the Greek Revival style in the latter part of the nineteenth century, to be replaced in turn by the California bungalow of the interwar years and the no-nonsense functionalism of the ranch style and split-level ramblers since World War II.

The cultural baggage of a group may affect the form and appearance of its structures, because different groups of people have their own distinctive ideas about how particular types of buildings should look. Some cultural geographers, in fact, have argued that house types are among the best indicators of cultural diffusion. A good example of a type of building that is associated with a particular cultural group is the Pennsylvania German barn, a massive two-level structure with a barn bank, or ramp, on one side and a forebay sticking out over the stockyard on the other: ⌂ . German farmers from southeastern Pennsylvania carried the idea of this barn with them when they migrated westward, and they built such barns wherever they settled. The Pennsylvania German barn was unnecessarily elaborate for the farming system that developed in the Corn Belt, however, and most non-German farmers in the Middle West preferred to build simpler feeder barns of the type that had originated in the Great Valley of northeastern Tennessee, but German farmers persisted in building barns of the familiar type.

Aesthetic and symbolic considerations undoubtedly affect the form and appearance of many human structures, but it is easy to assign too much importance to them. Most people are motivated by functional, not aesthetic, considerations when they erect a structure, and most ordinary human structures must be understood in terms of their functions. They are not intended as works of art, and any artistic quality they may happen to possess is unconscious, accidental, and incidental. People do not intentionally erect structures that are ugly, of course, but neither do they erect structures because they are beautiful; they erect them because they need them, and not because they will beautify the landscape and make aesthetes happy.

Most of us would like to live in a fine house, drive a fancy car, and wear the latest fashions, but few of us can afford the luxury of style, and the way we actually live is a compromise be-

Suburban Chicago. Photograph by Bob Thall, 1992.

tween our desires and our income. We like beauty—even though our perceptions of what is beautiful may not agree with the perceptions of others—but we are compelled to balance our desire for beauty against the dictates of our pocketbooks. Each of us harbors notions of rightness and propriety about the way things ought to be, and we try to implement our ideals, but we cannot always afford to do so. We do the best we can with what we have, and the results sometimes are quite handsome, but sometimes less so, and not everyone agrees about what is handsome. Some people, for example, like statues of pink flamingos, deer, and jockey boys in their front yards, whereas others prefer boxwood hedges, carpets of juniper, and brick walkways, and each is aghast at the awful taste of the other group.

Every August nearly 60,000 people attend the Clarke County Fair in Berryville, Virginia, the county seat. Photograph by George F. Thompson, 1987.

We must try to understand the human structures on the landscape in terms of their creators, inhabitants, and custodians, and in terms of the things with which these people are comfortable. For example, take Clarence Magnus's farmstead southeast of Slayton, Minnesota. The two-story white farmhouse sits at the back of a neatly manicured lawn, with enough trees to provide welcome relief from the scorching summer sun. Gleaming metal sheds and grain bins encircle the clean gravel farmyard back of the house. At the far corner, next to three cylindrical concrete silos, is a handsome old barn from which the white paint has started to fleck.

Southeast of the farmhouse, and hidden from it by a high hedge, but clearly visible from the highway, is a tatterdemalion collection of disc plows, chisel plows, field cultivators, stalk choppers, grain augers, wagons, and other equipment, all overgrown with weeds and apparently rusting away. At first glance it looks like a scrap-metal dealer's paradise, but when you take a closer look it is not nearly as unkempt and disorganized as it appears to the motorist speeding past on the highway.

Clarence is a splendid manager, and he carefully oiled each piece of equipment and gave it a protective coat of grease before he put it in the lot. His existing buildings simply do not have enough room to house all of the new machinery he needs to conduct a modern farm operation, and he has to leave some of his equipment outside, mostly the cheaper and hardier pieces. Does he need a new machine shed? Of course he does, and he will tell you so himself. He will also tell you, to the penny, what it will cost, including interest and the increase in his taxes because of what the new machine shed will do to the assessed valuation of his farm.

Clarence needs a new machine shed, but right now he can't afford it. One of these years he is going to get a good price for his corn or his beans or his beef cattle, and that's when he is going to build himself one. It will be a hulking metal affair, probably gleaming white with green trim. Aesthetes will consider it an eyesore, and Clarence quite frankly doesn't give a hoot whether some college professor or historic preservation officer happens to consider it an eyesore, because it is going to make his farm more efficient and his life easier.

Fred Kniffen, the cultural geographer, once remarked that no one is ever going to be able to wax sentimental over those ugly metal structures that are popping up all over the place. I disagreed with him then, and I still do. It probably will not happen in our lifetimes, and it is unlikely to happen until they have become old and rare, but eventually they will become old and rare, and then they will become precious. Everyone laughed at me back in the 1940s when I predicted we would live to see the formation of a Society for the Preservation of Victorian Monstrosities. Today everyone is far too busy snapping them up and stripping them and refinishing them and gentrifying them to have time to laugh at me any more. I am prepared to make the same prediction for Clarence Magnus's new metal machine shed, the one that hasn't even been built. One of these days it will be added to the National Register of Historic Places, but, of course, neither you nor I will be around long enough to find out whether my prediction will come true.

The real eyesore on the farm, as far as Clarence is concerned, is the barn, a fine old structure of white-painted wood, with a roof of cedar shingles that the years have gradually turned gray. When I asked him about it, over coffee and cookies in the cozy kitchen of his farmhouse, he said, "Oh, that old building has served its time. We used to use it back when we milked cows, but we don't need it any more, and one of these days I am going to tear it down. In fact, the place where it stands would be a good spot for the new machine shed."

What about the three silos, which form an aesthetically pleasing composition against the western skyline? Why did Clarence see fit to group them in that particular attractive fashion? "Well, two of them hold corn silage, and the third is sealed for high moisture corn. I have to mix the two to make a properly balanced ration for the steers in the feedlot, and then I have to throw in a sack of commercial protein. I placed the silos that way so I could drive a feed wagon right into the loading area and take the right amount from each silo without having to move the wagon." So much for aesthetics, at least on the Magnus farm.

A search for symbolism in the form and appearance of the human structures on the landscape makes me even more uneasy than a search for aesthetics. There is no question that structures can be symbolic, but for whom are they symbolic? Is their symbolism the same for everyone? I have the impression that symbolism is more important for the outsider than it is for the insider. The insider accepts structures as functional entities, whereas the outsider finds symbolism in them. A structure may indeed have symbolism for the insider, but that symbolism is rarely articulated, and I become uncomfortable when we start probing too deeply for symbolism that is subconscious at very best, and may actually exist only in the mind of the prober.

If I ask a farmer about one of his buildings, and he gives me an answer that goes beyond mere plausibility and makes real sense, I see no need to quiz him any farther. If I do go farther, in fact, I run the risk of imposing my own ideas, opinions, values, and beliefs on him. Some people, however, seem to need symbolism, and they have refined to a remarkable degree the knack of finding it where others do not even know it exists.

I am reminded of the story about Grandma, who had started to act a little bit flaky. The family members wondered if they shouldn't put her in a nursing home, but they were reluctant to submit her to the indignity of a trip to the psychiatrist's office, so they invited the psychiatrist to dinner, and asked him to check her out during the meal.

At one point he held up a spoon and asked her, "What's this?"

"By me," she said, "it's a spoon."

Later he held up a fork and asked the same question.

"By me," she said, "it's a fork."

Arcadia, Wisconsin, in August. Photograph by George F. Thompson, 1988.

When he asked her the same about the knife, she said, "By me, it's a knife."

The psychiatrist then asked her, "Why do you preface each of your answers with 'By me'?"

"That's easy," she said. "By me it's a spoon or a fork or a knife, but by you it's probably some kind of phallic symbol."

I sometimes wonder if psychiatrists have nervous breakdowns when they travel through the silo-studded dairy-farming areas of Wisconsin.

My reservations about searching for symbolism in the landscape apply with greater force to attempts to assign psychological power to it. No one can question the ability of the landscape to influence human attitudes, ideas, and behavior, but fashions in

Downtown Chicago. Photograph by Bob Thall, 1982.

the perception and appreciation of the landscape have changed greatly through time, and the psychological impact of the landscape varies enormously from person to person and from culture to culture. One of my friends, for example, complains about the boring monotony of endless fields of corn and soybeans on the flat plains of the Grand Prairie of east-central Illinois, but I find myself positively exhilarated by the vast open vistas of one of the finest farming areas on the face of the earth, and I feel uplifted and rejuvenated each time I travel across it. Who is to say that either of us is wrong?

There is a very real danger, I fear, of projecting our personal opinions and prejudices to the status of universal truths. Each one of us assumes we are perfectly normal human beings, and it is far too easy for us to project that assumption to the belief that all other normal human beings think and behave and react just as we do. In our heads, of course, we know they don't, but in our hearts we feel they should, and we become irritated when they are irrational, i.e., when they don't think or do as we would. The world would have been spared many blunders if planners and economic developers had been made to realize that their values are not universal nor everywhere wanted.

Different people perceive and assess the same landscape quite differently, and praiseworthy attempts have been made to measure differences in landscape assessment as objectively as possible, but the principal conclusion that emerges from such attempts is the complexity of the problem. We human beings are a cantankerous lot, and we seem to become increasingly cantankerous as we get farther from the constraints of having to make a living, and as we have greater freedom to indulge our personal whims and idiosyncrasies.

The form and appearance of human structures on the landscape are influenced by so many different considerations, from personal eccentricities to the necessities of making a living, that they have attracted the interest of scholars from many different disciplines. These scholars take different approaches to the study of landscape. They begin with different basic assumptions, they emphasize different aspects of structures (or whatever else they are investigating), they collect different kinds of evidence, and they lean toward different explanations. Although our approaches are different, each of us has an important job to do and a useful contribution to make, and we need to work together, in a spirit of mutual appreciation and respect, toward the common goal of a richer and fuller understanding of the landscapes that intrigue us all.

Some authors—I hesitate to call them scholars—have elected the aesthetic approach, and they have produced handsome volumes that make impressive decorations for coffee tables, but their excesses of enthusiasm fail to compensate for their inadequacies of insight. We need to learn to read the landscape, to understand its grammar and syntax and vocabulary, and not merely to rhapsodize over it. And the novice must realize that a considerable apprenticeship is necessary to become familiar with the basic vocabulary, which once mastered can grow like a snowball.

The landscape needs two types of research, detailed studies and extensive surveys, and it also needs two types of friends who feel quite passionately about it. It needs advocates, who are convinced they know why and how it should be preserved, or how and why it should be changed. It also needs scholar-teachers who are dedicated to trying to understand it, and to helping others understand it, but who are reluctant to advance their own personal opinions about it.

Advocates try to make the best possible case for the position they espouse. They emphasize the evidence that supports this position, and they ignore, belittle, or even try to discredit any evidence to the contrary. Advocates are necessary and important members of society, because they become involved in the hurly-burly of the decision-making process, and they can be responsible for inspiring great changes, but their credibility must inevitably be suspect, because everyone knows what they are going to say before they ever open their mouths.

The role of the scholar-teacher is to get people to think for themselves, instead of trying to convince them of the preferability of a particular position. Scholars have opinions of their own, to be sure, but they are hesitant about advancing them, and they would rather help others develop a sound and solid foundation for forming their own opinions. Scholars try to understand and appreciate all points of view, and they never cease their search for the one that is best. They challenge all opinions, including their own, and they demand the fullest possible evidence in support of all positions, with the goal of sifting through it in search of the position that is supported by the greatest weight of evidence.

Scholarship and teaching are inseparable. It is impossible to be a scholar without wanting to teach, and teaching that is not based on scholarship is pretty threadbare hand-me-down stuff. As a scholar I am eager to report my findings, both in person and in print, and to share with others what I have learned, but I find the role of advocate personally uncongenial, because I cherish the goal of scholarly objectivity in description and explanation. I appreciate the necessity and importance of advocacy, but I am happy to conclude this essay, as I began it, by agreeing once again with my good friend Brinck Jackson, who said: "[I]t is not the role of the student of landscape to make recommendations. If he [or she] has any role at all it is to teach people to learn by seeing."

John B. Jackson

# In Search of the Proto-Landscape

JOHN B. JACKSON was born in 1909 in France. He received an A.B. from Harvard University and an honorary Doctor of Fine Arts from the University of New Mexico. He served as a major in the U.S. Cavalry from 1940 to 1946, and in 1951 founded *Landscape* magazine, for which he served as editor and publisher until 1968. He has held numerous academic appointments while always maintaining his independence, including regular stints at the University of California, Berkeley, and at Harvard University. In 1986 the Association of American Geographers presented the first J. B. Jackson Award, given annually to the American geographer whose book best contributes to the public's understanding of human landscapes. Mr. Jackson's books include *Landscapes: Selected Writings of J. B. Jackson*, edited by Ervin H. Zube (Massachusetts, 1970), *American Space: The Centennial Years, 1865 to 1876* (Norton, 1972), *The Necessity for Ruins and Other Topics* (Massachusetts, 1980), *Discovering the Vernacular Landscape* (Yale, 1984), and *A Sense of PLACE, a Sense of TIME* (Yale, 1994). He resides near Santa Fe, New Mexico.

AS I DEFINE the word, a landscape is more than an area of attractive rural or natural scenery. It is a space or a collection of spaces made by a group of people who modify the natural environment to survive, to create order, and to produce a just and lasting society.

Natural environments are not everywhere equally hospitable, nor are all groups of people equally skilled in modifying them. The great diversity of landscapes has long been a matter of interest and study. Yet, since all of them derive from an intention to reveal an ordering of space and time, it follows that they all share certain basic characteristics.

In the past I spent much time studying the older, traditional landscapes of Europe and Anglo North America. I found they had many cultural and geographical traits in common. The landscapes of northwestern and central Europe and those of North America east of the Mississippi River are all situated in much the same kind of natural environment: one with a temperate climate, abundant rainfall, good soils, many navigable rivers, and few impenetrable mountain ranges. Furthermore, those who live in these landscapes on both sides of the Atlantic Ocean share a Christian-classical heritage, a stock of technical skills, a similar class structure, and, from a world perspective, the same historical evolution. Even the languages they speak are related. These are good reasons for their various landscapes being made alike.

Recently I undertook to study the landscapes of the prehistoric Pueblo Indian communities of New Mexico, where I live. At the time of the Spanish Conquest in the late sixteenth century the whole Southwestern region contained a population of not more than thirty thousand people, living in some one hundred fifty small, scattered farm villages. It was an isolated society, never powerful or rich, and it made little or no impact on the surrounding American world. It produced no literature, no fine art, and its original landscapes have long since vanished. But what survived in New Mexico were eighteen Pueblo villages; and from studying these villages, their religious practices, their social organization, and their myths and traditions, as well as from studying the many Pueblo ruins, scholars have learned much about that prehistoric Pueblo culture and even about the prehistoric Pueblo landscapes.

Like those of Europe and Anglo North America, these landscapes resembled one another in many ways. For the most part they were situated in the same natural environment: one which was mountainous, often very dry with great extremes of temperature, so that the scanty supply of rainfall had to be supplemented by irrigation from mountain streams. The inhabitants supported themselves by small-scale farming and gardening, and by hunting and gathering plants and fruit in the surrounding hills and valleys. They had no domestic animals, aside from the turkey and the dog, and they used no metals. With slight variations all Pueblos shared many ancient religious and social traditions, a solar calendar, and a number of symbols, myths, and legends. The prehistoric Pueblo Indians seem to have been a hardworking, peace-loving people who were closely involved in the life of their community and its religious ceremonies.

I was thus confronted by two very different sets of similar landscapes: those of Europe and Anglo North America and those of the prehistoric pueblos of New Mexico. Would it be possible to establish an overall similarity between the two, widely separated in space and time though they were? If so, then it might eventually be possible to come nearer to discerning the proto-landscape, the basic landscape from which all existing landscapes are mere variations. Yet, which landscape features ought I try to compare? Which forms and which relationships?

In visualizing a landscape as a human-made space or a collection of spaces, two features capture our attention: the focal point (or center) and the boundary. The prehistoric Pueblo Indians conceived of the boundary of their territory or world as marked by four Sacred Mountains, one at each point of the compass. The basin, the area surrounded by these mountains, was created by the gods as the home of the pueblo; the mountains were designed to protect and contain the powers and forces emanating from the center; so the landscape as space, as container, existed before the pueblo itself. In many cases these four mountains were more than fifty miles distant, and played no part in the daily life of the people. They were sacred for several reasons: they had been placed there by the gods for protection, each contained a lake or pond that was associated with the spirits of the ancestors, each had a sacred shrine, and each on occasion was the object of a solemn pilgrimage. Furthermore, they not only protected the community from contact with the forces of chaos and evil in the world beyond, but also served to reflect the beneficent spirits coming from the center. The landscape thus demonstrated the Pueblo belief that the spirits, or powers, emerging from the center ultimately returned to that center; just as the first human beings emerged from the underworld at a certain opening, and would, according to myth, return to the underworld at the same place. This pulsation was characteristic of all life. "Although the earth is believed to have no rotary movement," Rik Pinxten remarks in his book, *Anthropology of Space,* on the natural philosophy of the Navajo, "it is subjected to long-term expansions and contractions on a cosmic scale. After creation, it is said, the earth (and the sky) was stretched from the center toward the periphery. . . . It is likely that the end of the world will see its shrinking back into the center, thus realizing a perfectly symmetrical, pulsating movement over the whole period."

The boundary as the container of psychic power is not our modern way of defining or delimiting a landscape. Yet, in our remoter, European past, the same kind of wilderness boundary with the same magical properties seems to have prevailed: the primeval forest—half natural frontier and half mythical barrier— was common in the concept of the *March* (or mark). It was not to be penetrated by outsiders and only on sacred errands could it be visited by the members of the landscape community. The divinely ordained boundary is typical of the group that seeks to isolate itself from contact with others and considers itself as the product, the offspring, of a particular spot on the face of the earth. In the prehistoric European landscape there is, however, no suggestion of "pulsation": expansion, slow but persistent, is the destiny of our landscapes; the boundary eventually becomes an instrument of contact and confrontation.

The frontier of mountain and forest could be called the outermost of the three zones (or rings) surrounding and protecting the most sacred of spaces—the shrine in the village itself. The frontier region, partly because of its remoteness and possible danger, was exclusively the domain of the village men, who went there to cut logs that were used in roofing their houses, to hunt big game in the autumn, and to honor and maintain those special shrines and lakes that were identified with the ancestors. Closer to the village was the more open area of brush and grass and what we would now call rangeland—a vast region of foothills, canyons, and hidden valleys. Here it was that the men and women of the pueblo, usually in groups and on scheduled days or weeks, went to collect the various plants, stones, and kinds of earth they used in their crafts, or in their cooking, or as medicine—herbs, grasses, berries, flowers, as well as small game. Ortiz, in *The Tewa World,* calls this the zone of the flat-topped hills, of which each "has a cave and/or tunnels running through it," and all are inhabited by certain supernatural beings. He identifies the hills with labyrinths, and quotes from Mircea Eliade to the effect that "often the object of the labyrinth is to defend a 'centre' in the first and strictest sense of the word, it represented access to the sacred, to immortality, to absolute reality, by means of initiation." And he adds: "There is a firmly grounded belief in Tewa thought that women and children should never venture beyond that area of the Tewa world bounded by [the sacred flat-topped hills and their supernatural inhabitants]. Ecologically this works out quite well, for the types of subsistence activities in which women and children are permitted to participate are almost entirely limited to the river valley and foothills—well within this boundary."

The third of these concentric rings (or zones) in the prehistoric landscape was much smaller. It contained the irrigated garden plots or fields of the villages, the stream that watered them, and the abundance of grass and trees in the valley. The last zone, actually the center of the whole landscape, was the pueblo, the village itself, in the heart of which was the most sacred of shrines: called the Earth Mother, Earth Navel, Middle Place. This was in the village plaza.

Although the pueblo inhabitants perceived a concentric ordering of their landscape, with the four cardinal directions clearly defined, in actuality such an order was rarely visible. Yet, because by divine decision it *did* exist, its presence was assumed. The three rings—four if the village itself is included—differed ecologically, but resembled one another and merged into a unit, inasmuch as they served to protect the center, although different elements in the population used each of them. The garden (or farming zone) was identified with the various households. It is to be remembered, however, that each of the concentric zones had a divine, not a human, origin. It was a god who first planted corn in the irrigated garden plot, and the cultivated land belonged not to the individual cultivator, but to the community and ultimately to the central shrine.

Although largely fictitious, this concentric organization of natural (or god-created) spaces seems totally foreign to our Western ways of organizing landscape spaces. But again it resembles the system that once existed in much of medieval Europe, where there were three, instead of four, rings: first came the village with its fence or enclosure, then the plowed fields, then the open grazing land merging into the margin of the forest (or *March*) which surrounded the human-made landscape. This composition of three rings of diminishing intensity of use was seen as duplicating the cosmic order: the Almighty in the center, surrounded by heaven, which in turn rested on the earth. The difference between the two schemes (and it is a profound difference) is that, in the European version, the center, the heart of the village, represented temporal power that is dominated by the urge to expand.

Economic historians will point out that this expansionism in the European landscape was partly the result of the presence of domestic animals. The European villager possessed cows, horses, pigs, and sheep. The open space, the equivalent of the Pueblo ring of sacred, flat-topped hills, was used as a public area for grazing livestock and for the collecting of those small resources; as farming consumed more and more land, the grazing and small-scale exploitation invaded and helped to destroy the nearby forest. Yet, from a different perspective, it is possible to see a strong similarity between the way the large open space of each landscape was put to popular use. What both landscapes have is a *common:* an area open to all bona fide inhabitants of the community, where they can satisfy their basic domestic needs. The common is never divided, it is never permanently cultivated, and nothing taken from the common can be sold or bartered. It is the place where nature's bounty is available to all who live nearby. It is the place where a villager is reminded of the humble origins of the community: the coming together of people for survival. Both the European common and the area of "sacred, flat-topped hills" are infinitely rich in tradition, but perhaps the most vivid picture we retain of them is the peaceful presence of the women and children of the village, the atmosphere of work and play combined, and the unseen presence of the guardian spirits.

The parallel between that innermost ring of the Pueblo landscape and the ring of medieval farmlands is striking. In both cases the land under cultivation was allotted to the various families according to their needs. In both cases the village authorities regulated the crops grown and the dates of planting and harvesting. Just as the clearing and opening of the Pueblo irrigation ditch was celebrated as a public rite, the church bell in Europe announced when work was to begin and the appropriate service held.

As for the pueblo (or, strictly speaking, the village), that is a subject for architects and urbanists to explore. Of all the spaces in the prehistoric landscape, this one seems the easiest to interpret, though there are, I suspect, profound differences between them regarding the location of the dwellings and their function.

I have suggested that, despite the undeniable distinctions between the two sets of landscapes, there are strong similarities: in both the same part-mythical and part-topographical-strategic boundary; the same veneration and fear of the forest with its ancestral associations; the same areas of common, undivided land; and the same isolation from neighbors and the wider world. In brief, the landscapes resemble one another in terms of large-scale, spatial organization. This is no new discovery. Many modern theories of community planning and land use have maintained that the central village (or town) is always the focal point in any traditional landscape. It occupies the site of the original settlement and inherits some of its sanctity. It is the first area to be provided with defenses; it is the seat of legal authority, often of church authority, and the headquarters of administration and of wealth; it is the coming together of all communications, and all power radiates from this town into the surrounding forest or wasteland, transforming it into productive countryside. It was thus that J. H. von Thünen in the early nineteenth century defined the "Isolated State" and that W. Cristaller demonstrated his theory of his Central Place: a centripetal landscape composed of concentric zones (or rings) about the local capital.

Yet, when we look at the two kinds of landscape and compare them as pictures, as images, as glimpses of the human-made world, we see at once that they are, in fact, totally dissimilar. And we have no trouble in pinpointing the source of dissimilarity: the prehistoric Pueblo landscape, having no domestic animals, has no roads, no fences, no plowed fields, no fields devoted to grazing or the raising of feed; its impact on the environment surrounding the village and its fields is minimal.

I have long been a strong advocate of learning about landscapes from firsthand experience: by looking at it, traveling through it, even living in it, however briefly. But I assume that this immediate contact is a preliminary, and *only* a preliminary, inquiry to another, more thoughtful, contemplation. A certain kind of photography has encouraged many of us to rely exclusively on the instantaneous approach to the landscape as aesthetic object, just as a certain kind of travel writing has encouraged a hasty economic or cultural appraisal that is oriented to the tourist. If the study of landscapes is to acquire intellectual appeal, then it must venture into the field of cultural comparisons, and into the philosophical origins of these patterns that are inscribed on the surface of the earth.

I said in the beginning of the essay that, in my view, a landscape is not simply an organization of space, but also an organization of time. It is more accurate to say that every landscape reveals, often in indirect ways, a concept of time as it relates to space. Over the past generation we have grown acutely aware of how these concepts differ from one culture, and one period, to another, though it remains difficult to see how these differences influence the character of the landscape. E. T. Hall, in his book, *The Dance of Life,* brilliantly analyzes the manner in which societies have measured and defined time, philosophically and scientifically. But when we ask ourselves the question, "How does his or her concept of time affect the way the Pueblo farmer goes about daily work?" we find no easy answer. In his essay, "An American Indian Model of the Universe" from *Language, Thought and Reality,* Benjamin Lee Whorf states: "The Hopi language contains no reference to 'time' either explicit or implicit." He adds that the Hopi language is nevertheless "capable of describing correctly . . . all observable phenomena in the universe." For our purpose it is simpler to say that the Hopi have none of our sense of history. Fred Eggan, in *New Perspectives on the Pueblos,* remarks that, in the Pueblo worldview, "in contrast to the organization of space, time is less important. There is little speculation on origins beyond the emergence, and beyond the yearly cycles based on solar and lunar movements, there is little concern for the passage of time." The Pueblo calendar, like that of many agricultural societies, is based on recurrent celestial or natural events, such as the solstice sunrise, the alternation of summer and winter, the growth of crops, and the need for rain. It recognizes a *cyclical* notion of time, the yearly repetition of certain occurrences.

Compared with eternity, the passage of years and decades is irrelevant and illusory. Change and innovation are unwelcome and, when possible, ignored. Thus, any unusual action or happening in the Pueblo world is dismissed as actually the repetition of some similar event in the past. In a like manner, all modifications of the natural environment, or of the creatures in it, are justified as a restoration, a return to the original form as it is determined by the gods.

As a matter of fact, the Pueblo Indians modified the natural order in their various landscapes in several important ways. They introduced irrigation (a respectable engineering accomplishment in itself), developed several varieties of corn suited to the Southwestern climate, developed a variety of short-fibered cotton, and planted beans in containers, kept in the relatively warm and frost-free kivas during the latter part of the winter so the sprouts could later be transplanted to their gardens. Yet each of these revolutionary interventions was subsequently integrated into the cyclic religious calendar, and none was allowed to alter the agricultural routine, just as the turkey, which the Pueblo Indians (or perhaps their Mexican forebears) domesticated, was seen simply as the source of a supply of feathers for ceremonial use.

By contrast the prehistoric farmers of northwestern Europe learned at an early date to alter the composition of the soil in their small fields, and learned to ditch and drain marshlands, to say nothing of breeding livestock for special attributes. Time, and the slow process of growth and evolution, were thus outwitted by human intervention.

In short, the two landscapes each possessed their own concept of time. It has often been remarked that the Pueblo ceremonial calendar paid little or no attention to such private or individual events as birth or marriage or the passage of years or even to an individual's death, and, in fact, the absence of well-defined graveyards or grave markers in the Pueblo landscape confirms this characteristic. But, for the individual, time was a *linear* quality, a progress toward a definite goal or event, and it is this linear concept of time, acknowledged in Christian doctrine and especially in the concept of a last judgment, that has characterized our European-American culture. Our landscape, in theory at least, is tended and perfected for that ultimate end, the ultimate accounting. And on the individual scale it has for centuries been characterized by concern for both the future and for the past: by the presence of monuments and reminders and by unceasing preparations for the future in the form of community storage facilities, concern for family perpetuation, and, of course, incessant expansion in spatial terms. No more common expression of this linear concept of time can be found than in the church bell, telling not only the passage of cyclical time, but marking the human-made hours that remind us they are to be spent profitably and piously.

While it is obvious that neither landscape was exclusively loyal to one notion of time, that each of them observed, however intermittently, the other concept—cyclical or linear—it is no less obvious that the distinction between them is, to a large degree, based on two diametrically opposed concepts of reality: *timeless eternity*, manifesting itself in the yearly recurrence of the seasons; and *time as a gift*, to be accounted for when history finally comes to an end.

Calvin W. Stillman

# Learning from Landscape and Nature

CALVIN W. STILLMAN was born in 1915 in New York City, and was raised there. He received an A.B. in economics from Harvard College, an M.S. in agricultural economics from Iowa State College, and a Ph.D. in economics from the University of Chicago. He was a lecturer in economics at Roosevelt College in Chicago from 1948 to 1951, an instructor and assistant professor of social sciences at the University of Chicago from 1951 to 1956, a faculty member of the New School for Social Research in New York City from 1963 to 1967, and a professor of environmental resources at Rutgers University from 1968 to 1978. "To be on the University of Chicago faculty is my greatest single lifetime satisfaction; to have implanted the idea at Rutgers that nature is a humanity, rather than a science, is also gratifying." Retired since 1978, Professor Stillman resides in New York City.

I CAN DISCUSS "landscape" only in terms of my own reactions to those I have seen and experienced, either in a particular place or in reproduction, and I have come to appreciate two types: those that are familiar, and those that are worth traveling to—let us say simply, unfamiliar sights.

A familiar landscape belongs in a personal sense of the natural. Everything is where it ought to be. Details of landscapes have associations. They can arouse memories of persons and events long past. We all know the rising elation of coming home after a time away; of seeing familiar detail after familiar detail as home itself is approached. Such a landscape is a continuity, as I have heard Alan Gussow say. (Of course, few of these details aroused any reaction at all while one lived among them.) The home landscape can offer stability, reassurance, propriety, the familiar, a profound sense of belonging—feelings that are personal and idiosyncratic. No two persons will see a home environment in the same way. The bits are integrated into a single mind.

A landscape exists only for its viewer or listener. What one sees or hears is a function of what is going on in that person's mind at the moment, and of what memories and associations a landscape has for the individual, whether that landscape is real or imagined. "Nature always wears the color of the spirit," Emerson wrote.

One is always aware of one's environment. If a segment is particularly pleasing, such as a landscape is, that is fine. At times an individual is forced to exploit the environment for all the succor it can give. This has happened to me at times of great crisis: I have stared out at whatever was around me as if to ask my environment for some sign of meaning, for some sign that life will go on. I have always in such instances sought to run away to a bit of natural environment, to take a walk, to go somewhere with a view where I could reflect and collect myself. I have scoured the landscape for symbols of support. This is "reading the landscape" in a very special way, at a time of great personal need.

Once I was caught in an ocean current and found myself unable to swim back to shore. What little I could see—waves to eye level, a bit of distant beach, a fringe of trees, a figure or two—and my personal inability to get from here to there gave me a sense of identity in a landscape of such lasting clarity that I wonder if this is the root of the folktale that before the eyes of a drowning man passes his entire life.

Great landscapes always involve a personal response. This can have startling manifestations.

A few years ago I took two professors of landscape architecture on a walk in the Highlands along the Hudson River in New York. I led them up an undistinguished path through scraggly woods. I did not tell them my objective. The trail ended abruptly on a ledge that yielded a magnificent view over rolling hills and distant terrain, without a sign of human habitat in sight except for the two World Trade Center towers we knew to be at the lower end of Manhattan, forty-five miles to the south. Each professor was startled. One said nothing. The other leapt to the highest point, flung out his arms, and cried out, "I want to preach!"

Let us say the landscape intensified the professor's proclivity of the moment. Any broad-scale experience can have the same effect—the sea from a moving vessel, the sky on those rare occasions when one is made aware of it. I think a landscape leads us to see into ourselves, to feel a personal relation with something profound and mercifully transitory, and in the process to value ourselves anew. Not to be uplifted by a lovely view may be a symptom of emotional troubles. I cannot speak for those who cannot see.

I find all familiar landscapes very relaxing, gruntling perhaps, reminiscent of a seventeenth-century Flemish painting. Because in every familiar view I know where I am, I know my place, I know my relationship to the objects and the people I can see. This, after all, is the essence of the function of nature; of order in a personally supportive arrangement. With a familiar view, as in any natural setting, one is in contact with one's own subconscious. What is felt cannot be verbalized. Susanne Langer points out, in *Mind: An Essay on Human Feeling,* the essential similarity between "enjoyment of nature" and "appreciation of music." Neither can be verbalized.

A familiar view seen from an accustomed and comfortable place—a hammock, a penthouse, or an armchair on a porch—can have an effect that is relaxing to a fault. It can become soporific, addictive, perhaps more so than anything else in a landscape. A particularly frightening form of landscape addiction occurs in night driving on freeways, with little traffic. The white line on the right shoulder makes artistic curves as it bends gently to the right or left, and disappears beyond the headlights' beams. The red spots of taillights ahead can be part of an aesthetic design that appeals for itself, and that distracts entirely from the lethal potentials of high speed, heavy objects, and the need to be in control of the situation. I find that, in these lovely and sometimes charming night compositions, my mind wanders—just as it does when I look at a lovely view—to subjects far removed from the situation at hand. Each setting—looking at a lovely landscape, and sitting in the front seat of a car at night—is conducive to really serious conversation with a chosen companion, or with the self.

Drug users have told me of magnificent landscapes they have seen on their hallucinogenic "trips." The mechanics of this I do not understand. Are these memories akin to dreams, fictions of individual minds at rest, or is there a physiological explanation? At any rate, drug users are not the only addicts around. Persons who use landscapes for reverie solve for a while their problems of identity. They may take leave of reality and dream dreams. If they do it on a lonely highway with white lines and little red dots far away in front, they may be doing it at their peril. Over forty thousand people die each year on these U.S. landscapes, many of them at night.

Familiar views are understandable. The viewer knows his or her relation to what is in sight. Familiar views often are taken for granted. They are particularly useful in stressful situations—in times of emotional need, in homecomings. Views less familiar need something special to tie the viewer to the landscape. Chief of these may be repute. We all know we should be impressed by the Rocky Mountains and the Alps or by Milford Sound in New Zealand. Structural elements help: something interesting in the foreground; a winding road or a stream that ties foreground to background.

It takes effort to get to an unfamiliar landscape. The anticipated experience must be worth it. People pay money to go on tours to look at things in a landscape, and expect value in exchange. They come to see "the sights." A sight, I submit, is gobbled down in one gulp; it is a whole. It isn't read as a familiar landscape is, with its multiplicity of details, each with its own meaning. A sight is eminently photographic. Many tourists seek snapshots as good as the ones they remember from the travel brochures. They do not linger over the scene; they go on to the next photo opportunity. Such landscapes are discontinuous and episodic, because they are basically without personal associations.

I suppose the most dramatic unfamiliar landscape I ever saw was that from Dharmsāla in northern Punjab State, India. I had

*"Just do me one favor, will you? Don't tell me
what it reminds you of."*

gone there to have a look at the Dalai Lama. The village sits on
a high ridge, with a grand view to the north across a valley to
the main body of the Himalayas. As I sipped buttered tea in a
shop in the village, I could see countless peaks, all in the five-to-
seven-thousand-meter range, marching across the skyline. They
reminded me of a group of saws, lined up at eye level to have their
teeth sharpened. The distance between the mountains and men,
across the intervening valley, deprived me of personal contact
with any of the peaks. They were just shapes, no better than a
picture in a travel brochure.

I really do not enjoy looking at a mountain unless I have a
chance to get my feet and hands on it. I like to look at whatever I

am planning to scramble up, and I like to look down at where I came from. I feel humbled on the way up, and proud on the way down. I cannot be impersonal about any differences in relief in which I am involved in autolocomotion. It doesn't take a very large hill to attract my interest.

Most of my life has been spent in the well-watered northeast of the United States, and most of that time in hard-rock country—the New England Upland with its rugged shores and granite hills. Of particular importance to me has been the Upland's long and narrow extension through the Hudson River Highlands to Reading, Pennsylvania. I bore my friends with accounts of the Reading Spur—of the similarities of geology, road patterns, tree species, relict mines, Presbyterian churches, failed farms, forgotten large estates, religious institutions, summer camps for children, and large tracts held for years for no apparent rational purpose whatsoever. What appeals to me most about this country is the least visible element—the bedrock, exposed only here and there. The bedrock is in long ridges, crumpled perpendicularly to the collision hundreds of millions of years ago of Africa with North America. Now these ridges block the northwestward expansion of the New York metropolitan region. They are crossed by few highways. They have bankrupted railroads. Thanks to recent glaciers, they have little soil for farming. They discourage developers; building sites are too rough and rocky; soil percolation tests fail regularly. With the passing of the railroad-tie industry, and charcoal burning, these hills are resuming their appearance of 1609, as Robert Juet noted it in his journal. Juet was first mate of a ship named *Half Moon* (Hendrick Hudson, Captain).

I have lived in other North American environments: among the sands and pines of the Southeast, on the prairies of Iowa, among the winding rivers of eastern Maryland, in Chicago, Savannah, St. Louis, and New York City. The only environment that resonates "home" to me, other than the New England Upland, is that of the Mogollon Rim in east-central Arizona, where I spent the summer of 1937 on a birding expedition. Affection for this landscape I attribute to hands-on experience, scrambling up mesas, camping in difficult sites, getting the car across roadless spaces, digging it out of soggy arroyos. It was an environment with which I learned to cope. It was unlike my experience at the edge of the Himalayas.

The meanings of the word "nature" are legion. The same word can mean the intrinsic qualities of anything, the order of the physical universe, or a primitive state of existence. For most people, nature means primarily the nonhuman world. In the vernacular, it is a system of order that appeals to many of us who seek a larger and comfortable understanding of the world, but who are not excited by the strictures of the scientific method.

My own view is that nature is a personal sense of supportive propriety, and that having an effective personal view of nature always involves three elements: living things, a feeling of reciprocal relations with those living things, and an escape to "infinity"—in space, or in time. I am most assured about the importance of a personal view of nature when I read Goethe's statement about the same:

> *Nature surrounds us and entwines us; we cannot leave her, we cannot penetrate her further. Without invitation or warning she gathers us up into the cycles of her dance, and propels us along with herself until, exhausted, we fall from her arm. She appears eternally in new forms. What exists now has never been before. What once was shall never reappear. Everything is new, yet is long-established.*
>
> *We are apart from nature, but we live in her midst. She communicates with us continuously, but still keeps her secret. We continue to affect Nature, and yet have no control over her. Her entire thrust seems to favor individuality, but her concern is not with individuals. Nature is forever building and destroying; there is no way to enter her workshop. . . .*[1]

A great symbol of the order that is found in nature is the tree, which may be useful for its fruit and for its shade, but mostly because it belongs where it stands freely, has always been where its roots fall. The tree as a symbol in Western society has never been explored fully, by the writer or the scholar.

The tree as a symbol for the order in nature should not be confused with the forest. The forest derives from the royal hunting preserves of medieval times, and from the wilderness, that bane of early European settlers who were determined to establish themselves on the western shores of the Atlantic. Wilderness has a wholly new role in contemporary society, however, as it represents the last resort of untrammeled nature, that place where no one should be allowed to enter, for any human impact would be destructive.

For years I have suggested that we should create an imaginary national park, and publicize it in coffee-table books with lovely color photographs. But its location would be kept secret, so no person could enter its sacred grounds and thus despoil the sanctuary. The park's greatest asset would be its tangible absence from human life.

1. The quotation is taken from the essay he sent to Anna Amalia, Duchess of Weimer. The translation is by Elfriede M. Roth-Poirier.

Instead, worship of the tree has come down to us in those relict plantations of pine we see on private estates and surrounding reservoirs, most notably in New England, but also in the South and the Middle West. It comes down to us via America's national forests, and in the profession of forestry, which has become increasingly perplexed over its proper "management" role in the world. Multiple use can be a confusing concept when it involves a piece of land.

Nature, by my definition, is important as an emotional support for anyone, whatever happens to be the chosen instrument. I have mentioned familiar places, familiar people, and nonhuman living things. This sort of support is vital for emotional stability, and for growth and learning. This sort of support, consequently, should be of special interest to teachers who introduce students to the art of reading and interpreting landscapes and places.

My favorite definition of education (and I cannot recall to whom I owe it) is that education is the enhancement of the possible. This establishes education as the matter of facilitating an individual's growth toward a higher level of competence in dealing with the student's own particular personal environment; with the opportunities and the constraints she or he faces. This disestablishes education as a simple purveyor of facts. It avoids the question, "What is a fact?"

How can a teacher use nature, in general, and landscape, in particular, to enhance, for his or her students, their realms of the possible? A teacher can draw attention to the importance of "the natural," first, by sympathetic presentation of appealing elements in the proximate environment—landscapes being high on the list—and, second, by an historical presentation of the meanings of natural forms to peoples over time. This unlocks feelings which may have been repressed.

My aim in teaching college undergraduates was not to arouse them, to "increase their awareness," or to persuade them of an environmental value. I encouraged them, simply, to release their own feelings, and to learn what others have said, sung, danced, or otherwise depicted on the subject of nonhuman living things over the years. I treated feelings regarding nature as one of the humanities; one of the great good things of life, bringing in when I could literature, painting, music, dance, and sculpture. Then to keep the class in the real world, I introduced advocates of quite other values—exploitation of minerals, damming rivers for power and recreation, spraying crops and forests for insect "control"—and required the class to deal with these lively current perceptions which might seriously be at variance with their own. I wanted the students to deal with the whole world, the real world, not the private world of their satisfactions.

We read together in class such books as *The Urban Villagers* by Herbert J. Gans, an account of the elimination of a North Boston slum on the initiative of the local Brahmins. Gans reported the shattering effect on the residents of their familiar urban landscapes being reduced to rubble. Their neighborhood had been loved; their houses had flowers and window boxes, and tiny backyard gardens. The people had their familiar places, and above all they had each other, a supportive and family-oriented grouping of people learning to adapt, though transplanted from their village life in Italy.

I asked each student to complete a project on some aspect of nature that had meaning for her or him, and to present it to the entire class for comment and criticism. I wanted to encourage exploration, discovery, and reflection of one's self.

I experimented with centering attention on reading and interpreting landscape. This had the great value of getting all eyes to look out, together. It avoided the problems of identity in the classroom. Students are very sensitive beings, particularly in the presence of their peers. With everyone looking at the same objective bit of environment—even if it is just the blackboard, partly obscured by the teacher's back—I found it easy to talk about what is out there. I tried to do it in personal terms, to demonstrate my own vulnerabilities, feelings, appreciations, human responses to the landscape or other object under consideration. If a blackboard is all there is to use, it's a great time to try sketching; no one will care if you are no Rembrandt or Cézanne.

I tried always to present a personal feeling for the object under consideration. I never allowed to intrude any extraneous system such as nomenclature, or a scientific discipline. I used whatever associations came to mind. For instance, here is how I might have run on with a class on a field trip in the Highlands near the Hudson River:

*There's the river, flowing through all you can see. It used to be the only "roadway" through this countryside. Indian remains have been found down there, on that point. Do you see where I am pointing? They must have come here for the shad every spring, for many years. You can find fishhooks and arrowheads. The terraces you see off to the north—marked by the slightly different vegetation—were once shorelines of a lake, when the glacier had dammed the gorge there, and was melting slowly, tens of thousands of years ago. To the left was a protected route that George Washington used to get supplies up here for his*

*Continental Army from Easton, Pennsylvania. The British were never able to cut off his lines. The whole valley was being farmed a century and a half ago. The peak of agriculture marked by the opening of the Erie Canal; land has been "brushing up" ever since. Can you tell what the landscape right here looked like when Henry Hudson's men first saw it? The evidence is all in the trees around us.*

Or I might have taken a class to an urban area, and said something like this:

*All of these houses were built a bit over a century ago. Only one family lived in each one, at first. The owners were prosperous merchants and manufacturers. At that time there was much manufacturing done in the city. Labor was cheap. All the mansions had servants living in; that's why each house had two entrances from the street; one for upstairs, one for downstairs. There were very few telephones and fewer, if any, cars back then. Some of the larger houses had room for carriages and horses; most horses were kept in stables a few blocks away. Houses were heated by furnaces. Coal was delivered by wagons, then carried on men's backs in sacks across the sidewalk to a coal chute in the front wall. You can see where the chute has been bricked up in most of these houses. How are the houses heated now? How do people cook? Streets were all two-way then. Do you know why traffic moves to the right side of center? In the mother country it always moved to the left, so a mounted man could have his sword-arm free on the dangerous side. Construction in those days was of stone and brick. Brick was cheaper; it was made up the river where good red clay was available, and brought down by barge. Stone was used largely for decoration; it's an expensive material. None of these buildings had steel frames, or steel beams. Wooden beams hold up floors and roofs. That's one reason firefighters don't like to enter here when a house is on fire; the whole structure can collapse if a beam burns through.*

I do not hold with the South Asian doctrine that "all is illusion." I do, however, suspect that a great deal of what each of us sees around us, as in a landscape, is symbolic or representative of something important. These symbols must be respected by the teacher, though it is easy to see how symbols can be misused if carried too far.

Once I was a member of New York State's Hudson River Valley Commission. We were charged with protecting the scenic values of the shorelines from the ravages of commercial development. Our powers were limited, but we used them as best we could. At most, we could delay developments for a while, which gave us time to suggest compromises. One plan that came before the commission was to erect an apartment house on Warburton Avenue in Yonkers, New York. Warburton Avenue at that point had a lovely view across the Hudson River to the Palisades in New Jersey. Citizens strolling by had assumed the steep slope from the avenue down to the river's edge was parkland. It was assumed to be safely "natural." Unfortunately the land was privately owned, and developers found a way to build on what was a very awkward site. Their structure would block the view completely.

Our commission held a hearing, and many people came to state their opinions. All but two were opposed to the project, bitterly. Of the exceptions, one represented the building-trade workers of affluent Westchester County, New York. He wanted the jobs the building would provide. The other was an elderly gentleman of Italian extraction who spoke late in the proceedings. He favored the project, he said, because it would replace an area that "just had trees in it" with a fine brick wall. He did not mention the view past the trees.

The next day I met my class on "Ideas of Nature," and I reported my experience of the evening before. After class two students waited to speak with me. "We're Italian," they said. "We think brick walls are beautiful. The old man was right."

Margaret Mead once suggested that learning opportunities should be modeled less on ladders than on landing nets. Both can lead up, but a ladder requires progress in one mode only. A landing net allows one to scramble sideways also; to find one's own way up.

A wise teacher recognizes that students have private lives, and personal satisfactions. (And, by extension, a wise planner recognizes that citizens in a community do, too.) Precious among these are assured feedback positions; a good home is one, a reassuring sense of nature is another. A sense of nature can become a microcosm for an individual of the larger, more real world. Within the private world an individual can work out some of the problems facing him or her in reality, get it all together, and emerge. We find individuals experimenting with introducing into "nature" many of the problems they face in the larger world: competition, predation, death. Among bird lovers there are specialists who admire raptors.

We need sensitive teachers who can deal imaginatively with students' perceptions of nature. The great frame in which nature is made evident is landscape. To read a landscape can become a means for reviewing one's inmost thoughts.

Dale F. Ritter

# The Geological Perception of Landscape

DALE F. RITTER was born in 1932 in Allentown, Pennsylvania, and was raised there. He received a B.S. in education and B.S. in geology from Franklin and Marshall College, and completed an M.A. and a Ph.D. in geology at Princeton University. His honors include the Christian R. and Mary F. Lindback Award for Distinguished Teaching from the Lindback Foundation in 1970, the AMOCO Foundation Outstanding Teacher Award at Southern Illinois University in 1979, and in 1985 the first Southern Illinois University Outstanding Scholar Award. Dr. Ritter served on the Panel of the Quaternary Geology/Geomorphology Division of the Geological Society of America from 1982 to 1984 and as chairman of the Division in 1988 and 1989. Professor Ritter has been on the editorial board of several geological journals, has contributed over fifty articles to refereed scholarly journals, and is the author of *Process Geomorphology* (William C. Brown, 1978; second edition, 1986). He was a member of the faculty at Franklin and Marshall College from 1964 to 1972 and at Southern Illinois University at Carbondale from 1972 to 1990, where he was a professor of geology. He is presently executive director of the Quaternary Sciences Center of the Desert Research Institute in Reno, Nevada.

IT IS PROBABLY apparent that the question addressed by this book (*What is landscape?*) is unanswerable. This assessment may be unsettling, but its truth rests in the fact that people look at landscapes in so many different ways. Some of us, for example, appreciate landscapes for their aesthetic qualities: landscape is simply there to be enjoyed and to instill in each of us certain feelings and emotions that are difficult to explain. Any work of scenic art or poetry represents one person's attempt to communicate those intangible feelings. In a different viewpoint, landscapes are there to be used in some practical way. Geographers understand how the ingredients of landscape control human activities such as trade, and how they prophesied the development of civilizations and the growth of nations. Military leaders use their understanding of landscapes for planning, supply routes, and topographic advantage in battle. Engineers and architects learn to use the landscape for structural design and, in some cases, to combine that design with the natural beauty surrounding a construction site.

The point is that practitioners in each of these human endeavors all look at the same landscape, but see something different and ask different questions. Some accept landscape as nature's gift to be viewed and enjoyed according to individual likes and dislikes. Others recognize landscape as something to be used in an efficient and purposeful manner. In light of these common perceptions of landscape, it is my purpose to point out that geologists consider landscape in an entirely different way. Geologists are not concerned primarily with landscape aesthetics (though we, like others, enjoy its beauty), nor with how best to utilize its character (though we, like others, are conscious of and concerned about our environment). Instead, we view landscapes as physical entities that are amenable to scientific investigation. We try to understand how and why any landscape got to be the way it is, and therefore our fundamental goal is to determine the *reason* for landscape. Because we know that the clues to achieving that goal rest within the landscapes themselves, in essence they become our natural laboratories. Clearly, landscapes are not there to be enjoyed or used; they are there to be studied. This perception of landscape is not given as an apology or confession, but merely as a revelation of fact. Neither is it intended to suggest that our concept of landscape is somehow better than the others. It is simply different.

Anyone who has traveled across the United States knows that large portions of our country have characteristics that set them apart from other regions. Landscapes, therefore, change from one place to another, often so gradually and imperceptibly that we cannot be sure where the change begins. The reason for this variability is that the building blocks of a landscape, called *landforms*, are reflecting the gradual change of external factors such as climate and rock type. Major landforms are features such as mountains, plains, and plateaus. Each of these, however, may be dotted with smaller landforms which result from the action of some local phenomenon such as a glacier or river. Thus, landscapes come in a variety of packages, the internal contents of which consist of a hierarchy of landforms.

In the United States about forty broad areas have landscape properties that are unique enough to set them apart as coherent units. These areas or surficial units are called *physiographic provinces,* and maps showing their boundaries can be found in almost every textbook of physiography. Each province is unique because it has a special combination of underlying rocks and prevailing climate, and it has experienced its own peculiar geologic history in terms of the time needed for its development and the types of events which occurred. Thus, each province displays landforms and other characteristics, such as relief, elevation, drainage pattern, and soils, which make it different from its neighbor. Even so, the distinction between one province and another may be very subtle. In fact, it may be something as simple as average elevation or prevailing vegetation. Clearly, some province differences may be apparent only to someone with a trained eye, or may require the use of analytical tools such as aerial photographs or topographic maps before they can be revealed. For example, most of you can easily note the landscape change from the Great Plains Province in Kansas to the Southern Rocky Mountains of Colorado and New Mexico, but it may be more difficult for you to ascertain differences between those same Kansas plains and the Central Lowlands Province of Illinois and Indiana. Nonetheless, they are different, and considerably so in the geological sense.

Although geologists have used physiographic provinces for decades as the initial step in making regional geological interpretations, it is probably unclear to you what physiographic provinces have to do with the geological perception of landscapes. After all, a province is hardly more than a region characterized by a peculiar set of building blocks. Artists can still find beauty in any physiographic province, and engineers can use province characteristics to make initial guesses as to how difficult it might be to build roads or bridges across the Rocky Mountains, for example, in comparison to the Great Plains. Therefore, at this juncture it is critical for you to understand that the primary reason for the existence of separate and tangible physiographic provinces *is* geology. In other words, the combination of traits that gives physiographic provinces their unique character is a function of phenomena that are distinctly geologic. In essence then, landscapes become the windows through which geologists can observe the more fundamental factors that control landscape character. Thus, the landscape itself is of secondary concern to geologists. The geological ingredients that are reflected in landscapes, however, are extremely important, and probably represent the primary and perhaps only reason that geologists ever consider landscapes at all.

Having said all this, it is now incumbent on me to explain how these geologic ingredients are transformed into the landforms that constitute the landscape. The study of landforms and the processes of their genesis is the concern of a scientific discipline called *geomorphology* (*geo* meaning earth, *morpho* meaning form). Since the beginning of the twentieth century, geologists have accepted the proposition by the great American geomorphologist, William Morris Davis (1850–1934), that landforms are a function of three things: structure, process, and time. In the Davisian sense, structure refers to two factors: (1) the type of rock underlying any given region; and (2) whether these rocks have been deformed (folded, faulted, or tilted) or still maintain horizontal rock layers, although they may have experienced an increase in elevation by vertical uplift.

Most of you probably know that geologists recognize three major categories of rocks, which are called *igneous, metamorphic,* and *sedimentary*. Rocks in these groups have significantly different modes of origin. Igneous rocks form when their constituent parts (minerals) crystallize during the cooling of molten liquids. The molten liquid might cool slowly within the earth or quickly if the liquid is extruded as the lava you have seen during a volcanic eruption. Sedimentary rocks are considerably different. Some sedimentary rocks, such as sandstones and shale, are created when mineral particles or rock fragments are eroded from older rocks and transported elsewhere. Eventually these particles are deposited, usually as a grain-by-grain accumulation that develops a distinct layering. Some sedimentary rocks, such as coal, form their layers by accumulation of organic debris, and others, such as limestone, by precipitation of minerals from bodies of standing water. Metamorphic rocks differ because they originate from older igneous or sedimentary rocks that are placed under increased heat or pressure. The older rocks simply change their properties and mineral composition while remaining in the solid state as they try to reach an equilibrium with the new heat and pressure conditions.

These different modes of origin give rocks a variety of mineral compositions and internal arrangements of their mineral grains. This is very significant because these factors determine how easily any rock at the surface will succumb to the ravages of weathering and erosion. Rocks that are rich in silica minerals and have tightly bound grains will strongly resist those processes, while other rocks having soluble minerals might only be weakly resistant. The variations produced allow the topography to be etched differentially with time, leaving areas of resistant rocks standing at high elevations and, conversely, the weak rocks occupying lower elevations. High standing mountains, for example (Sierra Nevada, Rocky Mountains, Blue Ridge of the Apapalachians), are commonly held up by granite, a tightly bound siliceous rock. Lowlands are often underlain by limestones (Great Valley of Pennsylvania, Shenandoah Valley of Virginia) which are very soluble in humid climates. It is noteworthy, however, that the same limestones placed in an arid climate may be highly resistant because not enough water is available to drive solution in an accelerated manner. This indicates that rock characteristics in and by themselves will not determine landscape—their interrelationships with other factors, in this case process mechanics driven by climate, are equally important.

The second major component of geomorphic structure is the degree of deformation which the rocks have experienced. In most cases, the basic frameworks of physiographic provinces are very large landforms that are intimately related to the regional style of deformation. In fact, these features have commonly been referred to as *forms of structure*. For example, three major plains areas occupy about half of the United States: (1) the Coastal Plain along the Atlantic Ocean and the Gulf Coast, (2) the Central Lowland and Great Plains Provinces stretching from Ohio to Wyoming, and (3) the Central Valley of California. Plains are formed of nearly horizontal sedimentary rocks which are usually close to sea level or, like the Great Plains west of the Mississippi River, rise very gradually to higher elevations. For all practical purposes they are undeformed and have not even undergone ver-

Columnar jointing on the Appalachian Trail near Compton Peak, south of Front Royal, Virginia, in Shenandoah National Park. Photograph by George F. Thompson, 1988.

The Platte River near Kearney, Nebraska. Photograph by Gregory Conniff, 1990.

tical uplift. Because of this, rivers traversing these areas (the Platte rivers in Nebraska) are not deeply entrenched, and the resulting topography has rather low relief. In contrast, plateaus, which are also underlain by flat-lying sedimentary rocks, usually stand at much higher elevations because they have been affected by vertical movements of the earth's crust. These regions, occupying about twenty-five percent of the United States, are characterized by deeply incised rivers and considerable topographic relief. For example, the Colorado Plateau Province stands well above five thousand feet in elevation and is crisscrossed with major canyons which formed because rivers developed increased erosive energy as the land surface rose. The Grand Canyon is an excellent example of this phenomenon.

Mountains, which also occupy twenty-five percent of the United States, are the most complex of the major landforms and structural styles. In some cases, they reflect major folds in the rocks caused by forces tending to squeeze the crust together (Southern Rocky Mountains, folded Appalachian Mountains of Pennsylvania). In other mountains, the forces involved caused large fractures, called *faults,* along which some blocks of the crust rose relative to other blocks (Central Rocky Mountains, Sierra Nevada, Basin and Range of Nevada). It is even possible that some mountain provinces (Cascade Range in the Pacific Northwest) are the result of volcanic activity. Mountains here are simply built up as large volcanic cones rising above the general level of the landscape.

We see, then, that major blocks of the earth's surface and the prevailing character of physiographic provinces are basically reflections of the fundamental geologic control which we call *geomorphic structure.* The embellishments impressed on those major frameworks are landforms (called *forms of process*) and physical properties that readily respond to process.

This brings us to the second factor in the Davisian triad of landform control, which we call process. *Geomorphic process* is defined as the action produced when a force induces a change, either chemical or physical, in the materials or forms at the earth's surface. In other words, process is the method by which one thing is produced from something else. Processes are logically divided into two major groups: those that function at the earth's surface, called *exogenic processes,* and those that operate inside the earth, known as *endogenic processes.* Some processes alter the surface configuration by deposition of materials, and therefore produce what are commonly known as constructional or depositional landscapes. Other processes modify the surface by erosion, which creates a destructional or erosional landscape.

Processes are driven by forces that emanate from some energy source and control the magnitude and rate of the action. The primary forces that control exogenic processes are climate and gravity. Most endogenic forces arise, of course, from the heat which ultimately drives the volcanic machine and determines the distribution and character of volcanic terrains. In addition, spatial variations in rock properties within the earth require adjustments such that each vertical column of rocks has the same total mass as its adjacent neighbor. In order to maintain this remarkable balance, large blocks of the earth are elevated or depressed by a significant internal process known as *isostasy*. It is isostatic adjustment that produces the uplift of large plateau provinces and provides the final gasp of mountain building. Isostasy also creates the vertical movements in regions that were covered by large glaciers during the most recent Pleistocene glacial stage, which ended about ten thousand years ago. Removal of the ice during deglaciation, or stripping of the land surface by erosion, leaves a regional deficiency in mass which is brought back into balance by isostatic uplift. Incidentally, the concept of isostasy was first recognized, but not named, by Leonardo da Vinci (1452–1519). Clearly, he was a gifted thinker who could comfortably perceive landscapes in any of the ways we have discussed.

Exogenic processes are accomplished by surficial agents such as rivers, glaciers, wind, groundwater, and ocean waves. What these agents do and how effectively they carry on erosive work depends on the balance between the magnitude of driving forces and the resistance provided in the geologic framework. Thus, erosional forms directly reflect an accommodation between process and geomorphic structure. For example, any given river may easily erode a shale or limestone but find it enormously difficult to erode a granite. The resulting landforms will be significantly different, although the process magnitude is the same. Conversely, different processes or processes operating at various magnitudes will produce landforms of variable character, although they are being impressed on a geological framework having the same geomorphic structure.

A similar control exists in the formation of depositional landforms. In these situations, the agent is expected to accomplish more work than is possible with the force provided to it. In most cases, the work involved is the transport of sediment load. If the load provided to the river or glacier is too great, deposition will occur and constructional landforms will result.

The third major control on landscapes is the factor of time. It is significant in a way that is very difficult for any of us to imagine, because human life expectancy is miniscule compared to

Photographer Frank Gohlke climbs the lava dome inside the crater of Mount St. Helens, Washington. Photograph by George F. Thompson, 1990.

the geologic time available to form or modify a landscape. A simple example will demonstrate this point. Suppose erosive processes remove 1.2 inches of rock from the top of the Rocky Mountains in a thousand years. Obviously that change in elevation is indiscernible during the lifetime of any single person. Yet, at that rate, one foot will be removed during ten thousand years, one hundred feet in a million years, and, significantly, ten thousand feet of surface lowering will be accomplished in one hundred million years. Thus, at a humanly imperceptible rate of erosion, it is possible not only to change the landscape of the Rocky Mountains, but also to eliminate them totally during a time interval that is minor compared to the total length of geological time. After all, we know that the earth is older than four billion years, indicating that the one-hundred-million-year interval needed to obliterate the Rocky Mountains is but a minor spasm in the enormity of geologic time.

Having vast amounts of time during which process work can be accomplished leads to the basic tenet of geoscience that *landscapes are subject to change.* Furthermore, it suggests that we should address several ancillary concepts which derive from the relationship between time and the geologic perception of landscape.

First, we can say with certainty that *regions occupied by particular landscapes have histories.* These histories are best revealed when the processes shaping the surface have occurred recently. For example, the landforms created during the last great stage of the Pleistocene epoch still dominate many of the landscapes in North America. Features such as moraines, formed by deposition of debris carried by ice sheets or mountain glaciers, are common in the Middle West region of the United States and in the piedmont zones of our great mountain systems. Additionally, the spectacular scenery in most of the mountain provinces is the result of accelerated glacial erosion which occurred during that same period. These landforms are not in equilibrium with modern climate, and therefore represent vestiges of the past, when conditions were different. They clearly are part of landscape history, and provide us with pieces of evidence needed to reconstruct geologic events that have long since ended. Unfortunately, as time passes and a new generation of landforms develops, the landscape, like human history, loses its focus, and the details of older events become fuzzy and finally lost.

Second, our simple analysis given above concerning time and erosion begs the question as to why we have any distinct landscapes at all. In other words, given the fact that minor erosion rates can remove the Rocky Mountains in a blink of the geologic eye, why isn't the earth's surface as featureless and monotonous as a billiard ball? The answer is that the exogenic processes that remove mass and gravitational energy as they lower the surface are counteracted by endogenic processes (isostasy, mountain building, volcanism) which replenish surface systems with new mass and energy. Thus, we are dealing with the greatest of earth cycles, one in which landmasses are created and destroyed as materials are transferred internally and externally from one place to another. This allows plains that existed in one period of time to be converted into mountains at some other time. Mountains, of course, must relinquish themselves to a similar but converse fate.

Because traces of history are lost from a landscape with time, the reconstruction of ancient landscapes is accomplished from clues recorded in the rocks. It is therefore pure geological interpretation which allows us to suggest that our modern Rocky Mountains and Colorado Plateau were once covered by shallow inland seas, and that mammoth dinosaurs roamed the coastal plains landscape adjacent to those vast bodies of water. Thus, visitors to Dinosaur National Monument in northwest Colorado and northeast Utah stand several thousand feet above the modern ocean. What they see in the rocks, however, is evidence of a shoreline landscape that has been changed in character and position by the effects of geological processes and time.

The third corollary of the time/landscape relationship springs logically from the others. To many, creation of landscape is analogous to the sculptor chipping away with mallet and chisel at earth materials. This follows because processes are nothing more than geological work that molds a discernable configuration from the same earth materials. Actually, however, the comparison is unreal because, *unlike the work of a sculptor, landscape never culminates as a finished product*. The work can never be completely done because the design is continuously altered as geomorphic processes and structures change with time. What we see in landscape today is merely a fleeting glimpse, a snapshot that freezes its character for a short moment in time. It hints at what it might have been at some earlier time and teases us into believing that we can predict what it will be in the future. But behind the conceptual facade is the nagging realization that it never was and never will be precisely the same as we see it now.

To summarize, geologists find in the landscape a challenge to their interpretive skills. The features we see tell us something, but the message is garbled by the maze of interrelationships that exist between the controlling factors. Rarely do we all agree about the geological meaning of a landscape, and arguments concerning various interpretations are common in the literature. Nonetheless,

The sculpted shoreline of Monterey Bay and peninsula with its famous Lone Cyprus and Seventeen-Mile Drive, Carmel, California. Photograph by Joseph Courtney White, 1992.

there is little dispute in the geological discipline about our perception of landscape. We believe that the landscapes admired by the artist and writer and used by the engineer and architect all begin with geology. This conclusion could easily be construed as the highest level of arrogance except for the undeniable fact it is true.

Landscapes are, for better or worse, significant parts of our natural earth. They were not dropped on us from outer space nor constructed by a breed of early human beings long since lost in the ashes of history. Instead, they are the surface manifestations of earth materials, dynamic earth processes, and time. Geologists can justifiably claim that phenomena within the realm of their discipline constitute the production lines of landscapes. As such they become the necessary forerunners of this remarkable surface quality that each of us inherited and all of us own.

# PART II

# Landscape as History

*The great lesson of history—*
*and this applies to all the arts—*
*is that the past cannot be recaptured*
*except in spirit.*

—LEWIS MUMFORD

# The Range of Vision: Landscape and the Far West, 1803 to 1850

E. N. Feltskog

E. N. FELTSKOG was born in 1935 in Chicago, Illinois, and was raised in that city. He received a B.A. in English and history from Augustana College, and completed an M.S. in history and English at Washington State University and a Ph.D. in literature and history at the University of Illinois, Urbana. His edition of Francis Parkman's *The Oregon Trail* (Wisconsin, 1969) was a Book-of-the-Month Club selection in 1975 and a History Book Club selection from 1982 to 1984. He has also served as editor for *Mahoment and His Successors* by Washington Irving (Wisconsin, 1971), *The Last of the Mohicans* by James Fenimore Cooper (State University of New York, 1982), and *The Two Admirals* by James Fenimore Cooper (State University of New York, 1990). He is a professor of English at the University of Wisconsin-Madison.

"IN THE BEGINNING," John Locke observed, "all the world was America"—without form to European eyes, and void of history and time. Two centuries of westward expansion beyond the first American experience of wilderness in the "Virginian Enterprize" brought "the American, this new man" (in Crèvecoeur's enduring phrase) to the western passes of the Appalachians and down toward the Kentucky and Ohio countries; as Virginians and Massachusetts men alike agreed, two centuries of westering had been barely long enough to draw designs of purpose and futurity upon these settled landscapes of the East, to sink savage origins in the progressive triumphs of "the rising glory of America." For New Englanders especially, as William Cronon has noted in *Changes in the Land*, "the shape of the landscape was a confirmation of the state of human society. Both underwent an evolutionary development from savagery to civilization."[1] Though James Fenimore Cooper recalled vagrant Indians and white squatters in Cooperstown as late as 1793, he and his generation lived in and by the promise of westward expansion, "betterments" spreading across the continent in a national program of physical and moral improvement. "Republican virtue" proposed the American farmer as the standard-bearer of democracy and progress, the real basis in wealth and idealism for successive stages or generations of civilization. To Thomas Jefferson and John Adams, to Cullen Bryant and Cooper no less than to Boone and Harrod in frontier Kentucky, landscape was both "virgin land" and the Great Mother of Republics, pregnant with history and futurity; to Jefferson's yeoman democrat as to Cooper's Leatherstocking or to Henry David Thoreau, East was time past and West was time to come: "Eastward I go only by force; but westward I go free," wrote Thoreau in his essay, "Walking."

By 1803, when (as his critics claimed) Jefferson "took" Louisiana for the freehold Republic and Virginian land-claims, the common ways of freedom and transformation lay westward. There the de-

1. William Cronon, *Changes in the Land: Indians, Colonists, and the Ecology of New England* (Hill and Wang, 1983), page 6.

spised squatter, relic of an earlier wilderness anarchy, became heroic in his solitude (like Boone himself), breaking a path for the very civilization he had fled in dismay. Like Leatherstocking, escaping from "the sound of the hammers" in Cooperstown to the western plains "beyond the Platte," the lonely borderer (like Boone on the Missouri frontier) might await the coming of those who, just as the Astorians, were bound on farther journeys than he could undertake:

*Here they met with Daniel Boone, the renowned patriarch of Kentucky, who had kept in the advance of civilization, and on the borders of the wilderness, still leading a hunter's life, though now in his eighty-fifth year. He had but recently returned from a hunting and trapping expedition, and had brought nearly sixty beaver skins as trophies of his skill. The old man was still erect in form, strong in limb, and unflinching in spirit; and as he stood on the river bank, watching the departure of an expedition destined to traverse the wilderness to the very shores of the Pacific, very probably felt a throb of his old pioneer spirit, impelling him to shoulder his rifle and join the adventurous band.*[2]

Though he was speaking of American Indians, John Quincy Adams might equally have been denouncing the wilderness seclusion of a Boone or a Crockett when he demanded: "What is the right of a huntsman to the forest of a thousand miles over which he has accidentally ranged in quest of prey? . . . Shall the fields and valleys, which a beneficent God has formed to teem with the life of innumerable multitudes, be condemned to everlasting barrenness?" Both Leatherstocking and Boone had fled beyond the great river; only the trans-Mississippi West seemed in Jefferson's eye to lie beyond the immediate thrust of American settlement. Perhaps "Louisiana" had strategic value only as a great land-bridge to the Columbia River and the marts of the Orient, so that his principal "Instructions" to Lewis and Clark conceived a single portage from the headwaters of the Missouri to the sources of the Columbia: "The object of your mission is to explore the Missouri river, & such principal stream of it, as by it's course & communication with the waters of the Pacific Ocean, may offer the most direct & practicable water communication across the continent, for the purposes of commerce."[3] As Bernard DeVoto observed in his edition of the *Journals,* Jefferson's geopolitical assumptions were based on what was known about the western half of the continent and on what was apprehended of British and Spanish intentions from the north and south. For him and his contemporaries, the great watersheds of the interior, the valleys of the Co-

2. Washington Irving, *Astoria, or Anecdotes of an Enterprise Beyond the Rocky Mountains,* edited by Edgeley W. Todd (Oklahoma, 1964), page 146. All subsequent references to *Astoria* in my essay refer to Todd's edition and are self-evident in their context.

3. See Bernard DeVoto's edition of *The Journals of Lewis and Clark* (Houghton Mifflin, 1953), page 484. All subsequent references to the *Journals* (and to Jefferson's "Instructions") rest upon this edition, save for the transcription of Lewis's account of the Great Falls in John Conron, editor, *The American Landscape: A Critical Anthology of Prose and Poetry* (Oxford, 1974), pages 323–324. I have kept the captains' original orthographies as they appear in DeVoto in passages self-evident in context.

lumbia, the Missouri, the Platte, and the Arkansas, were themselves only vaguely known and then only by dim memories dating back to the Vérendryes and their narrative of the "Shining Mountains" to the west or by more recent commercial ventures in the fur-trade up the Missouri toward the Mandans and Arikaras and the Platte as far westward as Grand Island (Nebraska) and the Pawnees. Even as Jefferson was writing to his captains, English and Scots fur-traders were consolidating their monopoly of the North-West trade, and to the south and west Spain held a tenuous grip on settlements already some centuries old. In summary, Jefferson's imagination leaped at a bound from the Potomac to the mouth of the Columbia; the virgin landscapes along the Ohio and the Mississippi awaited the slow and hard-won progress of civilization, but Jefferson conceived a continental landscape beyond the vaguely realized topographies of plain and mountain, of lonely river and unmapped desert.

It remained for Lewis and Clark to find the Rocky Mountains in their way and the two hundred twenty miles of stony traverse that Jefferson's grand design had overlooked in his ambition to contract all previous American history westward to the three years of the captains' journey to and from the mouth of the Columbia. Jefferson chose his officers, of course, with an attentive eye to their backwoods skills *and* "literary" abilities; if their expedition was meant to open a road to the Pacific, it was also intended to be scientific and empirical, embracing both the physical geographies of the Missouri-Columbia passage and the ethnographies of the almost entirely unknown tribes of basin and range: "And considering the interest which every nation has in extending & strengthening the authority of reason & justice among the people around them, it will be useful to acquire what knoledge you can of the state of morality, religion & information among them, as it may better enable those who endeavor to civilize & instruct them, to adapt their measures to the existing notions & practices of those on whom they are to operate."

Our own historical distance from Jefferson and his America and its manifestly evolving destinies (as they partly reveal themselves in his "Instructions") somewhat conceals the cultural effects of the Expedition's ethnographic reports from Fort Mandan published as "A Statistical View of the Indian Nations Inhabiting the Territory of Louisiana . . ." or Nicholas Biddle's edition of their overland *Journals* in 1814.[4] Most obviously, their passage of the mountains and the subsequent reports from trappers following the captains' trail into virgin hunting-grounds expanded the fur-trade already long established at St. Louis; for a larger audience in the East, even then looking beyond the vague boundaries of

4. Lewis and Clark established winter quarters in 1804–1805 at Fort Mandan, now an historical site. Fort Mandan is located on the Missouri River in North Dakota, between present-day Stanton and Fort Clark. Upstream a short distance is the Great Plains Garrison Diversion Project, one of the largest and most expensive public works projects ever undertaken in the United States, which caused an uproar among conservationists during the 1960s and 1970s.

the Old Northwest and the old Southwest, the Expedition provided a broad outline of physical reality beyond the Great Bend of the Missouri River *and* a first rhetoric of wonder and discovery, a language for a landscape which held, in bewildering juxtaposition, plenitude and emptiness, empirical truth and psychic displacement, gardens in the wilderness and the complete *tabula rasa* of savage nature. Though *The Journals of Lewis and Clark* testify again and again to their hard-edged competence in prairie travel, still the explorers often found their "scientific" engagement with the widespread realities around them momentarily withdrawn before a landscape potent with wonder and sublimity, as when Lewis drew upon his reading for a "grand" view of the Great Falls of the Missouri, a "scene" which elaborated and transformed his earlier account of the physical dimensions of the contract:

*After writing this imperfect description, I again viewed the Falls, and was so much disgusted with the imperfect idea which it conveyed of the scene, that I determined to draw my pen across it and begin again; but then reflected that I could not perhaps succeed better than penning the first impressions of the mind. I wished for the pencil of Salvator Rosa, or Titian, or the pen of Thomson, that I might be enabled to give to the enlightened world some just idea of this truly magnificent and sublimely grand object which has, from the commencement of time, been concealed from the view of civilized man. But this was fruitless and vain. I most sincerely regretted that I had not brought a camera obscura with me, by the assistance of which even I could have hoped to have done better, but alas, this was also out of my reach.*

Lewis obviously wrote for an audience beyond Jefferson and his Congress; only literary allusion and image can clarify the sublimity of the Missouri's power and beauty, and only masters of complexity and contrast (like the painters) and of stasis and mutability (like James Thomson, the Scottish poet) can offer an analogy in aesthetic or psychological association for Lewis's emotions here, emotions which already demanded an "American School" of painterly vision for the Great West. Lewis's appeal to the painters and the poet, students of landscape may observe, shows his need for a framing perspective, a formal prospect-view from above or beyond the physical realities he faced directly. Like others before and after him, Lewis found his order of composition from the heights. For him and for Clark, climbing *above* the landscape gave them pattern and design in expanded vision; the "scene" became synthetic and resolved, even and implicitly an emotion, as Lewis discovered near the Maria's River: "between the time of my A.M. and meridian [observations] Capt. C. and myself stroled out to the top of the hights in the fork of those rivers from whence we had an extensive and most inchanting view . . . the country in every derection around us was one vast plain in which innumerable herds of Buffalow were seen attended by their shepperds the wolves; the solatary antelope which now had their young were distributed over it's face; some herds of Elk were also seen . . . the verdure perfectly cloathed the ground, the weather was pleasant and fair."

Such prospect-views diminished as the Expedition descended the Columbia and established winter quarters (1805–1806) at Fort Clatsop;[5] there the pressure of survival and the evidences of earlier white contact with the West Coast Indians dominate their narrative (Clark saw a "squar" with "*J. Bowman*" picked out on her arm). The immediate present was all their concern, and the "romantic" associations that Lewis had entered in his part of the journals on the upriver journey early in 1805 almost entirely passed from view. But that landscape *had* shown a timeworn look at the "Mauvaises Terres" and beyond; no merely physical description could hold the implicit associations of an immemorial past buried in the wilderness, a wasteland pregnant with the eighteenth century's obsession with the ruins of time and the inevitable images of fallen grandeur and buried empires. Even in the Far West Lewis found the fragments of an ancient time, images which landscape held suspended for a consciousness in history:

*The hills and river Clifts which we passed today exhibit a most romantic appearance. . . . The water in the course of time in decending from those hills and plains on either side of the river has trickled down the soft sand clifts and woarn it into a thousand grotesque figures, which with the help of a little imagination and an oblique view, at a distance are made to represent eligant ranges of lofty freestone buildings, having their parapets well stocked with statuary; collumns of various sculpture both grooved and plain, are also seen supporting long galleries in front of those buildings. . . . As we passed on it seemed as if these seens of visionary inchantment would never have and end; for here it is too that nature presents to the view of the traveler vast ranges of walls of tolerable workmanship, so perfect indeed are those walls that I should have thought that nature had attempted here to rival the human art of masonry had I not recollected that she had first begun her work.*

5. Fort Clatsop is now a national memorial. It is located at the mouth of the Columbia River on the Oregon side, a few miles southeast of Warrenton, near Astoria.

The vision of temporal ruins in the wilderness thus overlaps and complements the perspective-views of an unfallen Eden in the West, perhaps even a separate creation, though both prospects must, in Lewis's own word, be "oblique" and more representative of the traveler's own focus of memory and desire than of the actual river scenery they saw. But the timeworn geologic chaos of the Upper Missouri sorted well with the truths of myth—the Ten Lost Tribes of Israel, for instance, or John Evans's quest for the "Welsh Indians" among the Mandans and beyond—in a landscape like no other Americans had seen or charted. The landscape at a distance offered outlines and comprehensible patterns in its maplike contours; more closely observed, the valley of the Missouri showed veins of ore, bison paths, "the remains or ruins of eligant buildings; some collumns standing and almost entire with their pedastals and capitals" in the Bad Lands. Prince Maximilian (1832–1867), a generation later, brought with him his own painter, Karl Bodmer (1809–1893), for a more finished observation of the landscapes of wonder:

*Towards nine o'clock the valley began to be particularly interesting, for its fantastic forms were more and more numerous; every moment, as we proceeded along, new white fairy-like castles appeared, and a painter who had leisure might fill whole volumes with these original landscapes. As proofs of this we may refer to some of these figures, which Mr. Bodmer sketched very accurately. . . . Long tracts of the sand-stone strata perfectly resembled a large blown-up fortress, because the stratification everywhere gave these walls a certain regularity, while, at the same time, they bore marks of having been destroyed by violence. In several places where the sand-stone summit appeared plainly to represent an ancient knight's castle, another remarkable rock was seen to traverse the mountain in narrow perpendicular strata, like regularly built walls.*[6]

A rhetoric foreign to American realities, a language of time past and buried, here found its realization and reference in the broken landscapes of the great Missouri River.

But neither distant prospect nor imaginative reconstructions like Lewis's (or Maximilian's) brought the Expedition back to St. Louis. Lewis and Clark's *Journals* themselves are a complex guide to survival measured in azimuthal variations, new species and genera, and tribal languages and territories; and it was perhaps the very wonder and peril of the northern route that so engrossed the captains' contemporaries, who saw that the landscapes toward the headwaters of the Missouri and the Columbia

6. Maximilian, Prince of Wied-Neuwied, *Travels in the Interior of North America* (Cleveland: Arthur R. Clark Co., 1906), 23:78–79.

"The White Castles on the Upper Missouri," a watercolor by Charles Bodmer, appeared as Plate XVIII in Bernard DeVoto's *Across the Wide Missouri* (Houghton Mifflin, 1947). Devoto's legend states: "Both this and Plate XV ['Confluence of the Yellowstone and the Missouri'] show typical scenes in the Missouri badlands between Fort Union and Fort McKenzie." Fort McKenzie was located at the confluence of the Marias, Missouri, and Teton rivers in present-day Loma, Montana. Fort Union was a trading post located at the confluence of the Missouri and Yellowstone rivers on the Montana/North Dakota border; it is now a national historic site.

were not, after all, beyond the imaginative scale of their own earlier conquest of the Alleghenies. The more southerly routes following the valleys of the Arkansas and the Platte, and the trace
which the overland Astorians broke west of the Mandan villages,
opened a third range of landscape views as these routes drew fron-
tiersmen and trappers, traders and soldiers and scouts due west
toward the unknown and the incomprehensible.

Beyond the Ninety-Eighth Meridian the landscape extended
beyond all familiar bounds; the vastness opened a range of vision
alien to American eyes and therefore perilous. Zebulon Pike
(1779–1813), the American general and explorer, warned that the
eastern approaches to the Front Range of the Rocky Mountains
were a sterile emptiness like the sandy wastes of Arabia, and fixed
the unrelenting image of "the Great American Desert" firmly in
the American westering consciousness. Here the wilderness of
desert and mountain seemed to bar the triumphant expansion of
American history and progress; here might Jefferson's project of
a perpetual Indian Territory be bounded in a tract inhospitable to
national ideals and inviolable by the otherwise all-conquering axe
and plow. As Henry Brackenridge observed in his *Views of Louisiana* (1817), the absolute *fact* of the Desert refuted "the prevailing
idea, with which we have so much flattered ourselves, of these
western regions being like the rest of the United States, suscep-
tible of cultivation, and offering endless outlets to settlements. . . .
The [Indian] nations will continue to wander over those plains,
and the wild animals, the elk, the buffaloe, will long be found
there; for until our country becomes supercharged with population, there is scarcely any probability of settlers venturing far into
these regions."

Edwin James's *Account* of the Long Expedition (1823) reinforced these images of emptiness and trackless desolation, a landscape of mirage and sandstorm, barren, sterile, and void. By 1827
Fenimore Cooper could draw on both Pike and James for his narrative of a nomadic band of "hardy squatters" ranging far beyond
the Mississippi in criminal flight from civilization and laws; the
opening pages of *The Prairie* addressed an audience already well
aware of the blasted landscapes of the farthest West:

*In the little valleys which, in the regular formation of the land,
occurred at every mile of their progress, the view was bounded
on two of the sides by the gradual and low elevations which give
name to the description of prairie we have mentioned; while on
the others, the meagre prospect ran off in long, narrow, barren
perspectives but slightly relieved by a pitiful show of coarse
though somewhat luxuriant vegetation. From the summit of the*

*swells, the eye became fatigued with the sameness and chilling
dreariness of the landscape. The earth was not unlike the
ocean. . . . There was the same moving and regular surface, the
same absence of foreign objects, and the same boundless extent
to the view.*

In so indeterminate a wilderness, one so empty of the pastoral associations of a garden or the reconstructive vision of the
ruins of time, both the prairie traveler and the western historian
were driven to project upon the empty landscape the perils of
cultural displacement—the constant *threat* of "the perfect freedom of the wilderness"—and the deeply felt solitude of some two
hundred years of American westering. "The Great American Desert" was as much an apprehension of illimitable space and time in
the American imagination as it was a fixed sign for some sixty
years on the maps of the Great West. For the two generations of
Americans who discovered that reality in the pages of Nuttall and
Bradbury, Pike and Edwin James, Cooper and Irving and Cullen
Bryant and a thousand newspaper-letters and traveler's guides, the
Desert *was* the Great West, a constant limit to American expansion and a proof—if proof were needed—that even an empty
landscape might be cursed with a primal barrenness. In that eternal and unchanging *now* of the farthest West, only the Indians
and the bison moved in their endless migrations to obscure des-
tinations; the very emptiness of these wastes compelled the prairie
traveler to metaphors of separation and alienation, to reflections
upon Tartary or Stony Arabia, the Saharan Desert, and the Rus-
sian steppe. A party of overland Astorians was made to bear the
full weight of Irving's own cultural and psychic displacement, an
emotion founded on his own slightest actual experience of that
wilderness: "A part of their route would lay across an immense
tract, stretching north and south for hundreds of miles along
the foot of the Rocky Mountains, and drained by the tributary
streams of the Missouri and the Mississippi. This region, which
resembles one of the immeasurable steppes of Asia, has not in-
aptly been termed 'the Great American Desert.' It spreads forth
into undulating and treeless plains, and desolate sandy wastes
wearisome to the eye from their extent and monotony. . . ."[7] Such
a desolation opened no garden views or associations from imaginative "history"; if the Great American Desert dissolved time past
in "boundless wastes," then its possible futures offered no comprehensible purpose or design.

Thus, as the landscape broadened and lengthened before the
weary Astorians, the "scenic present"—the *void*—became an inevitable prospect of dislocation and exhaustion; the emptiness of

7. Students and teachers of landscape will be interested to know that
Irving's description is almost entirely
reconstructed from earlier reports and
the scattered topographical references
in his own primary sources. He saw
the Great American Desert mostly
with his mind's eye.

the wasteland invited a rush of compensatory "associations" from within for the prairie travelers and their historian, involuntary and internal images of wildness and chaos, fragmentation and collapse in the wilderness and the aboriginal peoples within it:

*Such is the nature of this immense wilderness of the far West; which apparently defies cultivation, and the habitation of civilized life. Some portions of it along the rivers may partially be subdued by agriculture, others may form vast pastoral tracts, like those of the East; but it is to be feared that a great part of it will form a lawless interval between the abodes of civilized man, like the wastes of the ocean or the deserts of Arabia; and, like them, be subject to the depredations of the marauder. Here may spring up new and mongrel races, like new formations in geology, the amalgamation of the "debris" and "abrasions" of former races, civilized and savage; the remains of broken and almost extinguished tribes; the descendants of wandering hunters and trappers; of fugitives from the Spanish and American frontiers; of adventurers and desperadoes of every class and country, yearly ejected from the bosom of society into the wilderness. We are contributing incessantly to swell this singular and heterogeneous cloud of wild population that is to hang about our frontier, by the transfer of whole tribes of savages from the east of the Mississippi to the great wastes of the far West. Many of these bear with them the smart of real or fancied injuries; many consider themselves expatriated beings, wrongfully exiled from their hereditary homes, and the sepulchres of their fathers, and cherish a deep and abiding animosity against the race that dispossessed them. Some may gradually become pastoral hordes, like those rude and migratory people, half shepherd, half warrior, who, with their flocks and herds, roam the plains of upper Asia; but others, it is to be apprehended, will become predatory bands, mounted on the fleet steeds of the prairies, with the open plains for their marauding grounds, and the mountains for their retreats and lurking-places. Here they may resemble those great hordes of the north; "Gog and Magog with their bands," that haunted the gloomy imaginations of the prophets.*

Irving's vision is apocalyptic: in this farthest West ultimate space annihilates time and consciousness; "the perfect freedom of the wilderness" points steadily to entropy and death. On these prairies and atop the Rockies Thomas Hart Benton's "statue of the fabled god, Terminus, should be raised . . . never to be thrown down" against the expansion of the Great Republic westward. Francis Parkman (1823–1893), the American historian, drew upon the same ideas of closure and denitiation to mark his discovery of the wastelands along the valley of the Platte: "Should any of my readers ever be impelled to visit the prairies, and should he choose the route of the Platte . . . I can assure him that he need not think to enter at once upon the paradise of his imagination. A dreary preliminary, a protracted crossing of the threshold, awaits him before he finds himself upon the verge of the 'great American desert,'—those barren wastes, the haunts of the buffalo and the Indian, where the very shadow of civilization lies a hundred leagues behind him."[8] Only bison skulls and the occasional lonely grave of an emigrant—and the wheel-ruts of the Trail—marked the journey he had to take alone.

The long passage westward and the steady ascent up the valleys of the Missouri, the Platte, and the Arkansas were thus both an induction to wonder and distance *and* a denitiation from the past, from time and memory, from design and culture and history. In a journey without maps into a landscape without definition, the inevitable psychological process (as Irving's chaotic prospect of wilderness and wilderness humanity makes clear) was displacement from familiar landscapes and established identities, an ultimate sense of loss and of *being* "lost" physically at first and emotionally and consciously at last. From Lewis and Clark to Ramsey Crooks and Wilson Price Hunt down to James O. Pattie and Osborne Russell and the "lost trappers" to Parkman himself and John Charles Frémont, the West's landscapes drove down bodies and fragmented and emptied consciousness itself; the prairie traveler found his and her own psychic boundaries opening and emptying into the illimitable wilderness. In part these dislocations came with the country; "mountain fever" was pandemic among the overland emigrants, a part of the "seasoning" of every greenhorn in high altitudes forced to devour wild meat badly cooked in its own grease. But physical illness and even starvation (and the recurrent horror of cannibalism from the Astorians down to the Donner Party and well beyond the period of this essay) were only accompaniments to the terrible isolation forced upon the solitary self in that immense landscape of prairie and sky. Even American poet and editor William Cullen Bryant (1794–1878), meditating upon the mingled images of garden and ruin in "The Prairies" of Illinois, woke from a vision of an imaginary "Indian" past to a solitary present and inevitably found himself "in the wilderness alone."

The course of Francis Parkman's journey toward Fort Laramie and the uncorrupted Oglalas—"to become, as it were, one of them"—was a series of wrong turnings and blind passages concluding in the complete blankness of the Laramie Basin:

8. See my edition of *The Oregon Trail* (Wisconsin, 1969), pages 34–35. All subsequent references from Parkman are drawn from the same text.

"Chimney Rock," a watercolor by Alfred Jacob Miller, appeared as Plate I in Bernard DeVoto's *Across the Wide Missouri* (Houghton Mifflin, 1947). DeVoto's legend states: "The Platte was also known as the Nebraska (from a Sioux word meaning shallow) and its valley was poetically referred to as the Coasts of Nebraska. As one traveled up that valley the grade inclined gently but steadily upward, the country grew drier, and the plains changed to a transition land that would merge with the mountains. About five hundred and fifty miles out of Independence [Missouri] a group of fragmented hills, buttes, and mesas signalized that the transition was beginning. Chimney Rock or The Chimney, a column of core rock whose softer covering had been worn away, was among the first of these nightmare formations. It was a landmark to all travelers of the Platte route." Chimney Rock is now a national historic site, and is located near present-day Bayard, Nebraska.

"Scene Near Fort Laramie," a watercolor by Alfred Jacob Miller, appeared as Plate VII in Bernard DeVoto's *Across the Wide Missouri* (Houghton Mifflin, 1947). DeVoto's legend states: "Laramie Fork, at a very low stage, is in the foreground. The Platte, out of sight here, runs approximately parallel with the hills in the right background, about a mile from the fort. The high summit is Laramie Peak. Compare this site with that of Fort Union in Plate XVI ['View of Fort Union; the Assiniboins Breaking Up Their Camp' by Charles Bodmer]." Fort Laramie was located at the confluence of the Laramie and North Platte rivers near present-day Fort Laramie, Wyoming; it is now a national historic site.

*On the fifth day after leaving Bisonette's camp, we saw, late in the afternoon, what we supposed to be a considerable stream, but on approaching it, we found to our disappointment, nothing but a dry bed of sand, into which the water had sunk and disappeared. We separated, some riding in one direction and some in another, along its course. Still we found no traces of water, not even so much as a wet spot in the sand. The old cotton-wood trees that grew along the bank, lamentably abused by lightning and tempest, were withering with the drought, and on the dead limbs, at the summit of the tallest, half a dozen crows were hoarsely cawing, like birds of evil omen. We had no alternative but to keep on. . . . We moved on, angry and silent, over a desert as flat as the widespread ocean.*

That metaphor of oceanic vastness and emptiness had served Parkman well for vision before; on the eastern stretches of the Oregon Trail he had found himself lost after a bison chase: "I looked about for some indications to show me where I was, and what course I ought to pursue; I might as well have looked for landmarks in the midst of the ocean. . . . I began now to think myself in danger of being lost," like the runaway slave, "Jack," whom he found at an Oglala village: "His cheeks were shrunken in the hollow of his jaws; his eyes were unnaturally dilated, and his lips shrivelled and drawn back from his teeth like those of a corpse. . . . The wretch was starving to death. For thirty-three days he had wandered alone on the prairie, without weapon of any kind; without shoes, moccasins, or any other clothing but an old jacket and trousers; without intelligence to guide his course, or any knowledge of the productions of the prairie." The runaway's physical degradation mirrored his psychological collapse: "He had not seen a human being. Bewildered in the boundless, hopeless desert that stretched around him, he had walked on in despair, till he could walk no longer, and then crawled on his knees" through the desolations of the wilderness and his own abandonment. Parkman would himself approach the same climactic meeting with landscape and death as his "summer's journey out of bounds" penetrated ever more deeply into barren ground; the end of his initiation was a submergence, a sinking into it and into the depthless superstition and fatality of an Oglala village in the Black Hills of northeastern Wyoming. For Parkman wilderness was absorption and surrender and death.

By the middle 1840s, when the images of ruin and garden had proven irrelevant to the realities of the most remote basins and ranges, the language of displacement and collapse had begun to

"The Lost Greenhorn," by Alfred Jacob Miller. Original in the Warner Collection of Gulf States Paper Corporation, Tuscaloosa, Alabama.

form the American experience of landscape and freedom. The very names on the land itself only repeated long ordeals by solitude and despair, the memories of wilderness heroes who had passed into the mountain man's mythology within a few years of their long journeys and lonely deaths: Sergeant Floyd and John Day and Hoback and Reznor, Hugh Glass and Hiram Scott and the Donners had died in winter snow and starving times, on nameless hills and empty prairies. As trapper James O. Pattie recalled, "Here on these remote plains, far from their friends, they had fallen by the bloody arrow or spear" of the Indians or perished of thirst and starvation. The last emotion of that landscape was fear. When George Kendall published his narrative of the Santa Fé Expedition in 1845, the national cry was "On to Oregon!" and "Manifest Destiny"; but Kendall's discovery of the wilderness—the object and vision of all American expansion in those brave years of decision westward—was terror:

*Gentle reader, you have never been lost on a wide ocean of prairies, unskilled in border life, and little gifted with the power of first adopting a course to follow and then not deviating from it.*

*You must recollect that there, as on the wide ocean, you find no trees, no friendly landmarks, to guide you—all is a wide waste of eternal sameness. To be lost, as I and others have experienced, has a complex and fearful meaning. It is not merely to stray from your path, but from yourself. With your way you lose your presence of mind. You attempt to reason, but the rudder and compass of your reflective faculties are gone. Self-confidence, too, is lost—in a word all is lost, except a maniacal impulse to despair, that is peculiar and indescribable.*[9]

Beyond that extremity he could not go; within that landscape mind and matter are annealed.

For the great overland emigrations of the 1840s following the traces of the fur caravans and the traders to Santa Fé, the wilderness and its enduring values in desire and will as garden and desert—"those flowery seas, the prairies," by one contemporaneous account—became the matter of newspaper-letters and journals and journals and travel books. Perhaps the wagons pointing toward Oregon City and Lassen's Ranch had no other language for their wonder and astonishment and dismay;[10] they saw the Indian and the bison as emblems of the landscape just as Lewis and Clark and the Astorians identified the grizzly bear as the totem of the wilderness. For the overlanders, moreover, the trappers and traders of the isolated posts—Fort Laramie and Bridger's Fort in Wyoming and Fort Hall in Idaho—were themselves savage and alien, a foreboding of their own destinies farther out on the road to Oregon and California. Those wild Westerners were called "French Indians" in Parkman's hearing at Fort Laramie, a confirmation of the "white savage" in Pattie's observation that wilderness was both liberation and metamorphosis for the mountain men who felt "the mere love of roving in the wild license of the forests, and a capacity to become hardened by these scenes to a perfect callousness to all fear and sense of danger, until it actually comes. . . ."[11] Jim Clyman saw that the speed of white regression to savagery, under the implacable pressure of the Desert, was rapid and inevitable and *certain:* "But I will not bore you with details of the savage habits of Indians to their enemies but I will merely state that it is easy to make a savage of a civilized man but impossible to make a civilized man of a savage in one generation."[12] The Noble Savage had become the Ignoble Westerner; and white men and women on the Trail outran the laws of their culture and the constraints of their history. The wagon-roads were littered with the cast-off possessions—and the identities—which the emigrants could no longer carry with them. For the individual members of "this strange migration" (as Parkman called it), the realities of

9. George W. Kendall, *Narrative of the Texan Santa Fé Expedition,* edited by Milo M. Quaife (Chicago: Lakeside Press, 1929), pages 204–205.

10. Oregon City was the terminus of the Oregon Trail and the first capital of the Oregon Territory (1849–1852); Lassen's Ranch is named for Peter Lassen, who settled during the 1840s in the area east of present-day Lassen Volcanic National Park in northeastern California.

11. James O. Pattie, *The Personal Narrative of James O. Pattie,* edited by W. H. Goetzmann (Lippincott, 1962), page 123. All other quotations and references to Pattie's *Narrative* derive from Goetzmann's edition. Pattie was the son of a frontier family and trapped in the trans-Missouri West. The original *Narrative* was edited by Timothy Flint (Cincinnati, 1831).

12. Charles L. Camp, editor, *James Clyman, Frontiersman . . .* (Portland: Champoeg Press, 1960), page 14. Clyman's journals and memoirs are very probably the best narrative we have of the mountain man's frontier.

"View of the Wind River Mountains," a "topographical sketch" by Charles Preuss in 1842, originally appeared, facing page 66, in Brevet Captain J. C. Frémont's *Report of the Exploring Expedition to the Rocky Mountains in the Year 1842, and to Oregon and North California in the Years 1843–'44* (Washington: Gales and Seaton, Printers, 1845; reprinted by Readex Microprint Corporation, 1966).

physical travail became obsessive; the day's journey reduced the hardy pioneer to the level of his beasts:

*To enjoy such a trip along with such a crowd of emigration, a man must be able to endure heat like a Salamander, mud and water like a muskrat, dust like a toad, and labor like a jackass. He must learn to eat with his unwashed fingers, drink out of the same vessel with his mules, sleep on the ground when it rains, and share his blanket with vermin, and have patience with mus-ketoes, who don't know any difference between the face of a man and the face of a mule, but dash without ceremony from one into the other. He must cease to think, except as to where he may find grass and water and a good camping place. It is a hardship without glory, to be sick without a home, to die and be buried like a dog.*[13]

13. *The St. Joseph Gazette* (27 October 1852), quoted in John D. Unruh, Jr., *The Plains Across* (Illinois, 1979), page 414.

*There* is the last authentic voice of "the course of Empire" westward.

Through the rest of the nineteenth century, the stark realities of the Great West coexisted uneasily with the public fantasy and willed illusion of an unfallen Eden, of another Virgin Land where rain followed the plow and democratic principles sprang up with the golden harvests of the new land. Whitman's "Passage to India" soared over the wilderness without pausing long for the instructive details; much earlier John Charles Frémont (1813–1890), the American general and explorer, had determined the altitudes of transcendence by climbing far above the barren landscapes—the old and familiar strategy of oversight—toward the summit of the mountains, at a place where in fact and in reconstructive rhetoric the great rivers of the West proved a grand and comprehensible design: "On one side we overlooked innumerable lakes and streams, the spring of the Colorado of the Gulf of California; and on the other was the Wind River valley, where were the heads of the Yellowstone branch of the Missouri; far to the north, we just could discover the snowy heads of the *Trois Tetons*, where were the sources of the Missouri and Columbia rivers; and at the southern extremity of the ridge, the peaks were plainly visible, among which were some of the springs of the Nebraska or Platte river." [14]

At a summit high enough and arduous enough, the West spread before Frémont and outward *from* him; it was for him that the immense landscape formed for composition and meaning—for coherence and design. The world lay spread before him and his ragged band of scouts and soldiers didn't know where to go. That vision of landscape never left him; it restored and renewed him and his men from the fatigues and the terrors of the trail; it gave him (and us) the wonder and the power and the transcendence which *West*—reality and dream—had always promised the American imagination of freedom and transformation.

14. Excerpted from the entry of 15 August 1842 in Brevet Captain J. C. Frémont, *The Exploring Expedition to the Rocky Mountains, Oregon and California* (New York: Miller, Orton, & Mulligan, 1856, as reprinted from the edition of 1845), page 104.

Frederick Law Olmsted, the founder of landscape architecture in the United States, managed the Mariposa gold-mining estate in California, where he encountered in Frémont a different kind of man than the hero figure he was perceived to be by most Americans at the time. See *The Papers of Frederick Law Olmsted, Volume V: The California Frontier, 1863–1865*, edited by Victoria Post Ranney, Gerard J. Rauluk, and Carolyn F. Hoffman (Johns Hopkins, 1990).

David Schuyler

# The Sanctified Landscape: The Hudson River Valley, 1820 to 1850

*How rapidly is civilization treading on the footsteps of nature!*

—JAMES FENIMORE COOPER *

DAVID SCHUYLER was born in 1950 in Albany, New York, and was raised in the mid-Hudson River valley city of New-burgh. He holds a Ph.D. in history from Columbia University, where his disserta-tion was awarded the Richard B. Morris Prize. Professor Schuyler serves as a con-sulting editor to the *Creating the North American Landscape* series (Johns Hop-kins University Press) and as a member of the Editorial Board of the Frederick Law Olmsted Papers publication project. Schuyler is author of *The New Urban Landscape: The Redefinition of City Form in Nineteenth-Century America* (Johns Hopkins, 1986) and coeditor of three volumes of *The Papers of Freder-ick Law Olmsted,* the most recent of which is *The Years of Olmsted, Vaux & Company, 1865–1874* (Johns Hopkins, 1992). He is professor of American stud-ies at Franklin and Marshall College.

* From James Fenimore Cooper, *The Pioneers: Or, The Sources of the Susque-hanna* (1823; New York, 1964), page 202.

1. Auguste Levasseur, *Lafayette in America in 1824 and 1825: Or, Journal of a Voyage to the United States,* trans. J. D. Godham, 2 vols. (Philadelphia, 1829), 1:99–100, passim.

2. Ibid.

IN 1824 the Marquis de Lafayette returned to the United States to visit familiar places and to observe the changes that had taken place in the nation whose independence he had helped to cre-ate. Shortly after arriving in New York Lafayette and his party boarded the steamboat *James Kent* for a journey up the Hudson. Everywhere the aged republican went, throngs of people greeted him. In Newburgh, for example, citizens erected five triumphal arches, hosted Lafayette at a festive dinner, and showered him with wreathes, flowers, and assorted gifts. The same outpouring of respect and generosity greeted the gallant Frenchman every-where he went in the United States: to a nation experiencing great change, Lafayette represented continuity, a link with the stirring events of the Revolutionary past and a commitment to republicanism that many commentators believed was being lost amid the pursuit of wealth.[1]

Lafayette's secretary, Auguste Levasseur, recorded the de-tails of their journey up the Hudson. They traveled past Tarry-town, where Major André had been captured, and other sites notable for events that occurred during the struggle for inde-pendence. But Levasseur was especially struck by the scenery of the Highlands, a place "where nature only shows herself under strange forms, and in sombre colours," and which evoked "phan-toms" and "sinister sighings" not unlike the legends Washington Irving had created. Although someone who cherished the rem-nants of feudalism and the castles of the Middle Ages might favor the scenery of the Rhine, Levasseur wrote, "for one who prefers nature still virgin and wild, there is nothing so beautiful as the banks of the Hudson."[2]

The English-born landscape painter Thomas Cole arrived in New York in 1825. Although the Erie Canal extended to Buffalo that year, ensuring the prosperity of the merchants who in the future would provide the patronage essential to an artistic com-munity, according to Cole's first biographer, Louis Legrande Noble, the artist was more captivated by the scenery than by evidence of a robust commercial economy. "From the moment when his eyes first caught the rural beauties clustering round the cliffs of Weehawken, and glanced up the distance of the Palisades," Noble wrote, "Cole's heart had been wandering in the Highlands, and nestling in the bosom of the Catskills."[3]

Lafayette's visit was an occasion both for reflection and for celebration. As Levasseur observed, the Frenchman's presence provided the opportunity for reverent acknowledgment of the historical events that had taken place during the Revolutionary era and also to measure the nation's progress since independence. Cole's arrival in New York was unheralded, though in later years it would be considered a starting point in the maturation of landscape painting in the United States. Despite his and Levasseur's celebration of the scenery, the age of sail was rapidly giving way to steam, and economic development was transforming the cultural geography of the Hudson Valley. Levasseur was astonished by the volume of commerce on the river. "It would be difficult," he observed, "to enumerate the boats of all sorts and sizes which carry on the trade between Albany and New York; the river is continually covered with them, and you can rarely sail for a quarter of an hour without meeting a long succession of them." Cole, who lamented the impact of civilization on his beloved wilderness, could do little to forestall the march of progress. Yet the celebration of the domesticated landscape he championed, and the evidence that civilization was destroying both natural beauty and the physical remains of the nation's history, led to the sanctification of the Hudson River valley. In the middle of the nineteenth century, contemporaries combined an appreciation of landscape with an increasing awareness of the importance of history to urge the preservation of a simple vernacular farmhouse that had been associated with important events of the Revolutionary War. That building became the first structure in the United States preserved for its historic significance.[4]

The domestication of landscape, the achievement of a balance between nature and the human presence, was a necessary precondition for the sanctification of the Hudson Valley. Andrew Jackson Downing, the Newburgh, New York, nurseryman and landscape gardener who became the preeminent arbiter of taste in the mid-nineteenth century, chronicled the cultivation of the land and the symbolic impress of civilization upon it. Two of his earliest essays, published in the *New-York Mirror* in 1835, proclaimed the superiority of cultivated nature over the sublime, of pastoral civilization over wilderness. The first, "Beacon Hill," led readers to the summit of Mount Beacon, which was directly across the

3. Louis Legrande Noble, *The Life and Works of Thomas Cole,* edited by Elliot S. Vesell (1853; Cambridge, MA, 1964), page 34. There are numerous works devoted to the culture of the Hudson River valley during the mid-nineteenth century, but see especially James T. Callow, *Kindred Spirits: Knickerbocker Writers and American Artists, 1807–1855* (Chapel Hill, 1967); Barbara Novak, *Nature and Culture: American Landscape and Painting 1825–1875* (New York, 1980); Raymond J. O'Brien, *American Sublime: Landscape and Scenery of the Lower Hudson Valley* (New York, 1981); and Walter L. Creese, *The Crowning of the American Landscape: Eight Great Spaces and their Buildings* (Princeton, 1985).

4. A. Levasseur, *Lafayette in America,* 1:100. See also Charles B. Hosmer, Jr., *Presence of the Past: A History of the Historic Preservation Movement in the United States Before Williamsburg* (New York, 1965), pages 29–51. Barbara Novak has similarly argued that "America's search for some sense of the past in the raw new world focused on an idea of landscape that was at once strongly nationalistic and moralistic." See Novak, *American Painting of the Nineteenth Century* (New York, 1979), page 61.

Hudson from Newburgh. Named because of the beacon fires that alerted Washington's troops to the movements of the British army in the long months between the battle of Yorktown and completion of the negotiations in Paris that ended the War for Independence, Mount Beacon was, to the young Downing's untraveled eye, one of nature's "most majestick thrones." He compared the view favorably to better-known prospects in the Catskills, which were too sublime for his taste. From Mount Beacon, by contrast, "In every direction the country is full of beauty, and presents a luxurient and cultivated appearance." Downing noted that visitors could enjoy the scenery because settlement had eliminated the dangers traditionally associated with wilderness, which increased the appeal of the landscape: "none of the fashionable," he wrote, "think their summer's tour complete until they have loitered away a day or two at 'Cozzens' [Hotel], falling in raptures with the captivating, though (at that place) stern and majestick beauty of the Highlands."[5]

The second of Downing's essays was a "reverie" at Dans Kamer, a flat rock that projected into the Hudson several miles above Newburgh. The northernmost point of Newburgh Bay, this was a locale celebrated by Washington Irving as a ceremonial powwow ground for Native Americans. Downing, who praised Irving for preserving the "rich old legends and antiquarian scraps" of the river's history, amply described the autumnal splendor of the vicinity and reiterated Knickerbocker's tale of how the "wild yell of the savage" had alarmed Peter Stuyvesant's crew. The age of the canoe had given way to the tall sloop and the steamboat, however, and where wigwams once stood were "a thousand cheerful homes gleaming in the sunshine." What best characterized the changes wrought by civilization, Downing implied, was the domestication of the landscape, the establishment of homes, farms, and villages: the "once dense wilderness," he wrote approvingly, "has disappeared under the hand of civilized man."[6]

Taken together, Downing's later writings on architecture and landscape gardening are a prescriptive treatise on the domestication of nature. In his more famous books Downing provided illustrations of the Beautiful (or Graceful) and the Picturesque, but not of the Sublime, the state of nature at its rawest and most powerful, and which evoked associations of awe and terror. He supplied plans for country houses and their gardens, and for dwellings in small towns and villages, but none for large cities. He also promoted the suburb as a place of residence for those persons who were compelled to work in urban areas but who wished to raise their families in landscaped surroundings more

5. [A. J. Downing], "American Highland Scenery. Beacon Hill," *New-York Mirror* 12 (14 March 1835): 293–294. See also George B. Tatum and Elisabeth B. MacDougall, eds., *Prophet With Honor: The Career of Andrew Jackson Downing 1815–1852* (Washington, D.C., 1989).

6. A. J. D[owning]., "The Dans-Kamer. A Reverie in the Highlands," *New-York Mirror* 13 (10 October 1835):117–118. Washington Irving's tale described how Stuyvesant's crew "were most horribly frightened, on going ashore above the [Hudson] highlands, by a gang of merry roistering devils, frisking and curveting on a flay rock, which projected into the river, and which is called the *Duyvel's Dans-Kamer* to this very day." Diedrich Knickerbocker, *A History of New York, From the Beginning of the World to the End of the Dutch Dynasty* . . . (1819; Philadelphia, 1871), pages 392–393.

"Landscape Gardening, in the Graceful School" (above) and "Landscape Gardening, in the Picturesque School" (below). Engravings appeared as figures 12 and 13 in the second edition of Andrew Jackson Downing's *A Treatise on the Theory and Practice of Landscape Gardening Adapted to North America* (New York: Wiley and Putnam, 1844). Courtesy of the Shadek-Fackenthal Library, Franklin and Marshall College, Lancaster, Pennsylvania.

appropriate to the new culture of domesticity. As Downing's writings indicate, by the second quarter of the nineteenth century nature and civilization had achieved a harmonious equilibrium in the Hudson River valley. Thomas Cole presented a similar assessment in his "Essay on American Scenery," which he published in the same year as Downing's writings in the *New-York Mirror.* A "cultivated" landscape, Cole wrote, "encompasses our homes, and though devoid of the stern sublimity of the wild, its quieter spirit steals tenderly into our bosoms mingled with a thousand domestic affections and heart-touching associations."[7]

The Hudson River landscape not only was domesticated, but also was considered by contemporaries an important element in the nation's collective identity. Because of the short time that had passed since independence, the United States lacked the monuments, ruins, and centuries of tradition that provided Europeans with a sense of identity in place and time. James Fenimore Cooper, Nathaniel Hawthorne, and other writers complained about the absence of historical associations in the New World. But if the United States lacked the physical remains of the past, it had nature in abundance—a landscape older than all the institutions of European civilization. In *Home As Found,* Cooper's fictional character Eve Effingham described the "Silent Pine" that stood in "solitary glory" on the bank of Lake Otsego:

*It is indeed eloquent; one hears it speak even now of the fierce storms that have whistled round its tops—of the seasons that have passed since it extricated that verdant cap from the throng of sisters that grew beneath it, and of all that has passed on the Otsego, when this limpid lake lay like a gem embedded in the forest. When William the Conqueror first landed in England this tree stood on the spot where it now stands! Here, then, is at last an American antiquity!*

As if following Cooper's assertion of the supremacy of nature over civilization, in an era dominated by romanticism, artists and writers found in the domesticated landscape a source of inspiration and the guarantor of America's distinctiveness as a culture. "The painter of American scenery," Cole noted in his journal, "has privileges superior to any other. All nature here is new to art." While Cole was preparing to depart on a visit to Europe in 1829, newspaper editor and poet William Cullen Bryant warned the artist that "Thine eyes shall see the light of distant skies." The last six lines of Bryant's sonnet cast the landscapes of the Old and New Worlds in dramatic contrast:

7. G. B. Tatum and E. B. Mac-Dougall, eds., *Prophet With Honor,* passim; Thomas Cole, "Essay on American Scenery" (1835), in John W. McCoubrey, ed., *American Art 1700–1960: Sources and Documents* (Englewood Cliffs, NJ, 1965), page 100.

The domesticated landscape: "The Hudson at Newburgh," an oil on canvas by W. G. Wall. The painting appeared in *Hudson River Portfolio* (1825). Courtesy of the Henry Francis du Pont Winterthur Museum Library: Collection of Printed Books.

*Fair scenes shall greet thee where thou goest—fair*
*But different—everywhere the trace of men.*
*Paths, homes, graves, ruins, from the lowest glen*
*To where life shrinks from the fierce Alpine air.*
*Gaze on them, till the tears shall dim thy sight,*
*But keep that earlier, wilder image bright.*

Bryant's poem warned his friend Cole to avoid the temptations of an overcivilized Europe and to keep nature, the birthright of the American continent, foremost in his paintings.[8]

8. J. F. Cooper, *Home As Found* (1838; New York, 1961), page 202; T. Cole, journal, quoted in L. L. Noble, *Life and Works of Thomas Cole*, page 148; W. C. Bryant, "To Cole, the Painter, Departing for Europe," in J. W. McCoubrey, ed., *American Art 1700–1960*, page 96. See also Nathaniel Hawthorne, *The Marble Faun* (1859; New York, 1961), page vi.

A host of other writers echoed the same theme. Writing in the *Literary World,* for example, a correspondent asserted that landscape was the "first field and the best field for our painters," as it guaranteed originality and "distinguished success." Another suggested that American artists who traveled to Europe left behind "GOD'S landscape," while Asher B. Durand's "Letters on Landscape Painting" advised aspiring artists to study American nature rather than the masterpieces of the art of the past. Following these injunctions, and undoubtedly inspired by Cole's commercial success, numerous artists set out to explore the aesthetic potential of the Hudson Valley. Many of their prosperous countrymen, predominantly from large cities, shared the artists' appreciation of the domesticated landscape. During the second quarter of the nineteenth century the pages of literary magazines filled with reveries on the Hudson Highlands and the Catskills, while engravers produced hundreds of illustrations of handsome scenes of natural beauty for popular gift books and souvenirs. As the environmental impact of the emerging industrial cities was becoming evident, those who could afford the cost and who shared an enthusiasm for landscape began patronizing such well-known establishments as Cozzens Hotel and the Catskill Mountain House to partake the beauties of nearby scenery. Hartford merchant John Olmsted took his son Frederick on numerous "tours in search of the picturesque," and years later the son recalled how deeply the perception of nature had affected his father and shaped his own career as a landscape architect:

> On a Sunday evening we were crossing the meadows alone.
> I was tired and he had taken me in his arms. I soon
> noticed that he was inattentive to my prattle and
> looking in his face saw in it something unusual.
> Following the direction of his eyes, I said: "Oh!
> there's a star." Then he said something of Infinite
> Love with a tone and manner which really moved me,
> chick that I was, so much so that it has ever since
> remained in my heart.

Only the ineffable beauties of nature could evoke such a response from the normally stolid John Olmsted, a response the son later attempted to make possible for visitors to the urban public parks he designed throughout the United States. For John Olmsted and for numerous other members of his generation, during the second quarter of the nineteenth century nature had become a source of inspiration, a place not for the rigors of agriculture, which neces-

"Below Cozzens," an engraving that appeared in William Cullen Bryant's *Picturesque America* (New York, 1874), illustrates what Downing termed the "stern and majestick beauty" of the Hudson Highlands. The engraver and the date of the engraving are unknown. Courtesy of the Henry Francis du Pont Winterthur Museum Library: Collection of Printed Books.

sitated the transformation of the land, but for contemplation, for tranquility, for renewal that was impossible within the confines of cities and the routine of daily life.[9]

A corollary to the impress of civilization was the sacralization of the landscape. Ralph Waldo Emerson, for example, described nature as "these plantations of God" and asserted that "In the woods, we return to reason and faith." This investing of landscape with religious significance was not necessarily an expression of pantheism, as some critics suggested at the time. Instead, as James T. Callow has pointed out, Knickerbocker writers and artists "used nature to supplement rather than supplant formal religion in their lives." Other Americans, tired of theological disputes or the institutional trappings of religion, turned toward nature as a more immediate expression of the divine. Geology, the most popular science in the first half of the nineteenth century, became in some respects a new theology. Experts debated the age of rocks and of Niagara Falls, to be sure, but found in everything proof of the Creator's immanence. Artists and writers inspired by the scenery of the Hudson Valley in the second quarter of the nineteenth century contributed to the sacralization of the landscape. The poet Bryant entitled one of his verses "Forest Hymn"—a title laden with religious connotations and reverence for nature—which includes the phrase "The groves were God's first temple." Similarly did editor and litterateur Nathaniel Parker Willis observe sabbath in what he termed nature's "Vast cathedral." Like the solitary hunter in Thomas Doughty's painting, *In Nature's Wonderland* (1835), who stands in awe before a scene of ineffable beauty, these celebrants of nature found in the landscape proof of the Creator's existence.[10]

Perhaps the best example of the religious connotations of nature is the career of Thomas Cole. In his "Essay on American Scenery" Cole pointed out that "the good, the enlightened of all ages and nations, have found pleasure and consolation in the beauty of the rural earth." Old Testament prophets found God in nature, he suggested, and so might latter day seekers of the divine: "that voice is YET heard among the mountains! . . . the wilderness is YET a fitting place to speak of God." Cole believed that, "in gazing on the pure creations of the Almighty, he feels a calm religious tone stealing through his mind." The painter's verse was still another means of expressing the divine in creation. In "The Wild" Cole wrote:

> *To kneel in nature's everlasting dome,*
> *Where not the voice of feeble man does teach,*
> *But His, who in the rolling thunder speaks.*

9. "The Fine Arts. Exhibition at the National Academy," *Literary World* 1 (15 May 1847):347–348; ibid., 6 (4 May 1850):448; A. B. Durand, "Letters on Landscape Painting—II" (1855), in J. W. McCoubrey, ed., *American Art 1700–1960*, pages 110–113; R. J. O'Brien, *American Sublime*, pages 102–163; F. L. Olmsted, "Passages in the Life of an Unpractical Man," in *The Papers of Frederick Law Olmsted, Vol. I: The Formative Years, 1822–1852*, edited by Charles Capen McLaughlin and Charles E. Beveridge (Johns Hopkins, 1977), page 100. See also Betsy Blackmar and Elizabeth Cromley, *Resorts of the Catskills* (New York, 1979) and Roland Van Zandt, *The Catskill Mountain House* (New Brunswick, NJ, 1966).

10. R. W. Emerson, "Nature" (1836), in Reginald L. Cook, ed., *Ralph Waldo Emerson: Selected Prose and Poetry*, 2d ed. (New York, 1969), pages 5–6; J. T. Callow, *Kindred Spirits*, p. 120; W. C. Bryant, "Forest Hymn," quoted in Joshua C. Taylor, *America As Art* (Washington, D.C., 1976), page 104; N. P. Willis, *Out-Doors at Idlewild* (New York, 1855), page 28; R. J. O'Brien, *American Sublime*, pages 123–124; B. Novak, *Nature and Culture*, passim.

According to historian Joshua C. Taylor, Cole "succeeded in identifying the actual scenery of the countryside with a spiritual content acceptable to the most avid advocates of high moral purpose in art." Shortly after Cole's death in 1848, Asher B. Durand explained that his friend's paintings had demonstrated the "high moral capabilities" of landscape art. Perhaps fittingly, at the time of his death Cole was working on *The Cross and the World,* a series of allegorical paintings that attempted to convey didactically the truths the painter had learned through direct contact with nature.[11]

Even as nineteenth-century Americans invested profound cultural significance in the landscape, fundamentally dislocating change was reshaping the natural environment. Completion of the Erie Canal accelerated New York City's growth into the dominant American metropolis, while the availability of foodstuffs from distant regions dramatically altered agricultural practices in the Hudson Valley, resulting in a shift from grain and other staples to fruit and dairy farming. Steamboats made the transport of goods and people much easier, which contributed to the industrialization of river towns and the development of suburbs in the southern end of the valley. The Hudson River Railroad, which began service on the east bank in 1849 and which extended to Albany two years later, separated Washington Irving's beloved Sunnyside from the river, as the machine quite literally invaded the author's garden. More important, by increasing speed and telescoping distance the railroad altered people's perception of self in space and time.[12]

As an aggregation of individuals Americans seem peculiarly torn between the past and the future. This observation is not new: Thoreau based *Walden* upon it. Change was occurring so rapidly in Concord that after a midday nap a farmer would inquire, "What's the news?" Thoreau, who lamented the pace of modern life, urged contemporaries to foresake the thriftiness of Poor Richard, as well as the new inventions that were transforming society, and instead to save themselves by enjoying the process of living. More recently, other writers such as Edward Shils and David Lowenthal have investigated the importance of tradition and nostalgia as cultural expression. This tension between what was and what can be was particularly noticeable in the Hudson Valley during the second quarter of the nineteenth century. At that time residents simultaneously reached forward and backward, and in celebrating their past attempted to shape a future in ways that would make it less threatening.[13]

It is difficult now to comprehend how aware of the past Americans were in the nineteenth century. In the 1820s virtually

11. T. Cole, "Essay on American Scenery," pages 99–100; T. Cole, "The Wild," quoted in L. L. Noble, *Life and Works of Thomas Cole,* page 64; J. C. Taylor, *America As Art,* pages 106–108.

12. R. J. O'Brien, *American Sublime,* pages 127–163.

13. H. D. Thoreau, *Walden and Other Writings of Henry David Thoreau,* edited by Brooks Atkinson (1854; New York, 1950), page 84; Robert A. Gross, "'The Most Estimable Place in All the World': A Debate on Progress in Nineteenth-Century Concord," *Studies in the American Renaissance* 1 (1978):1–15; idem, "Culture and Cultivation: Agriculture and Society in Thoreau's Concord," *Journal of American History* 69 (June 1982): 42–61. See also Edward Shils, *Tradition* (Chicago, 1981) and David Lowenthal, *The Past is a Foreign Country* (Cambridge, 1985).

every eastern town and village boasted of at least one resident who was a veteran of the nation's struggle for independence, and these men, who so often were called upon to deliver the traditional Fourth of July oration, provided physical and psychological continuity with the past. An event such as Lafayette's visit was a stirring reminder of the sacrifices of the Revolutionary generation, while the simultaneous deaths of Thomas Jefferson and John Adams on 4 July 1826, fifty years to the day of the signing of the Declaration of Independence, was a symbolic reminder that Providence was indeed guiding the new nation.[14]

Nevertheless, with the passing of years the last of the veterans died—in 1825 John Quincy Adams praised the surviving soldiers of the Revolution as "these venerable relics of an age gone by"—and even the best intentioned plans to sanctify the sites and events of the War for Independence went uncompleted. Long before Lafayette's visit the steeple of Independence Hall had been damaged and removed, but to the Frenchman's dismay it had not been replaced. Residents in Newburgh intended to erect a monument "commemorative of that glorious termination of our revolutionary struggles" at Temple Hill, in nearby New Windsor, where the Continental Army had camped while Washington maintained his headquarters in the village. The best of intentions did not, however, protect significant structures or sites associated with the nation's past, even as venerable buildings were torn down and sacred ground turned to more prosaic use.[15]

The march of time and the march of progress made it imperative that antebellum Americans preserve the landscape that was so much a part of their collective heritage. Settlers on the frontier ravaged the environment. They cut trees with the enthusiasm of Cooper's fictional Billy Kirby, whose heroic efforts cleared forests in the name of "progress" with such efficiency that Natty Bumppo fled west to escape the settler's axe. Cole noted the same pattern of exploitation and development in the Hudson Valley. In his "Essay on American Scenery" he lamented that the "ravages of the axe are daily increasing—the most noble scenes are made desolate, and oftentimes with a wantonness and barbarism scarcely credible in a civilized nation." A year later, in a letter to his patron, New York merchant Luman Reed, he observed bitterly, "They are cutting down all the trees in the beautiful valley on which I have looked so often with a loving eye." At this time the artist was working on a series of paintings, *The Course of Empire,* that expressed his despair at the impact of development on the landscape. Following a cyclical theory of history closely associated with Bishop Berkeley, Cole portrayed the evolution of civilization from a savage to a pastoral state, then to a grandiose ur-

14. See Stanley J. Idzerda et al., *Lafayette, Hero of Two Worlds: The Art and Pageantry of His Farewell Tour of America, 1824–1825* (Flushing, NY, 1989), and Fred Somkin, *Unquiet Eagle: Memory and Desire in the Idea of American Freedom, 1815–1860* (Ithaca, 1967), pages 131–174.

15. J. Q. Adams, "First Annual Message," 6 December 1825, in James D. Richardson, ed., *A Compilation of the Messages and Papers of the Presidents,* 20 vols. (New York, 1897), 2:874; Samuel W. Eager, *An Outline History of Orange County . . .* (Newburgh, NY, 1846–1847), page 196; Michael Kammen, *Mystic Chords of Memory: The Transformation of Tradition in American Culture* (New York, 1991), pages 52–56, passim. Marc H. Miller has pointed out that shortly before Lafayette's visit the British earthworks at Yorktown, Virginia, had been destroyed. A newspaper commented, "As if we had not land enough already, and as if these works, the monuments of our glory, were not worth a million times the space they occupy." S. J. Idzerda, ed., *Lafayette, Hero of Two Worlds,* page 134.

ban setting, which was followed by destruction and reversion to the primitive. The pastoral or domesticated landscape, which depicted the human presence living in harmony with nature, was obviously best, while an unbalanced state—either overwhelmingly savage or urban—was not conducive to the highest development of society. Cole's allegory was obvious, that destruction would be the price exacted of the United States if it became an urban nation.[16]

Just as ominous a warning of the impact of civilization on nature was sounded a decade later by a critic in the *Literary World*. Reviewing the annual exhibition of the National Academy of Design in 1847, this anonymous author found special poignance in a pair of Staten Island landscapes painted by Jasper Francis Cropsey. There was an essential lesson in Cropsey's works:

> *The axe of civilization is busy with our old forests,*
> *and artisan ingenuity is fast sweeping away the relics*
> *of our national infancy. What were once the wild and*
> *picturesque haunts of the Red Man, and where the wild deer*
> *roamed in freedom, are becoming the abodes of commerce*
> *and the seats of manufacture. Our inland lakes, once*
> *sheltered and secluded in the midst of noble forests,*
> *are now laid bare and covered with busy craft; and even*
> *the old primordial hills, once bristling with shaggy pine*
> *and hemlock, like old Titans as they were, are being shorn*
> *of their locks, and left to blister in cold nakedness in the sun.*

This reviewer recognized that "Yankee enterprise has little sympathy with the picturesque," and charged American artists with the responsibility to "rescue from its grasp the little that is left, before it is for ever too late." The recording of the American landscape, this writer concluded, was the artist's "high and sacred mission." The advance of civilization was destroying nature, and it became the painter's mission—a word replete with religious connotations—to capture and preserve the beauties of the New World before they were sacrificed to Mammon.[17]

Little was done, however, to preserve the landscape of the Hudson Valley until the last quarter of the nineteenth century. In 1847 A. J. Downing advocated the formation of tree-planting associations in every town and village throughout New York State, but such efforts were hardly commensurate with the task of protecting the valley's scenic heritage from development. Californians initiated the preservation of the Yosemite Valley and the Mariposa big tree grove in 1864, while eight years later the federal govern-

16. J. F. Cooper, *The Pioneers,* passim; T. Cole, "Essay on American Scenery," page 109; T. Cole, letter to Luman Reed, 26 March 1836, in L. L. Noble, *Life and Works of Thomas Cole,* pages 147–148.

17. "The Fine Arts. Exhibition at the National Academy," *Literary World* 1 (15 May 1847):347–348.

ment established Yellowstone as the first national park. Perhaps ironically, the lineal descendants of Cole who served as artists on explorations in the West contributed to the establishment of national parks there, while residents in the East did little to preserve the landscape that was the setting for this national reorientation in attitudes toward nature. When conservation became a paramount concern in New York State at the end of the nineteenth century, the most successful efforts were directed toward the celebration of natural wonders (Niagara Falls) or were so couched in the Progressivist rhetoric of efficiency and expertise that traditional scenic values were almost totally absent (the Adirondacks). Only with the formation of the American Scenic and Historic Preservation Society in 1895 did New Yorkers act energetically to protect the landscape of the Hudson Valley.[18]

If few woodsmen and their contemporaries in antebellum America heeded the pleas of Cooper and poet George P. Morris to "spare that tree," at least on a scale necessary to protect the scenic heritage of the Hudson River basin, residents at the middle of the nineteenth century were more conscious of the need to preserve their past. They succeeded in large part because they sanctified the Hudson Valley, merging history with the landscape, which functioned both as the physical setting in which the stirring events of the past had taken place and as a sacred space in its own right. Thus, at the time when workers were hewing timber and laying iron for the railroad along the east bank of the river, which, when completed, would accelerate the rate of change, Samuel Eager was writing his *Outline History of Orange County*, John R. Brodhead and Edmund B. O'Callaghan were compiling their documentary histories of colony and state, and Benson J. Lossing was traveling with pen and sketchbook in hand preparing his *Pictorial Field-Book of the American Revolution*. In the subtitle of that magisterial work Lossing listed "scenery" with "relics" in the topics covered, an assertion of the interdependence of landscape and history. He described the mid–Hudson Valley as possessing "some of the finest scenery in the world," which was "enhanced by the associations which hallow it." As these and other books celebrated the American landscape and familiarized readers with scenes of the revolutionary past, residents of the Hudson Valley acted to preserve a modest fieldstone farmhouse Lossing praised for its historic significance, Washington's Headquarters at Newburgh.[19]

The preservationist impulse, which was nurtured and promoted by artists and writers, was an important element of what historian Daniel Walker Howe has called Whig political culture. It was a manifestation of a "proper sense of responsibility, both

18. A. J. Downing, "Trees, in Towns and Villages," reprinted in *Rural Essays. By A. J. Downing. Edited, With a Memoir of the Author, by George William Curtis; and a Letter to His Friends, by Fredrika Bremer* (New York, 1853), pages 303–310. See also R. J. O'Brien, *American Sublime*, pages 237–280; Roderick Nash, *Wilderness and the American Mind*, rev. ed. (New Haven, 1973), and Samuel P. Hays, *Conservation and the Gospel of Efficiency: The Progressive Conservation Movement, 1890–1920* (Cambridge, MA, 1959).

19. B. J. Lossing, *The Pictorial Field Book of the American Revolution; Or, Illustrations, by Pen and Pencil, of the History, Biography, Scenery, Relics, and Traditions of the War for Independence*, 2 vols. (New York, 1850), 2:98–102.

toward previous generations, whose sacrifices had made freedom possible, and toward subsequent generations, who depended on present exertions" to maintain continuity with the past. Thus, in 1834 Knickerbocker author Gulian C. Verplanck described the dwelling in Newburgh where Washington lived during the waning days of the American Revolution as "one of the most interesting relics of the first and heroic age of our republic." The significance of the building was not limited to the immediate vicinity: Verplanck recounted how, at a dinner honoring Lafayette, a French host replicated the principal room of the house. A surprised Lafayette recognized the room with "seven doors and one window" and exclaimed, "We are at Washington's Headquarters on the Hudson, fifty years ago!" This simple vernacular dwelling was not simply a monument to the past, Verplanck asserted, but it had didactic importance for present and future generations: "What shall we say of the American who feels no glow of patriotism," he inquired, "who kindles not into warmer love for his country, and her glorious institutions, who rises into no grand and fervent aspiration for the virtue and the happiness of this people, when he enters the humble, but venerable walls of the HEAD-QUARTERS AT NEWBURGH. [20]

For Verplanck what made this structure a venerable shrine was the interdependence of a landscape aesthetic and the historical consciousness it embodied. "The view from the house and grounds, as well as the whole neighbourhood around it," he wrote, "are rich alike in natural beauty and historical remembrances." A year later, in his "Essay on American Scenery," the artist Cole noted that the Hudson Valley was full of "historical and legendary associations" because "the great struggle for freedom has sanctified many a spot." Then, in 1839, Washington Irving, who was born in 1783 and appropriately named in honor of the man widely regarded as the father of the nation, and whose pen and fertile imagination invented many of the legends to which Cole had referred, joined a group of citizens of Newburgh in petitioning the state legislature to preserve Washington's headquarters as an historic site. [21]

This first successful preservationist effort moved closer to fruition when, in 1848, the owner of the house, Jonathan Hasbrouck, defaulted on a government loan. When the building was scheduled to be put up at auction, Andrew J. Caldwell, persuaded of its historical significance, corresponded with Governor Hamilton Fish and won his support for its preservation as an historic site. In November of 1849 the Orange County supervisors petitioned that the state purchase and maintain the house and

20. D. W. Howe, *The Political Culture of the American Whigs* (Chicago, 1979), pages 72, passim; Gulian C. Verplanck, "View of Washington's Head-Quarters," *New-York Mirror* 12 (27 December 1834):201–202.

21. G. C. Verplanck, "View of Washington's Head-Quarters," pages 201–202; T. Cole, "Essay on American Scenery," page 108. See also Daniel R. Porter, "The Knickerbockers and the Historic Site in New York State," *New York History* 64 (January 1983):35–50, and William G. Tyrrell, letter to the editor, ibid. 64 (July 1983):349–350.

The sanctified landscape: "Washington's Headquarters," an oil on canvas by Raphael Hoyle, 1830. Courtesy of the Historical Society of Newburgh Bay and the Highlands, Newburgh, New York.

grounds for the public. A legislative committee studying the question endorsed the petition the following year, noting that:

> *If our love of country is excited when we read*
> *the biography of our revolutionary heroes, or*
> *the history of revolutionary events, how much more*
> *will the flame of patriotism burn in our bosoms*
> *when we tread the ground where was shed the blood*
> *of our fathers, or when we move among the scenes*
> *where were conceived and consummated their*
> *noblest achievements.*

In their report the legislators predicted:

> *No traveler who touches upon the shores of*
> *Orange county will hesitate to make a pilgrimage*
> *to this beautiful spot, associated as it is*
> *with so many delightful reminiscences in our*
> *early history, and if he have an American heart*
> *in his bosom, he will feel himself a better man;*
> *his patriotism will kindle with deeper emotion;*
> *his aspirations for his country's good will ascend*
> *from a more devout mind for having visited*
> *the "Head-Quarters of Washington."*

The language of this report included the words "pilgrimage" and "devout," each conveying a religiosity that equated preservation with the sacred "mission" the reviewer for the *Literary World* earlier had ascribed to the landscape painter. The language must have been persuasive, because until this time the national and state governments had been reluctant to assume responsibility for constructing monuments or preserving historic sites. The great memorial at Bunker Hill in Boston and the Washington Monument in Baltimore, as well as the uncompleted obelisk in the District of Columbia, had been erected through private funding. At the middle of the nineteenth century, however, residents of the Hudson Valley requested that the state not only purchase, but also restore and maintain as an historic site what had been a private residence.[22]

The committee's report, together with mounting evidence of the "progress" that threatened to destroy the surviving relics of the Revolutionary era, led the state legislature to approve "an Act for the preservation of 'Washington's Head-Quarters'" on 10 April

22. Richard Caldwell, *A True History of the Acquisition of Washington's Headquarters . . .* (Salisbury Mills, NY, 1887), passim; A. Elwood Corning, *The Story of the Hasbrouck House* (Newburgh, NY, 1950); C. B. Hosmer, Jr., *Presence of the Past,* pages 35–36; M. Kammen, *Mystic Chords of Memory,* passim.

1850. On 4 July 1850, citizens throughout the Hudson Valley gathered at Washington's former residence to dedicate it as an historic shrine. A large military procession paraded through the town to the grounds, where General Winfield Scott, hero of the Mexican War, presided over the ceremonies. While a group of singers gave a spirited rendering of a celebratory ode, Scott raised the flag on what a newspaper described as a 135-foot liberty pole. Mrs. John J. Monell's thirty-line poem described the ground as "holy" and the building as "sacred," while charging listeners with the responsibility of cherishing the monument:

> *Brothers! to your care is given,*
> *Safe to keep this hallowed spot;*
> *Though our warriors rest in heaven,*
> *And these places see them not,*
> *see ye to it,*
> *That their deeds be ne'er forgot.*

Appropriately, an amateur poet's verse captured the religious connotations of the sanctified landscape, as well as of patriotism, at the very moment when "this venerated relic" of the past was preserved for the future.[23]

The preservationist impulse that culminated in the dedication of Washington's Newburgh headquarters as an historic shrine was the product of a broader cultural movement through which nineteenth-century Americans sanctified the landscape. This new landscape aesthetic combined with the historical consciousness that was becoming more compelling as time and economic development swept away the relics of the Revolutionary era. Nurtured by Knickerbocker writers and landscape painters who first explored the aesthetic potential of the Hudson Valley, the sanctification of landscape united attitudes toward scenery, history, political culture, and change into a conservative worldview that helped contemporaries adapt to the social and economic forces that were transforming their lives. Residents of the Hudson Valley recoiled from at least some of the implications of change and turned to the sanctified landscape as an alternative to industrialization, to the more secure ground of the past to find their identity as a nation.[24]

23. "4th of July in Newburgh," *Newburgh Gazette,* 10 July 1850; "The Fourth—The Celebration," *Newburgh Telegraph,* 4 July 1850. Mrs. Monell's ode was printed in the *Literary World* 7 (13 July 1850):36, and excerpted in B. J. Lossing, *Pictorial Field-Book of the Revolution,* page 99.

24. For this interpretation I am indebted to the writings of numerous historians and geographers, but see especially D. W. Howe's *Political Culture of the American Whigs* and David Lowenthal's "Past Time, Present Place: Landscape And Memory," *Geographical Review* 65 (January 1975):1–36.

*Someone who has encountered the deep backwoods*
*of Finland has no fear of the forest.*[1]

1. This 1887 quotation, which I have
translated from the original Finnish,
was made by an immigrant residing in
northern Minnesota; it appeared in
*Uusi Kotimaa* ("The New Homeland"), a newspaper published in New
York Mills, Minnesota. Many other
Finnish-language newspaper accounts
have been employed throughout this
essay, but they are not referenced.
Only selected English-language
sources appear in these notes.

Arnold R. Alanen

# Back to the Land: Immigrants and Image-Makers in the Lake Superior Region, 1865 to 1930

ARNOLD R. ALANEN was born in 1941 in west-central Minnesota (Menahga-Wadena) and spent his formative years on a hardscrabble farm in the Lawler-Tamarack area of northeastern Minnesota. He received a B.A. in architectural studies and an M.A. and a Ph.D. in geography from the University of Minnesota, Minneapolis. He was a Visiting Research Professor in 1982 at the University of Helsinki, Finland, a W. K. Kellogg Foundation National Fellow from 1980 to 1983, and in 1984 a recipient of the University of Wisconsin Alumni Foundation's Excellence in Teaching Award. He was a cofounder and editor of *Landscape Journal* from 1981 to 1989, for which he received an Award of Merit from the American Society of Landscape Architects in 1983 and an Award of Special Recognition from the Council of Educators in Landscape Architecture in 1990. Professor Alanen has published over three dozen articles in leading professional journals in the United States and abroad, and his book, *Main Street Ready-Made: The New Deal Community of Greendale, Wisconsin* (State Historical Society of Wisconsin, 1987), coauthored with Joseph A. Eden, won the Scholarly Book Award of the Wisconsin Council of Writers and the Gambrinus Prize of the Milwaukee Historical Society. Dr. Alanen is a professor of landscape architecture at the University of Wisconsin-Madison.

2. John Brinckerhoff Jackson, *Discovering the Vernacular Landscape* (New Haven: Yale University Press, 1984), page 5.

AMONG SCHOLARS and writers who study and interpret landscapes, there is agreement that the very term "landscape" is rather elusive and difficult to define. Despite such problems with semantics, people outside the field (many of whom are not remotely involved with the study of the earth's surface) use the word for a variety of reasons and purposes. We are told by book reviewers that certain authors have surveyed the "literary landscape" of a region, nation, or historical epoch; seasoned news reporters announce after a major election that the "political landscape" of America has changed; interior designers, in an effort to increase employee morale, productivity, and efficiency within an organization, create an "office (or interior) landscape"; and neurophysiologists, using high-powered magnification, describe their activities as exploring the "landscape" of the brain.

Perhaps we should not be too concerned when landscape is adopted as metaphor, as long as such usage helps us to comprehend what J. B. Jackson calls a "concrete, three-dimensional shared reality."[2] For those who are interested in the actual landscape, however, there is no doubt that continued attention should be given to the development of a better and more inclusive definition of landscape, one that considers physical settings, social behavior, and meaning. To gain such an understanding, a greater variety of historical and modern landscapes needs to be studied. In the past, the vast majority of landscape history has been concerned almost entirely with those spaces and places for which considerable documentary or field evidence is available. With new historiographical techniques and methods, however, along with a better use of imagination, the history of past landscapes can be described and portrayed more clearly.

This essay, therefore, in addressing the question *What is landscape?*, considers the behavior, experiences, and impressions of a group of people seldom studied by landscape historians, namely immigrants, within the physical setting of a specific North

American region, Lake Superior, one of the last frontiers to be settled in the continental United States. To do so, certain sources and approaches normally within the purview of social history are used and, as will become evident, consideration of the methods, techniques, tools, and sources of related disciplines can open new doors to understanding a landscape.

Overall, we know rather little about the landscape impressions of early pioneers and immigrants. One reason, of course, is that such people simply were too busy to record their thoughts and perceptions. Another is that not all immigrants were able to write and, even if they could, only small numbers of the total population were interested in, or could successfully articulate their attitudes toward, the landscape. Whereas relatively few of these emigrés were well educated, a number were at least familiar with the rudiments of reading and writing. As the historian Theodore Blegan said in 1947, America's immigrants may have been unlettered, but they were not inarticulate.[3]

If Blegan's observation is valid, and I believe it is, then it can be assumed that a number of non-English language sources—primarily almanacs, diaries, letters, journals, periodicals, oral histories, and newspapers—include descriptions of the "home landscapes" that immigrants perceived, encountered, and created in North America. Of this array, the immigrant newspaper appears to be a great source of information, given that more than 3,440 non-English language titles appeared in the United States between 1884 and 1920 alone.[4]

In the Lake Superior region, the largest immigrant group to inhabit the area during the late nineteenth and early twentieth centuries (the Finns) displayed virtual universal literacy. To be sure, few were well educated, but almost every Finnish immigrant, because of some basic Old World education via the church or traveling schools, was at least familiar with the essentials of reading and writing. With this rudimentary knowledge, the Finns, beginning in 1876, developed over 350 newspapers and serials in the United States and Canada; of these, the majority were published in Michigan, Minnesota, and Wisconsin.

When considering the typical English-language newspapers published in small-town, nineteenth-century America, it has been noted that they generally failed to comment on two important facets of local life: children and landscapes. Since both were "simply part of the scene," it is quite possible the editors assumed their readers were already so familiar with landscape-related features and the antics of children that these merited little attention in newspaper columns.[5]

3. Theodore Blegan, *Grassroots History* (Minneapolis: University of Minnesota Press, 1947), pages 18–19.

4. Jerzy Zubrzycki, "The Role of the Foreign-Language Press in Migrant Integration," *Population Studies* 12 (1958–1959), page 76.

5. See the chapter by John Stilgoe in this volume.

Finnish immigrant newspapers also gave little consideration to children, but landscapes were discussed more frequently—especially during their formative years when such journals often had networks of readers and correspondents who were scattered across a region, state, and nation. The most common points of discussion were job availability, wages, the weather, land costs, the arrival and departure of emigrés, the health of local residents, and even the shortage of suitable (i.e., Finnish) marriage partners, but numerous descriptions also featured landscapes and environments. Such discussions commonly were written by immigrants working as farmers, miners, lumberjacks, railroad section hands, laborers, and domestics. Their descriptions often portrayed local landscapes for the benefit of compatriots in Finland and the United States searching for employment opportunities and places to reside in the New World.[6]

For centuries, Finland's forests, lakes, and landscapes have been of great importance to its writers, artists, musicians, and scientists. During the 1850s, Finnish nationalist Sacharias Topelius recommended that the incipient discipline of geography provide a landscape-based view of Finland so as to foster greater national identity among the populace. (Finland was a Grand Duchy of Russia from 1809 to 1917.) According to one recent interpretation, Topelius believed that "the Finnish landscape was in effect the only thing held in common by a people apparently lacking in outstanding achievements either in its history or in the form of an authentic Finnish-language culture."[7] The major thrust of his message was directed towards Finland's cultural elite, but Topelius also sought to reach a wider audience by writing humorous little stories with geographical themes for publication in children's magazines, and he edited a number of school textbooks. From a landscape standpoint, the most important of these volumes was *Maamme kirja* ("The Book of Our Land"), first published in Finnish in 1876. Somewhat later, the verbal descriptions of Finnish landscapes given by Topelius were illustrated by a group of nine artists; these paintings were widely reproduced and used for instructional purposes in public schools during the early decades of the twentieth century.

Finnish novelists of the late nineteenth and early twentieth centuries are especially noted for their use of landscape imagery. Of these authors, none surpassed Aleksis Kivi in describing the natural and cultural features that formed the landscape of Finland. Excerpts from the first paragraph of Kivi's seminal work of 1870, *Seitsemän veljestä* ("Seven Brothers"), indicate why this volume has been termed "the first great forest novel in Finnish literature":

6. Some four thousand pages of newspapers were consulted in preparing this essay. These included most of the known extant copies of nineteenth-century Finnish-language newspapers published in the United States and a selective sample of every article or report that used specific words to describe features related to the landscape. Altogether, landscapes were mentioned in several hundred accounts. In addition to newspapers, sixty oral histories were consulted from two collections initiated in the early 1970s, one at Suomi College in Hancock, Michigan, and the other at the Iron Range Research Center in Chisholm, Minnesota. Since first-generation Finnish immigrants still resided in the region at that time, special efforts were made to record the conditions these pioneers experienced during their early years in North America. It should be mentioned that more traditional sources such as memoirs, letters, reports, and books were also used to flesh out this account. During the period covered in this essay, some 300,000 Finns immigrated to the United States, the majority to the Lake Superior region.

7. Hannele Rikkinen, "Development in the Status and Content of Geography Teaching in the Secondary Schools of Finland in 1770–1888," *Fennia* 160 (1982), page 87.

These paintings by Kustaa Heikkila in 1903 (left) and by Vihtori Ylinen in 1915 (right) depict typical scenes in Savo and Hämö, provinces in eastern and south-central Finland. They were two of several paintings used in the public schools in Finland during the early twentieth century to portray different regions of the country originally described by Finnish nationalist Sakarias Topelius. The illustrations are from a collection of the paintings that were reproduced in Kerkko Hakulinen and Pentii Yli-Jokippi, *Maame kuvat: valistuksen maantieteeliset opetustaulet, 1903–32* (Espoo, Finland: Weilin + Goos, 1983), pages 79 and 89, respectively.

*On a rocky north slope near the village of Toukola in the southern part of the province of Hame stands the Jukola house. Below it lie fields where full heads of grain once rippled in the wind before the farm went to ruin. Further down is another field fringed with clover and crossed by a zigzag ditch, which grew hay in abundance before it became a common pasture for the village cattle. Great expanses of wilderness lands, woods, and swamps also belong to the farm. . . .*[8]

8. Aleksis Kivi (translation of the original 1870 text by Richard A. Impola), *Seven Brothers* (New Platz, NY, 1991), page 1.

But what of the typical Finns, including those who emigrated to the New World? How did experience and limited educational opportunities affect their attitudes toward landscape, in both Europe and North America? Most Finns had little direct acquaintance with their country's literary and scientific works, but these are the individuals who resided in the very areas that Topelius, Kivi, and other writers and artists described and illustrated.

Since Finland was a land of forests, lakes, marshes, and small farms where folk traditions remained relatively unchanged for centuries prior to the early 1900s, the immigrants could call upon an extensive vocabulary to describe what they encountered in the Lake Superior region. The most commonly used terms to describe natural and cultural landscape elements were *aukko* (opening), *haavikko* (aspen grove), *järvi* (lake), *joki* (river), *laidun* (pasture), *luonto* (nature), *metsä* (forest), *pelto* (field), *metsikko* (grove), *räme* (bog), and *suo* (swamp). Three additional words, however, require special mention: *maisema* (landscape), *erämaa* (wilderness), and *korpi* (backwoods).

*Maisema*, or landscape, which was influenced by its antecedents in other European languages, began to be used in Finland during the 1830s to describe land, soil, terrain, district, place, or locality. By the late 1800s, the definition for the German term, *Landschaft*—which referred to an area or region—was utilized by Finnish scientific writers; and in the early 1900s the meaning of *maisema* was expanded further to include scenes illustrated in landscape paintings and to define descriptions of a view.[9]

The Finnish concept of *erämaa*, on the other hand, is somewhat unique, given that the original meaning differed from most definitions of wilderness expressed elsewhere in Europe and North America. Unlike "the western idea of wild nature in a 'natural' state," *erämaa* originally referred to forested areas of Finland used for utilitarian purposes; to a Finn, *erämaa* described wilderness as vital and familiar forested areas that frequently were visited and used—especially for hunting purposes.[10]

The ancient term, *korpi,* has been, and still is, used to describe remote, wild, backwoods areas. Typically, *korpi* referred to large spruce swamps and bogs; when such areas displayed some limited agricultural potential, it was commonly recognized that much time and effort were needed to make them productive.

In considering the perceptions of seventeenth-century and eighteenth-century explorers and missionaries who arrived in the Great Lakes region centuries before Finnish settlement began, it becomes clear that a very different situation prevailed. Peter Fritzell has noted that, despite their religious backgrounds, these individuals did not speak of the wilderness in metaphorical terms. In fact, the word "wilderness," whether used literally or metaphorically, can hardly be found in early accounts of the Great Lakes region. The region was, according to Fritzell, "treeless and forestless in published conception for two centuries."[11]

Explorer Jonathan Carver, in his 1778 account, was the first to mention the regional landscape, but even his interpretation was abstract. Carver's prose reflected traditional views of wilderness and landscape, and indicated an overriding preference for sparsely forested areas. Actual appreciation of the Great Lakes regional landscape developed somewhat slowly, but interpretations in language and art were firmly rooted in the sublime and picturesque.[12]

Henry Schoolcraft, in a famous expedition that led to the discovery of the headwaters of the Mississippi River in 1820–1821, gave the world its first scientific conception of the region's flora, fauna, and physical features; but even as late as the 1850s, "no one had authored a sociobiotic conception of the northern forest to suggest or indicate in some detail how incoming settlers would or could use the forest and its elements."[13] And no one at this time conceived of the aesthetic properties of the regional landscape.

9. Tarja Keisteri, "The Study of Changes in Cultural Landscapes," *Fennia* 168 (1990), pages 34–37. It is important to emphasize that Finnish immigrant writers rarely used so sophisticated a word as *maisema* (landscape) in their writings, probably because the word entered the common vocabulary so late.

10. Ari Aukusti Lehtinen, "The Northern Natures—A Study of the Forest Question Emerging within the Timber-Line Conflict in Finland," *Fennia* 169 (1991):136.

11. Peter Fritzell, "Changing Conceptions of the Great Lakes Forest: Jacques Cartier to Sigurd Olson," in Susan L. Flader, ed., *The Great Lakes Forest: An Environmental and Social History* (Minneapolis: University of Minnesota Press, 1983), page 278.

12. Ibid., pages 280–282.

13. Ibid., page 287.

The geologist and surveyor Douglas Houghton was the person most responsible for drawing significant numbers of people to the unsettled Lake Superior region in the early 1840s. Following his success in identifying and locating some of the major copper ore deposits of northern Michigan, thousands of prospectors and would-be residents descended upon the Keweenaw Peninsula in the years following 1842 and participated in the United States's first mining bonanza. Though Houghton drowned in an unfortunate accident on Lake Superior in 1843 and never lived to see the development and activity his efforts engendered, other geologists and scientists continued his work from the 1850s onward, surveying and mapping out the extent of the Copper Range, or "Copper Country," and the six iron ore districts of the region— the Marquette, Menominee, Gogebic, Vermilion, Mesabi, and Cuyuna ranges.

The development of the region's ore deposits throughout the latter 1800s was accompanied by the exploitation of the forest cover. Soon, the white pine of the Great Lakes region was synonymous with one word throughout America: lumber.[14] Fritzell contends that, once the noticeable presence of timber operators, railroad companies, and agriculture settlers was evident by the 1870s and the 1880s, descriptions of the regional forest were seldom given in hostile terms, with few accounts portraying the process of "hewing, blasting, and burning a way of life from a slowly yielding, recalcitrant wilderness."[15] We do not learn from Fritzell whether there were significant differences between the views of "outsiders" and of "insiders." It is quite possible, for example, that the rather limited number of explorers, prospectors, timber cruisers, scientists, and other outsiders whom Fritzell included in his useful review failed to recognize or chose to ignore the unceasing toil that the hundreds of thousands of insiders—primarily farmers, loggers, miners, and laborers—regularly encountered on a firsthand basis.

At first timber removal was based on the myth that the forest was inexhaustible. Later, as the finite limitations of this resource became evident, a utilitarian attitude was adopted: removal of the pine, it was argued, contributed to the land clearance that was necessary before agriculture could emerge. In northern Wisconsin alone, where 130 billion board-feet of virgin white pine once stood, only sixteen billion remained by 1898. As the twentieth century dawned, all major pineries in the three states had been decimated, only a few scattered and low-yielding areas remained to be harvested, and a "cutover" landscape of slash, stumps, and brush had emerged as the dominant visual image throughout the region.[16] This is the same legacy that eventually landed in the Pa-

14. William Cronon, *Nature's Metropolis: Chicago and the Great West* (New York: W. W. Norton & Co., 1991), page 152.

15. Fritzell, "Changing Conceptions of the Great Lakes Forest," page 287.

16. Initially used as an adjective, the term "Cutover" began to be employed as a proper noun to describe the region during the 1930s.

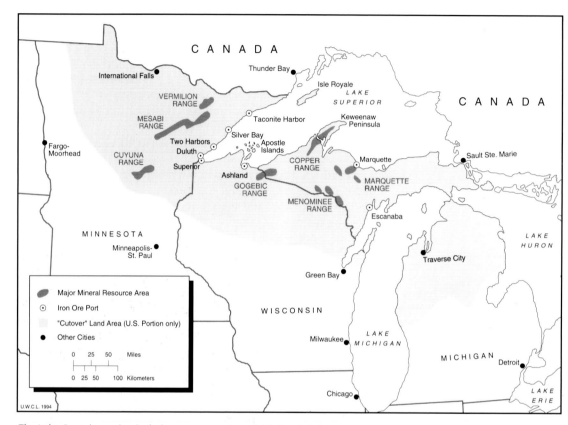

The Lake Superior region includes one copper ore district and six iron ore ranges. The far northern section of Michigan's Upper Peninsula is known as the Keweenaw; in 1992 a portion of the area was designated the Keweenaw National Historic Park. Since its discovery in the 1890s, the Mesabi Range has served as the single most important source of iron ore in the United States. Bob Dylan, the musician, was born and raised on the Mesabi Iron Range in Hibbing, Minnesota. The northern Wisconsin islands that extend into Lake Superior near Ashland were designated the Apostle Islands National Lakeshore in 1970, at the initiative of Gaylord Nelson, then United States Senator from Wisconsin and now counselor of the Wilderness Society. Cartography by the University of Wisconsin-Madison Cartographic Laboratory, 1994.

cific Northwest where, by 1990, less than five percent of the old growth forest was left.

Soon questions began to be raised as to how the land might be utilized after the logging era ended. As early as the 1850s, a transplanted New Yorker claimed that, once northern Wisconsin's better lands were converted to farms, the region would "sustain a more dense population than any country of prairie and openings can do."[17] After the prime stands of pine had been harvested, a number of large landholders, primary lumber and railroad companies, started to dispose of their properties by promoting the agricultural potential of the region. Eventually, community and governmental officials, representatives of colonization companies, speculators, and other individuals and groups encouraged settlement on the cutover land.

State-sponsored agencies were developed to induce European immigrants to the region, and a series of publications prepared by several agricultural researchers in the land grant universities of Wisconsin, Minnesota, and Michigan gave a sense of scientific legitimacy to the farming ventures. Undoubtedly the best-known and most prestigious of these image-makers was Dean William A. Henry of the College of Agriculture at the University of Wisconsin in Madison. The key document completed under Henry's direction was a promotional booklet entitled, *Northern Wisconsin: A Hand-Book for the Homeseeker*, a lavishly illustrated tome that touted the agricultural potential of the region. To Henry, and to the Wisconsin State Legislature which authorized the document, it was essential that the cycle from wilderness to cutover lands be completed by achieving the final phase of development, the middle landscape, or garden:[18]

> *With farms supplanting the forest northern Wisconsin will not revert to a wilderness with the passing of the lumber industry, but will be occupied by a thrifty class of farmers whose direct, intelligent efforts bring substantial, satisfactory returns from fields, flocks and herds.*[19]

Other Wisconsin scientists voiced the opinion that, since "farms follow stumps," hard work and perseverance would reward resourceful settlers with security and happiness. In Minnesota, university personnel voiced similar ideas, as illustrated by a statement of the director of an agricultural experiment station in the northern area of the state. To him it was necessary that the potential of the region be announced until "there is a farmer on every eighty acres of land, till every swamp is drained and every needed road is built."[20]

17. Albert G. Ellis, "Northern Wisconsin—Its Capacities and Its Wants." *Transactions of the Wisconsin Agricultural Society* (1852), page 329.

18. Historian Leo Marx, geographer Yi-Fu Tuan, and several other scholars who are interested in tracing the evolution of environmental themes note that the rural countryside often has been termed the ideal middle ground between city and wildness (or wilderness). The middle landscape, especially when represented in the form of cultivated fields and bucolic scenes (i.e., the image of the garden), becomes, according to Marx in his *The Machine in the Garden* (1964), "the symbolic repository of value of all kinds—economic, political, aesthetic, religious."

19. William A. Henry, *Northern Wisconsin: A Hand-Book for the Homeseeker* (Madison: Democrat Printing Co., 1896), page 18.

20. "Farms Follow Stumps," *University of Wisconsin Experiment Station Bulletin* 332 (Madison: College of Agriculture, University of Wisconsin, 1921); A. J. McGuire, "Report of the Northeast Experiment Farm at Grand Rapids, Minnesota," *University of Minnesota Experiment Station Bulletin* 116 (St. Paul: College of Agriculture, University of Minnesota, 1909), page 2.

The attributes of agricultural areas and settlements were touted regularly in English-language and foreign-language newspapers during the early twentieth century. This advertisement appeared in *Mesabi Ore and Hibbing News* (Hibbing, Minnesota), 2 December 1911.

Advertisements in Finnish-American newspapers used verbal and visual images to induce immigrants to purchase land and become farmers. This advertisement appeared in *Amerikan Suomalainen* (Duluth, Minnesota), 1909.

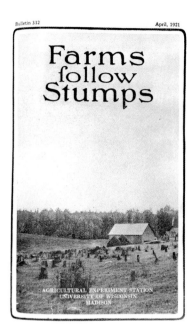

Bulletins published by early twentieth-century agricultural scientists in Wisconsin, Minnesota, and Michigan argued that, once fields had been cleared of stumps and rocks, the Lake Superior wilderness and Cutover region could be converted into a northern garden. "Farms follow Stumps" appeared in Bulletin 332 (April of 1922), and was published by the Agricultural Experiment Station at the University of Wisconsin-Madison.

BULLETIN No. 196                                     JULY, 1910

## THE UNIVERSITY OF WISCONSIN

## Agricultural Experiment Station

The variety and excellence of the roots and vegetables which may be grown in northern Wisconsin furnish ample evidence of its possibilities as a farming country.

## OPPORTUNITIES FOR PROFITABLE FARMING IN NORTHERN WISCONSIN

BY

E. J. DELWICHE

"Opportunities for Profitable Farming" appeared as Bulletin 196 (July of 1910) and was published by the Agricultural Experiment Station at the University of Wisconsin-Madison.

To carry out such a monumental task, no settler was considered more appropriate than the immigrant Finn. Marveling at the tenacity and stoicism of the Finns in carrying out an existence in such a refractory area, claims were made that these pioneers would be "the makers of history" in the new agricultural empire of the Lake Superior region. Other commentators stated that Finns thrived best when conditions were most severe, and an agricultural agent, reviewing his forty years of interaction with these immigrants, said the Finnish farmer really was an engineer: "His ability to make things, not only buildings but tools as well, enables him to succeed where others fail."[21]

To explain why so many Finnish immigrants settled in the region (56,300 individuals, or forty-three percent of all Finns residing in the United States by 1910), a number of early twentieth-century scholarly and popular accounts used deterministic arguments to explain their presence. Stating that Finns emigrated to the Lake Superior region because it "reminded them of Finland," these environmental determinists succeeded in promulgating a myth that exists to some extent in the region even today. One of the most influential scholars to promulgate this argument was geographer Eugene Van Cleef, who claimed that "given freedom and land the Finn in the United States will select an environment that reminds him of the home of his fathers."[22] The geographic factors that Van Cleef listed included similar topographic, soil, and climatic features.

Virtually all investigators now agree that, after the Finns established their earliest settlement nuclei in the region, economic opportunities in mining, logging, farming, and other occupations, along with the availability of land, were primarily responsible for attracting large numbers of Finns to the northern reaches of the three states. Once the Finns arrived in the Lake Superior region, however, they also were culturally "preadapted" to cope with the environment because of their previous experiences in a marginal agricultural region of Europe.[23]

Thousands of Finns and smaller numbers of other settlers were relatively successful in establishing farms and sustaining themselves, but the physical and economic limitations of the region led to widespread tax delinquency and land abandonment during the late 1920s and the 1930s. Just under two million acres of land had been cleared for agricultural purposes by 1930, but this represented less than one-fourth of the region's total area. As the conversion of private lands to public ownership occurred, a host of studies were prepared, some sponsored by the state governments and others by New Deal agencies created during the 1930s. These assessments, unlike those undertaken in previous

21. Mark Thompson, "Finnish Farmers in the Upper Lake States," (Duluth: Northeast Experiment Station, University of Minnesota, 1953).

22. Eugene Van Cleef, "The Finn in America," *Geographical Review* 6 (1918), page 203.

23. Matti Enn Kaups, "Finns in the Lake Superior Region," in Alan G. Noble, ed., *To Build in a New Land: Ethnic Landscape in North America* (Baltimore: Johns Hopkins University Press, 1992), page 249. For a similar argument about Finnish preadaptation to the eastern American frontier of the 1600s and 1700s, refer to Terry G. Jordan and Matti Kaups, *The American Backwoods Frontier: An Ethnic and Ecological Interpretation* (Baltimore: Johns Hopkins University Press, 1989), pp. 38–49.

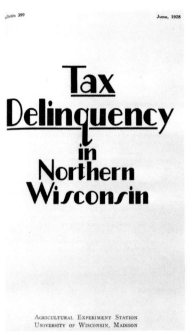

Bulletin 399                                    June, 1928

# Tax Delinquency in Northern Wisconsin

AGRICULTURAL EXPERIMENT STATION
UNIVERSITY OF WISCONSIN, MADISON

By the late 1920s, academics were beginning to understand the difficulties that prospective farmers encountered in the Lake Superior region. This bulletin compares nicely with the preceding illustrations: myth versus reality. "Tax Delinquency in Northern Wisconsin" appeared as Bulletin 399 (June of 1928) and was published by the Agricultural Experiment Station at the University of Wisconsin-Madison.

years, noted the hardships and difficulties that agrarians faced in the region. Whereas previous accounts envisioned the conversion of cutover lands to a middle landscape, these reports contained a more realistic message: Large areas of the cutover region might actually revert to forest again. Since then such a transition has occurred, albeit not uniformly throughout the entire three-state area.

Significant immigration to the Lake Superior region commenced in the mid-1840s, when the copper ore deposits of the Upper Peninsula of Michigan were initially explored and mined, followed by movement to the state's iron ore districts. At first the majority of immigrants were from England (Cornwall), Ireland, Germany, and Canada, but, in the mid-1860s, Scandinavians and a few Finns started to settle in the region; they were followed, in subsequent decades, by South Slavs, Poles, Italians, and other European ethnic groups—including many more Finns.

By the late 1890s, more than twenty-five major immigrant groups were evident in the mining districts, with Finns predominating in the majority of areas, including the agricultural sections of the region. Finns were attracted to the land for various reasons, yet once a parcel of property had been acquired, the same process of changing wilderness, marshland, and cutover forest into a cultivated landscape could begin for all. Many Finns who had arrived in the mining towns and subsequently moved to agricultural areas in the 1860s and the 1870s were able to develop farms in the mixed forest and prairie regions of Minnesota and South Dakota. Once large-scale emigration from Finland began in the 1890s, however, such sources of relatively fertile land were limited. It was at this time that the unsettled expanses of the Lake Superior frontier were considered for their agricultural potential and that the outside image-makers urged prospective settlers, and Finns in particular, to convert the region into a northern garden.

A distinction must be made between the two groups of immigrant Finns who developed the region. One group, the vast majority, consisted of the tens of thousands of mostly anonymous immigrants who provided the labor that transformed portions of the Lake Superior wilderness and cutover areas into fields and farms. The other group included no more than a few score of better-educated individuals (primarily newspaper editors and publishers, land agents, clergymen, and a few other professionals) who were especially important in promulgating the images and impressions that were formed of the region. Some of the image-makers, including the best-known members of the immigrant community, were profoundly concerned with the fate of their compatriots, and sought to understand and depict the conditions

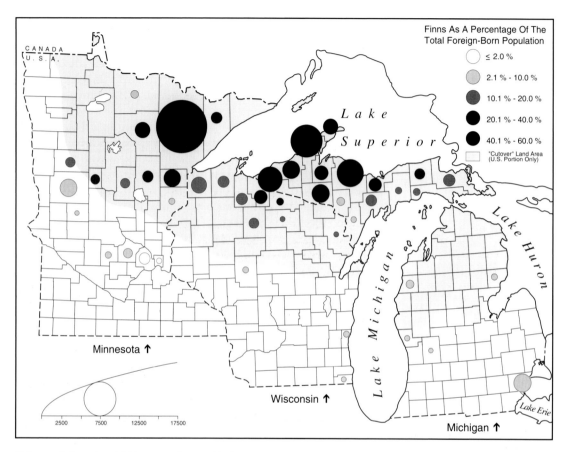

This map is based on 1920 census data and indicates the total number of Finns by county, as well as their proportion of the total foreign-born population, in Wisconsin, Minnesota, and Michigan. The data are derived from the U.S. Census Office, *Fourteenth Census of the United States, Taken in the Year 1920: Vol. 1, Population—Number and Distribution of Inhabitants* (Washington, D.C.: Government Printing Office). Cartography by the Department of Geography, University of Helsinki, Finland, and the Cartographic Laboratory, University of Wisconsin-Madison, 1994.

and environments that would be encountered in new areas of North America. In addition, they offered advice, usually in printed form, that was intended to improve the lot of the typical immigrant. Other members of this group, however, were little more than promoters who gave overly positive depictions of the region's potential for settlement in order to enhance their own pecuniary gain.

The Finns of the United States wished to become farmers for several reasons, although certain factors were clearly of greater importance. For the earliest immigrants, the majority of whom embraced a pietistic form of Finnish Lutheranism known as *Laestadianism*, farming and a rural way of life represented opportunities to protect and maintain their faith, language, and culture. Large numbers of immigrants, who were employed as miners, also looked to farming areas as havens where they could escape the ever-present danger of death, illness, and injury; other Finns retreated to the land in the early twentieth century when they were blacklisted for their leadership and participation in a series of major mining strikes and labor disturbances.

As often was the case, the Finns used Old World proverbs, homilies, and experiences to explain their attachment and movement to rural areas. One 1915 account, among many, claimed that farming was the natural occupation for Finns in America since they had a rural instinct born of generations of contact with the soil. Agriculture was acknowledged to demand considerable effort and hard labor, but prospective agrarians were reminded that the land produced even while one slept. "Why shouldn't the Finns," asked an immigrant, "who in the homeland gained their bread with the assistance of a plow, also do the same in this country?"

Another correspondent noted that "security for one's old age is found on the farm," while religious-minded immigrants believed that farming represented the best opportunity to be in close contact with God. "Why farm? Because God wants the Finns to do so," answered one writer from a rural enclave, whereas another person responded that agriculture was a spiritual calling since each individual had to rely and depend upon divine intervention for rain, sunshine, and warm days. "When God wanted to make a person completely happy," announced a Finn renowned for his strong religious beliefs and use of hyperbole, "he put him on a piece of land."

Other accounts proclaimed it was the patriotic duty of the new Americans to pursue farming in remote places. "Uncle Sam wants the land settled," stated one such recent immigrant, "and we want to till the backwoods." Some correspondents found it amazing that the Homestead Act of 1862 allowed a person to acquire free land in certain areas of the Lake Superior region; equally amazing to many was the amount of land (up to 160 acres) available for homesteading purposes: "Isn't it astounding when land is given for free," asked an incredulous observer, "and not sold for money?"

Since farming could be done at a considerably larger scale in the United States than in Finland, it was only natural, concluded several immigrants, that one's returns also would be significantly larger. Nonhomesteaders, however, usually had to be content with smaller parcels of land when they first acquired property. Often the parcel was no more than forty acres in size, but the immigrant could find solace in claims that said this amount was sufficient to support a family, as long as the land was properly maintained.

Stark contrasts often were drawn between the positive images of rural areas and the negative properties of mining, urban, and industrial centers. When a contingent of Finns, in 1883, left the copper mines surrounding Calumet, Michigan, to farm in Minnesota, the local newspaper editor announced that this was to be expected since men who had worked ten years underground needed to breathe the fresh air that existed on the earth's surface. Cities, it was claimed in 1917, could supply little more than blue milk for their unfortunate residents, while rural areas could provide yellow cream, fresh eggs, and fruit for a healthy population. Clean air and a simple way of life were not to be found in the factory or mine, argued many writers, and others pointed out that farmers could be especially happy whenever they heard that industrial facilities had been shut down because of strikes or reduced labor demands. After proclaiming the beauties and advantages of his own small town and its agricultural hinterland, one reporter stated that, in those places where greasy smoke filled the air, people could not even begin to understand the wonders of nature.

Not everyone agreed that farming was the best life for Finns to pursue in such a marginal agricultural region. Great concern was especially expressed in cases where unscrupulous boosters and promoters induced unsuspecting immigrants to settle in areas with minimal agricultural potential. Various accounts questioned the claims made about the advantages of farming, and others asked whether agriculture actually was a suitable occupation for large numbers of Finns. Not every Finn, they concurred, had the aptitude to succeed as a farmer: "God is the same, the land is the same, the sky is the same, and the opportunities are the same,"

Years of diligent work and effort were necessary to establish a farm and home in the Lake Superior region. This anonymous and undated photograph appeared in *Amerikan albumi: kuvia Amerikan Suomalaisten asuinpaikoilta* (Brooklyn, New York, 1903). The original legend states: "Minnesotan Farmimailta: J. Ojalan talo ja perhe, Swan River" ("Minnesota Farm Country: J. Ojala's home and family, Swan River").

said a concerned writer in 1898, "but even then the possibility of one person progressing like another is uncertain." Other writers with a socialist bent pointed out that farmers, just like their urban comrades, were affected by panics, depressions, and economic exploitation.

Finnish land agents and writers who were genuinely concerned with the fate of their colleagues agreed universally on one point: no man would be a successful farmer unless he had a good wife. J. H. Jasberg, a well-known immigrant who participated in a host of Finnish community activities, was employed as an agent for a railroad company disposing of its large land holdings, and he often used hyperbole to woo people to farming. While Jasberg stated, undoubtedly tongue-in-cheek, that the only language the stumps understood in the Cutover region was Finnish, he realized

While the advantages and disadvantages of farming in the Upper Middle
West were debated, on one point there was universal agreement: No man
would be a successful farmer without an industrious wife. This anonymous
and undated photograph appeared in *Amerikan albumi: kuvia Amerikan
Suomalaisten asuinpaikoilta* (Brooklyn, New York, 1903). The original
legend states: "Minnesotan Farmimailta: Mike Siermalan talo ja perhe,
Swan River" ("Minnesota Farm Country: Mike Siermala's home and family,
Swan River").

that one man alone would have great difficulty in establishing a
farm. Noting that the best potential settler was a "strong, steady
laborer with a large family," Jasberg claimed that the most vital
requirement for success was an "industrious wife." Even a lethar-
gic man with a diligent spouse could succeed as a farmer, he said,
but a land agent should "never attempt to sell a farm or cutover
farm land to a man whose wife objects to moving to the country."

Commentators portrayed the Finnish American farmwife's
daily schedule in America as involving an eight-hour regimen:
eight hours of work in the morning and eight more in the after-

noon and evening. Some writers noted that, on occasion, a particularly energetic and strong woman could actually clear more land than her husband. The wife of one agrarian, as reported in an early twentieth-century account, "plowed and sowed, hoed and harrowed, dug ditches, cut hay, and gathered the harvest better than her spouse," while another report claimed that "farming and cattle-raising were left in the hands of the wife, who in addition acted as the dairymaid, stableman, veterinarian, doctor, bookkeeper, tailor, shoemaker, carpenter, midwife, trapper, poultry specialist, and so on."

Despite the significant obstacles that prospective agrarians faced, close to one-half of America's total Finnish population was found in Michigan, Minnesota, and Wisconsin by the early twentieth century, and most of these immigrants were in the Lake Superior region of the three states. Thus, many of the land-hungry peasants from Finland who settled in North America heeded an age-old call: "Back to the land! Mother Earth will provide for all of us."

In addition to the Finnish terms that were employed to distinguish the features that characterized their new surroundings, the immigrants relied upon their rich folk traditions to describe the landscapes of the upper Middle West. The majority of this expressive vocabulary, much of it based upon descriptions and centuries of human interactions with the natural environment, are found in the folklore, proverbs, and riddles Finnish immigrants brought with them to the New World. Two riddles serve as examples:

> *A bride stands beautiful on the hill every*
> *summer, every winter she is nude.*
> [*a birch tree*]

> *They bring the maiden here, leave a seat there,*
> *strip the finery from her hair.*
> [*a log being brought home from the forest*] [24]

Coming from a country that has one of the richest and largest collections of folklore in the world, the Finnish immigrant could literally draw upon tens of thousands of statements to explain or describe situations she or he encountered in a new and often difficult environment.

To Finnish immigrants, the wilderness of the Lake Superior region certainly was not foreign in appearance or character, for

24. Leea Virtanen et al., eds., *Arvoitukset: Finnish Riddles* (Helsinki: Finnish Literature Society, 1977), pp. 172 and 178.

their homeland also was a place of forests, lakes, and marshes. (Even today, more than three-fourths of Finland is forested.) The reports on the wilderness of northern Michigan, Minnesota, and Wisconsin that were written by the immigrants can be divided into two general categories: (1) portrayals of a romantic or attractive wilderness where untrammeled nature could provide the perceptive observer with useful lessons and insights to guide one's life, and (2) wilderness viewed in more foreboding terms, although seldom with fear.

When the wilderness of the Lake Superior region was discussed favorably by these immigrants, comparisons often were made with impressions of Finland. One writer recalled that, after departing his cherished homeland and settling proximate to Lake Superior, it was difficult to imagine he was in America. Certain fragrances of the forest rekindled cherished memories of the past. Recalling the poignant odor of cedar was especially meaningful to one native of eastern Finland whenever she went into the woods of northeastern Minnesota to cut boughs for the *sauna*. Other Finns commented poetically on how inspiring it was to listen to songs of spring emerging from the edge of a dark spruce forest, whereas some stated that breezes spreading through the trees reminded them of the low notes conveyed on a *kantele*—an ancient stringed instrument that continues to be played by Finns and Finnish Americans. Lakes, ponds, streams, and brooks, especially when bordered by trees, were considered the most attractive elements in any natural setting; areas of the region were so rich in water, stated an 1890 account, that they gave the impression of small landscape pictures of Finland. Lake Superior and other large bodies of water, when bathed in a clear summer sun, were portrayed as mirrors that made adjacent forests greener and landscape views more beautiful than on typical days. Even mining communities, considered to be anything but attractive by most observers, were described somewhat positively when situated next to a water feature.

On several occasions the pioneers were impressed with the immensity of the region and wilderness they saw. One account reported that a group of newly arrived Finnish immigrant women, who were riding in a train on their way to their prospective homes, excitedly ran to the windows and peered out when Lake Superior first came into view. One day later, to their amazement, they were still paralleling the lake. Other thoughts were conveyed by a prospective settler who, before filing for his future homestead in Minnesota, climbed a tree and described the panorama and sounds that existed below:

*Suomalaisten*
**Vaski - Kantele.**

The sounds of nature in the American Middle West sometimes reminded Finnish immigrants of the *kantele*, a stringed instrument with a harplike sound. This illustration appeared originally in Anneli Asplund's *Kantele* (Helsinki: Suomen Kirjallisuuden Seura, 1983).

*[There was] wilderness all around, heavy green
timber on all sides, no marked trails anywhere,
and the nearest road eight miles distant. The baying
of the wolf, the growling of a bear, the shrill
whistle of a deer, and the scolding of a squirrel
were the only sounds that one could hear.*

To some, however, certain backwoods areas were viewed as forlorn, unproductive, and desolate. Swamps and lowlands were particularly singled out for being forbidding, flat, monotonous, and good for growing little more than tamarack trees and tough marsh grass that could exceed the height of a person. When approaching Michigamme, Michigan, in 1890, a commentator asked himself whether the view and the land could be termed attractive and beautiful. "No," the writer firmly replied, although he also made a distinction between his negative interpretation of the backwoods area and his positive view of nature's attractive features: "The terrain is very irregular, the hills are rocky and virtually treeless, the valleys wet, marshy, and situated in the deep backwoods; by no means do such areas appeal to an eye that enjoys nature." Such assessments, however, commonly were tied to the perceived agricultural limitations of an area. Certain areas altogether different from swamps, such as sandy uplands, were deemed suitable for growing jack pine trees and blueberries only.

While a Finnish proverb proclaimed that "stones are the gardener's seeds," the number and size of the glacially deposited boulders found in several sections of the Lake Superior region (from the last Ice Age, some 10,000 years ago) could overwhelm even the most experienced and energetic Finn. One immigrant woman, who had moved with her family to Finland, Minnesota, graphically portrayed an area so strewn with rocks that Finns throughout the region knew it as "stone country" (*kivi kontri*). Since there were no roads when they arrived in the wilderness, everything had to be carried on the backs of the prospective residents over a distance of several miles. "But children were born in the wilderness," she remarked vividly, "between the rocks and the strawberries." Another Finn wistfully recalled the isolation he experienced when first arriving at a forested site where he would establish a homestead: "At that time there were no friends to greet me warmly, no cow bells to sound in my ear, and no murmurings of neighbors to dispel my evening loneliness."

Themes involving the transition from wilderness to landscape and garden (i.e., to clearings and farms) were common in nineteenth-century and early twentieth-century Finnish-language literature, whether written in Europe or North America. In some novels, the movement of a character or characters deep into the wilderness represented a spiritual quest for freedom from the shackles of society and social convention. Even here, however, the protagonists had to make a small clearing and construct a log cabin so at least some semblance of conventional life could continue. Other novels were more explicit in their treatments of environments that had been changed from wilderness to fields and farms, be it a marsh that needed draining or a forest that had to be cleared. Landscape thus became a commonly used device to demonstrate the advance of civilization and civility in an area. Even Finland's most important post-World War II novel, *Täälä pohjan tähden alle* (*Beneath This Northern Star*), a trilogy written by Väinö Linna, begins with the line: "At first there was the swamp, a grub hoe—and Jussi [John]."

Many immigrant pioneers welcomed the opportunity to participate in the activities that transformed wilderness and cutover forest into an agricultural landscape. Such transformations, however, were tied to conscious human interventions that resulted in positive gains, while random events such as cataclysmic forest fires were described through the lens of negative imagery. A train passenger passing through eastern Minnesota, in 1884, not only noted the infertile, rocky, and wild land, but was especially affected by the black stumps and half-burned pine trees. Such a landscape, he claimed, looked similar to a sheared sheep, while another commentator stated that new farming areas often were anything but beautiful since burned forests and huge, charred stumps stood everywhere like ghosts and apparitions. Nevertheless, not all pioneers considered forest fires to be totally disastrous events. Even after his farm buildings, animals, crops, and cordwood had been destroyed totally and his cattle and horses killed by a major fire that claimed close to 500 human lives in northeastern Minnesota on Columbus Day in 1918, one farmer still stated optimistically that clearing the land would now be easier and could proceed more quickly![25]

When properly controlled, fire was considered an appropriate tool for land clearing. Burn beating (termed *huhta* and *kaski* in Finnish) had been practiced for centuries in Finland, and was employed by a small group of Finns who helped establish Sweden's Delaware Colony in North America during the 1600s.[26] Although burn beating wasn't used extensively by Finnish immigrants in the Lake Superior region, a farmer from Suomi, Michigan, clearly recalled the sights and smells of black smoke that re-

25. For a recent, book-length treatment of the conflagration, refer to Francis M. Carroll and Franklin R. Raiter, *The Fires of Autumn: The Cloquet-Moose Lake Disaster of 1918* (St. Paul: Minnesota Historical Society Press, 1990).

26. See Jordan and Kaups, *The American Backwoods Frontier*.

sulted when recent settlers fired the pine stumps, roots, and brush they had gathered into large piles.

Whereas Fritzell contends that few English-language reports mentioned the toil associated with land-clearing activities in the Great Lakes region, numerous Finnish-language accounts spelled out the arduous nature of the task. One writer, commenting on the actions of his neighbor in Thompson, Minnesota, used the experience to symbolize the rural settlement activities of many Finns:

> *The Finn comes to the site, puts his supplies down*
> *by the roots of a stump, and looks silently around*
> *at the possibilities and the problems. Finally he*
> *begins to speak to us in such sad Finnish about*
> *those rocks, stumps, and brush. In a little while*
> *the brush began to be gathered, stumps overturned,*
> *and rocks placed by the shore of the river. From*
> *this he attempts to make a living, and establish*
> *a successful farm, a satisfactory home, and often*
> *an independent way of life.*

A more poignant comment was made by an old-time resident of Wisconsin who recalled the effort he and his family made to develop a farm by Lake Superior in the early 1900s:

> *With the snow still on the ground in the spring,*
> *the whole family worked to clear the brush.*
> *We cleared out stone and blasted stumps.*
> *With the stone and stumps, we built a fence.*
> *The second year, we had three acres of potatoes*
> *to show the world. Everyone worked as hard as*
> *anyone can work.*

Clearing land obviously was a slow procedure in the Lake Superior region, even for a farmer with an industrious wife and several children. Homestead records reveal that, during the first six years of pioneering, the average Finnish farmer and his family were able to clear annually no more than one and one-half acres of land. Nevertheless, such difficulties did not faze all pioneers, for some Finns actually found the physical work enjoyable. One farmer recalled how his neighbor genuinely loved to pull up stumps and clear land—especially in preparing new ground for the potato field. When asked why, the land-clearer simply replied it was a secret his father had brought over from Finland. Likewise, a group of agrarians voiced an old Finnish proverb when describing their preferences in northern Wisconsin: "New uncleared land is better than an old, prepared field."[27]

Various techniques, generally dependent upon the economic resources of the farmer, were used to clear land. Newly arrived settlers, who often were penniless, first cut down the trees with an axe and crosscut saw and placed the remnants in piles. Potatoes were then planted between the stumps and rocks, or the cutover clearing was used as a cow pasture. Once the stumps had rotted somewhat (a large white pine stump can stand for well over 100 years before it deteriorates completely), they were removed by human effort or, if the farmer was fortunate, with the power of a team of horses owned by the immigrant or a neighbor. After the farmer had acquired sufficient funds, dynamite could be purchased to blast out the stumps. In Minnesota and Wisconsin special trains containing land-clearing specialists, who were equipped with machines and explosives, toured the northern counties to demonstrate "scientific dynamiting." Stump blasting contests were conducted, with each contestant loading and shooting a certain number of stumps; prizes were then awarded on the basis of speed, safety, skill, results, and the economical use of explosives. The Finns were especially enthusiastic users of dynamite, as evidenced by a 1920 account which stated that a railroad carload of explosives acquired wholesale by a large Finnish-sponsored co-operative in Superior, Wisconsin, had sold so quickly that only one-third of it remained after a few days. Some farmers also used stump pullers. After anchoring the device into a stump, a horse or team of horses walked around the remnant in a circular pattern to wind a cable onto a spool, thereby removing the object.

Once portions of wilderness and cutover land had given way to fields, farms, and *landscape,* many Finnish writers described the transformation in especially glowing terms. After visiting a new farming area in Minnesota, one journalist said it could no longer be compared to a wilderness since human enterprise was now evident everywhere. There were green fields and attractive farmsteads, reported the enthusiastic observer, and beautiful trees guarded each clearing and lake. Another writer praised a group of Michigan Finns for their labors: "Through your power the rocks and stumps disappeared, and the swamps and bogs became verdant fields of grain."

Other commentators remarked how pleasing a log house appeared when situated along the shoreline of a lake or set within a space enclosed by trees. A newspaper correspondent waxed elo-

27. To create a landscape of fields and farms from the refractory Cutover region, Finns often mentioned that such work required considerable *sisu.* Although there is no direct English-language equivalent that fully captures the meaning of *sisu,* the term refers to the intestinal fortitude that is required when one encounters significant obstacles or great adversity. Some translators interpret *sisu* as "guts."

Once the stumps had been rooted out of the ground they could be put in piles for burning, as this 1919 photograph from northern Minnesota attests. The author's grandfather is pictured on the far right. Photographer is unknown. Courtesy of Arnold R. Alanen.

quently over a new house that had been placed in the midst of an "attractive park," while a recent arrival from Finland was no less forceful in describing a dwelling that was enveloped by "shimmering groves" of birch trees. After discussing the "charming beauty" of a house situated on an upland peninsula, as well as the rich soil, the heavy forests, and the fish-stocked lake, a writer asked: "What else could be lacking?"

Some people used rather distinctive analogies and metaphors to portray certain landscapes. After visiting an emerging enclave situated along the Mississippi River in Aitkin County, Minnesota, newspaper editor J. W. Lahde announced that the Finns were creating "a small picture of their native land." The log houses dotting the landscape in another area of Minnesota appeared as if they had been dropped from the sky, while the haystacks in a nearby location rose like poised towers into the winter heavens. These landscape features were no less fascinating to some Finnish immigrant writers than similar cultural features had been to Claude Monet and the Impressionists in France.

Sounds, as well as views, added to the landscape experience of the immigrants. One newspaper editor, renowned for his bouts

Some commentators, when they described the emerging clearings and fields of the Lake Superior region, reported that the haystacks rose like towers into the sky. This anonymous photograph was taken in northern Wisconsin in 1896. Courtesy of the State Historical Society of Wisconsin, Iconography Section, the W. A. Henry Collection.

with Demon Rum, was especially prone to use romantic, sentimental imagery when comparing the rural upper Middle West to memories of his innocent childhood in Finland. "It is wonderful to walk on a spring morning in the lap of nature," he remarked, "where one hears the singing of several kinds of birds, the cow bell, and the wonderful songs of Finnish maidens." The ring of cow bells may have been the most common sound that awakened recollections of rural Finland among the American immigrants. One account, commenting on the beauty of Lake Superior in 1883, concluded that the visual delight was enhanced by the notes of familiar cow bells, whereas another newspaper column, written fifteen years later, announced that the singular tone of the bell invoked deep feelings and memories of a boyhood spent long ago in Finland.

The *sauna,* according to numerous reports, was *the* distinguishing feature of the farmsteads, and served as the Finns' "pet accommodation," but the entire farmstead complex represented the greatest sign of accomplishment to most immigrants. Claiming that "a home was not a real home until it became one's own," an early Finnish writer stated that, in America, people failed to believe they had a genuine residence unless they possessed a piece of land and a house and farm buildings surrounded by cattle and horses. Another Finn summarized his thoughts and undoubtedly those of many other immigrants when he wrote from isolated Arthyde, Minnesota, in 1913: "Far away from the big world, with its sweat-inducing and blood thirsty factories, I slowly built my own wonderful home." It is no wonder then that the saying, *Oma tupa, oma lupa* ("One's own home, one's own freedom"), was popular both in Finland and in North America; it was in the United States, however, where a transplanted peasant actually had genuine opportunities to pursue this dream.

In many ways, the attitudes of immigrant Finns resembled those of other groups that established agricultural enclaves throughout America. Virtually all frontier cultures have viewed the transformation from wilderness to an orderly middle or agricultural landscape as a logical, positive, and necessary endeavor. There was the sense that "one was somehow present at the creation of a new world." [28] The Finns' relationship to, and understanding of, traditional wilderness, however, differed somewhat from the majority of yeoman farmers who established themselves in a new homeland. Unlike many other individuals and groups associated with the settlement of the American frontier, Finnish immigrants seldom regarded wilderness with suspicion or hatred. As an insightful immigrant stated in 1887, a Finn "has no fear of the forest."

It should not be assumed that the Finns failed to recognize the difficulties associated with the taming of wilderness and cutover land throughout the Lake Superior region. While many Finnish-language accounts mentioned the constant toil that characterized all phases of rural life, a much larger number viewed the region's agricultural possibilities through the prism of optimism and hope. Even when told that certain areas of the Lake Superior region were unfit for cultivation, not all Finnish pioneers heeded the warning. An immigrant who settled by Palmer, Michigan, didn't accept such a viewpoint since he had arrived from Erijärvi, Finland—a place where "bread had to be derived under even more barren conditions and further north of the sunline."

28. William Cronon, George Miles, and Jay Gitlin, "Becoming West: Toward a New Meaning for Western History," in William Cronon, et al., eds., *Under an Open Sky: Rethinking America's Western Past* (New York: W. W. Norton & Co., 1992), p. 10.

Artistic representations, such as this anonymous and undated painting, concentrated a host of activities into a small area and presented an entirely positive assessment of life on a homestead. The painting originally appeared in *Koti-Home* (Duluth, Minnesota, 1922). The original legend states: "Vanha, suomalainen homesteadi Minnesotassa" ("An old Finnish homestead in Minnesota").

Since landscape historians are largely concerned with understanding the organization of common and ordinary exterior spaces that have developed in the past, one can study a virtually inexhaustible list of topics and themes. While this essay focuses upon a group of immigrants who resided in one region of the United States, very little is known about the landscape imagery of the millions of other immigrants in America who spoke and wrote in languages other than English. Nevertheless, given the veritable wealth of resources available to document the perceptions of Finns who settled in America, scholars should be able to undertake similar studies of other immigrant groups.

Although this Finnish family is justifiably proud of the work it has done on the frontier, this anonymous photograph, taken at the turn of the twentieth century, contrasts nicely with the previous painting and presents the real look of an established homestead in the Lake Superior region. The photograph originally appeared in *Amerikan albumi: kuvia Amerikan Suomalaisten asuinpaikoilta* (Brooklyn, New York, 1903). The original legend states: "Herman Granin asunto je perhe, Grand Rapids, Minnesota" ("Herman Gran's home and family, Grand Rapids, Minnesota").

Of course, one category of primary information that seldom is tapped by the landscape historian includes the foreign-language materials produced by these immigrants. Although some students and observers of landscape may not possess the necessary linguistic skills to make direct use of documents written by a specific immigrant group, greater attention can be given to those sources already translated into English. That list needs to be expanded, but one can consult a host of immigrant diaries, letters, and memoirs that are available in English and then apply the landscape historian's lens to this material for perspective, synthesis, and interpretation.

A larger array of documentation can be considered by those with the necessary foreign-language skills. The newspapers, oral histories, and other accounts used in preparing this essay have equivalents among many immigrant groups. Likewise, various sources, ranging from the novels written by immigrants to the ledgers and daybooks kept by farmers, are worthy of our attention. When supplemented with, and verified by, fieldwork, early photographs plat maps, and county atlases, homestead and census data, documents, and other traditional sources, the common landscapes of America can indeed be portrayed and interpreted in a much clearer light.[29]

To determine what landscape is, it is imperative to know what landscape was. This is the tenet of the landscape historian. If scholars, writers, and artists eventually connect the threads of the past to the present and create a fabric that displays the diversity and richness of America's regions and population groups, then the task of landscape assessment, understanding, interpretation, and preservation will be further enhanced. This is the challenge for those who study landscape in America.

29. Certain research questions come immediately to mind. For example, were the attitudes of Swedish and Norwegian immigrants, who also had a northern European forest culture background, similar to those of the Finns when they encountered and settled the Lake Superior region? Was gender a factor in these attitudes? Likewise, did the impressions of the three Nordic groups differ from central and southern European immigrants? What were the reactions of the Finns when they settled in regions totally unfamiliar to them such as the northern Great Plains? Perhaps it was in such treeless and strange environments that the Finns actually experienced "wilderness" (*erämaa*). Also, did any European group display even limited similarities with the original Native Americans? Preliminary evidence (see Jordan and Kaups, *The American Backwoods Frontier*) indicates that some commonalities existed between the environmental viewpoints of Finns and American Indians.

# PART III

# Landscape as Myth and Memory

*Light from the river brightens your old room.*
*The heron you called Pete returns still young*
*to sweep the river like a cloud. This bend's*
*the one the river loves to make, moving easy*
*to the bank and curving easy as the moon.*
*Your eyes ride water and your eyes climb trees.*
*Nights were filled with horses and each morning*
*all that final summer 20 years before*
*beaver crossed in wild herds to the island.*
*You saved your brother from the undertow.*

—RICHARD HUGO

# Home Landscape

**William Kittredge**

WILLIAM KITTREDGE was born in 1932 in Portland, Oregon, and was raised in Adel, Oregon, on the MC Ranch. He received a B.S. in general agriculture from Oregon State University, and completed an M.F.A. in creative writing at the University of Iowa. He was a National Endowment for the Arts Fellow in 1974 and 1981, won a PEN/NEA Syndicated Fiction Award in 1982 and 1984, was a writer on the film *Heartland,* for which he won the Neil Simon Award in 1984, and worked as a coproducer with the late Norman Maclean and with director Robert Redford on the movie *A River Runs through It* (1992). Professor Kittredge's books include *The Van Gogh Fields* (Missouri, 1979), which won the St. Lawrence Fiction Prize and the Fiction International Prize; *We Are Not in This Together* (Graywolf Press, 1984), which won the Northwest Booksellers Award and the Governor's Award for Literature; *Owning It All* (Graywolf Press, 1987); the edited collection *Montana Spaces* (Nick Lyons, 1988), with photographs by John Smart; *The Last Best Place: A Montana Anthology* (Montana Historical Society, 1988) co-edited with Annick Smith; and *Hole In the Sky: A Memoir* (Knopf, 1992). He is professor of English at the University of Montana.

EDITOR'S NOTE: This essay was commissioned and written for inclusion in this book. Another version also appears in Mr. Kittredge's book of essays, *Owning It All* (St. Paul: Graywolf Press, 1987), pages 3–19.

IN LATE SEPTEMBER of 1942 our dog named Victory was crushed under the rear duals of a semi-truck flatbed hauling one-hundred-pound burlap sacks of my father's newly combined oats some forty twisting miles of gravel road over the Warner Mountains to town and the railroad. My sister ran shrieking to the kitchen door, and my mother came to the roadside in her apron, and I was stoic and tough-minded as that poor animal panted and died. *Beyond the crystal sea, undreamed shores, precious angels.*

This was a time when our national life was gone to war against U-boats and Bataan and the death march, betrayal reeking everywhere. The death of that dog with cockleburrs matted into his coat must have seemed emblematic. We were American and proud, and we were steeled to deal with these matters.

So we unearthed a shallow grave in the good loam soil at the upper end of the huge rancher garden my father laid out each spring in those days before it became cheaper to feed our crews from truckloads of canned goods bought wholesale in the cities. We gathered late-blooming flowers from the border beneath my mother's bedroom window, we loaded the stiffening carcass of that dead dog on a red wagon, and we staged a funeral with full, symbolic honors.

My older cousin blew taps through his fist, my brother hid his face, and my six-year-old sister wept openly, which was all right since she was a little child. I waved a leafy bough of willow over the slope-sided grave while my other cousins shoveled the loose, dry soil down on the corpse.

It is impossible to know what the child who was myself can have felt, gazing across the valley which I can still envision so clearly: the ordered garden and the sage-covered slope running down to the slough-cut meadows of the Thompson Field, willows there concealing secret, hideaway places where I would burrow back away from the world for hours, imagining I was some animal, hidden and watching the stock cows graze the open islands of meadow grass.

On the far side of the valley lay the great level distances of the plow-ground fields that had so recently been tule swamps, reaching to the rise of barren, eastern ridges. That enclosed valley is the home I imagine walking in when I someday fall through the dream which is dying, my real, particular, vivid, and populated solace for that irrevocable moment of utter loss when the mind stops forever. The chill of that remembered September evening feels right as I imagine that boy, distant and correct as his heart.

It's hard to know where I got the notion of that willow branch unless I find it in this other memory, from along in the same time. A Paiute girl of roughly my own age died of measles in the ramshackle encampment her people maintained alongside the irrigation ditch which eventually led to our vast garden. A dozen or so people lived there, and nowadays, for my own dumb, ironic, political reasons (irony and satire being the silliest modes of rhetoric), I like to think of them as in touch with some remnant memories of hunting-and-gathering forebears who summered so many generations in the valley we had so recently come to own.

In the fall of 1890 a man named James Mooney went west under the auspices of the Bureau of Ethnology to investigate the rise of American Indian religious fervor which culminated in the massacre at Wounded Knee on 29 December. In Mooney's report, *The Ghost Dance Religion and the Sioux Outbreak of 1890,* there is a statement delivered by a Paiute man named Captain Dick at Fort Bidwell in Surprise Valley, California—right in the home territory I am talking about, at the junction on maps where California and Nevada come together at the Oregon border:

*All Indians must dance, everywhere, keep on dancing. Pretty soon in the next spring Big Man come. He bring back game of every kind. The game be thick everywhere. All dead Indians come back and live again. Old blind Indians see again and get young and have fine time. When the old man comes this way, then all the Indians go to the mountains, high up away from the whites. Whites can't hurt the Indians then. Then while Indians way up high, big flood comes like water and all white people die, get drowned. After that water go away and then nobody but Indians everywhere game all kinds thick. Then medicine-man tell Indians to send word to all Indians to keep up dancing and the good time will come. Indians who don't dance, who don't believe in this word, will grow little, just about a foot high, and stay that way. Some of them will turn into wood and will be burned in the fire.*

In the 1950s and the 1960s a Paiute named Conlan Dick lived in a cabin on our ranch in Warner Valley, and helped look after the irrigation and fences. Conlan was reputed to be a kind of medicine man in our local mythology, and related to the man who delivered that statement. His wife, whose name I cannot recall, did ironing for women in the valley. And there was a son, a young man named Virgil Dick, who sometimes came to Warner for a few weeks and helped his father with the field work.

In the early 1960s my cousin, the one who blew taps through his fist in 1942, was riding horseback across the swampy, spring meadows alongside Conlan. He asked if Virgil was Conlan's only child.

Conlan grinned. "Naw," he said. "But you know, those kids, they play outside, and they get sick and they die."

Story after interrelated story. Is it possible to claim that proceeding through some incidents from a childhood in this free-associative manner is a technique, a way of discovery? Quite probably. One of our model narrators these days is the patient on his couch, spinning and respinning the past until it makes sense.

". . . They get sick and they die." Once I had the romance in me to think that was the mature comment of a man who had grown up healed to wholeness and connected with the ways of nature in a degree I would never understand. Now I think it was more likely the statement of a man trying to forget his wounds, so many of which were inflicted by schoolyard warriors like us. A healthy culture could never have taught him to forgo sorrow.

In any event, Captain Dick's magic was dead.

All these stories are part of my landscape about a place called "Home." The girl who died was named Pearl. I recall her name with that particular exactness which occasionally hovers in memories. She was of enormous interest to us because she so obviously disdained our foolish play with make-believe weapons and miniature trucks. Or so it seemed. Maybe she was only shy, or warned away from us. But to our minds she lived with adults and shared in the realities of adult lives in ways we did not, and now she was being paid the attention of burial.

Try to imagine their singing on that spring morning. I cannot. I like to think our running brigade of warrior children might have been touched by dim, sorrow-filled wailing in the crystalline brightness of her morning, but the memory is silent.

Maybe it's enough to recall the sight of people she loved, carrying her elaborately clothed body in an open, home-built casket. Not that we saw it up close, or that we ever really saw a body, clothed or unclothed.

They were making their slow parade up a sandy path through the sagebrush to her burial in the brushy plot, loosely fenced with barbed wire, which we knew as the "Indian Graveyard." I see them high on the banking sand-hill behind our house, and beyond them the abrupt, two-thousand-foot lift of rimrock which formed the great western lip of our valley. That rim is always there, the table of lava-flow at the top breaking so abruptly, dropping long scree-slopes clustered with juniper. It is always at my back. The sun sets there, summer and winter. I can turn and squint my eyes, and see it.

From down amid the flowering trees in the homesteader's orchard behind our house we watched that astonishing processional through my father's binoculars; and then we ran out through the brush beyond the garden, tasting the perfect spring morning and leaping along the small animal trails, filled with thrilling purpose—silent and urgent. We had to be closer.

The procession was just above us on the sandy trail when we halted, those people paying us no mind but frightening us anyway, mourning men and women in their dark, castaway clothing and bright blankets and strange robes made of animal skins, clutching at spring blossoms and sweeping at the air with thick sheaves of willow in new leaf. It is now that I would like to hear the faint singsong of their chanting. I would like to think we studied them through the dancing waves of oncoming heat, and found in them the only models we had for such primal ceremonies.

But this landscape keeps becoming fiction. Ours was a rising class of agricultural people, and new to that part of the world, too preoccupied with an endless ambition toward perfection in work to care at all for any tradition or religion. No one in our immediate families had ever died, and never would as far as we knew. None of us, in those days, had any interest in religion or ritual.

So I have this story of those shrouded people proceeding through my imagination. I feel them celebrating as that young girl entered into the ripe fruit of some unknown paradise, lamenting the doleful exigencies of their own lives, some of them likely thinking she was lucky to have escaped.

But none of that really happened. Not to my knowledge. I don't really have much idea what was going on behind the story I've made of that morning for myself and you. It was as if those people were trailing along that sandy path toward never-never land themselves. Some of them, somewhere, are likely still alive.

In a book called *Shoshone,* the poet Ed Dorn tells of interviewing an ancient man and woman in a trailer house on the Duck Valley Indian Reservation, a few hundred miles to the east of us, but still deep in the high basin-and-range desert, along the border between southwestern Idaho and northeastern Nevada. They were more than one hundred years old, and told Dorn they never heard of white people until they were past the age of thirty (which was possible). Imagine that tribe (the Tsasaday) we've all heard about on Mindanao in the Philippines, supposedly living undisturbed, Stone Age lives until they were discovered a couple of decades ago. Think of them guessing at jet streams, even if their lives are fiction.

So those ancient people, living in an aluminum-sided trailer house on the Duck Valley Indian Reservation, with screens on the windows, must have understood stories. It's easy to imagine them grinning in what looks to be a toothless old way, and demanding cartons of cigarettes before they allow themselves to be photographed. The point is they were actual and yet willing to be part of any make-believe anyone could invent for them, willing to tell their stories and let us make of them what we could, but not for nothing. They knew that whatever story Dorn was imagining had something to do with the nature of storytelling itself, understanding that everything turns on make-believe at heart—stories being valuable precisely to the degree that they are, for the moment, useful in our ongoing task of making sense of ourselves in the world, good ones always worth the price of some smokes.

Let's go back to our children in the September landscape of 1942, the same year that girl named Pearl was buried. They have learned something about the emotional thrust of a warrior code as the dry news from the Zenith Trans-Oceanic radio is translated into singing in first-period music class, and they have loaded that dead dog named Victory in a red wagon, and they are trailing him toward burial at the upper end of the garden, and waving sweeps of willow over the ceremony while my cousin blows taps through his fist. As Borges says somewhere, in a phrase those ancient Paiute from Duck Valley might have appreciated, *reality invaded by dream.*

A few summers later my father's catskinners bulldozed the shacktown Indian camp with its willow-roofed ramada into a pile of old posts and lumber, and burned it, after the last of them was gone to wherever they went. All this is part of the place I know as "Home."

Let's hope T. S. Eliot was right:

*And the end of all our exploring*
*Will be to arrive where we started*
*And know the place for the first time.*

"LITTLE GIDDING"

We are talking about what Susanne Langer calls "virtual" events, happenings that are distinguished from "actual" events by the emotional, qualitative factor which is central in their constitution. Virtual events are actual events transformed and universalized by metaphor. They belong to that class of events we call "fictions."

In examining this series of virtual events I am talking about the relationship between those ongoing creative acts, through which we simultaneously invent and come to value both our most intimate selves and our landscapes, and the notion that each is a complexly interrelated part of the other, the base at rock bottom under that most encompassing fiction we call "reality."

During the late fall of 1958, after I had been gone from Warner Valley for eight years, I came back to participate in our agriculture, which, to use a metaphor that works in terms of either autobiography or landscape, might be thought of as the bulldozing of my own childhood. Over in that other world on the edge of rain forests, which is the fertile Willamette Valley of Oregon, I'd gone to school in General Agriculture, absorbed in a kind of County Agent/U.S. Army Corps of Engineers mentality, and straight from there I had gone to Photo Intelligence work in the Air Force. The last couple of those years were spent deep in jungle on the island of Guam in the Marianas, where we lived in a little compound of cleared land, in a Quonset hut.

They were basically happy, bookish years, newly married, with children. A hundred or so yards north of our Quonset hut, along a trail through the luxuriant undergrowth between coconut palms and banana trees, a ragged cliff of red, porous, volcanic rock fell directly to the ocean. When the strong Pacific typhoons came roaring in, our hut was washed with blowing spray from the great breakers. On calm days we would stand on the cliff at that absolute edge of our jungle and island, and gaze out across the waters to the island of Rota, and to the endlessness of ocean beyond, and I would marvel at my life, so far from southeastern Oregon.

It is impossible to recall how consciously I reacted to metaphors of landscape when we came back in 1958. It was indeed another place, in a number of senses. I had seen something of the world, and the valley had changed. The road in had been paved, we had Bonneville Power on lines from the Columbia River, and high atop the western rim of the valley there was a TV translator, which beamed fluttering pictures from the Great World directly to us.

Standing at elevation beside that translator tower, looking down maybe three thousand feet into Warner, and across to the beginnings of the high basin-and-range desert where we summered our cattle, it was no doubt absolutely natural to feel myself drawn to that fertile, childhood *homeplace* as one would be drawn to any oasis in the vast, sagebrush territory that rolled on for several hundred literal miles beyond what I could see. No doubt most of us would intuit all the watered places in such country as standing in the imagination like islands in the sea of desert, sacred enclaves in the wilderness, like Guam out there in the western Pacific.

Such a mute, iconographic sense of landscape seems always to exist as a subtext behind our understanding of the intricate textures of real deserts and islands and valleys and seas. Innate responses to place are likely as biological as the inherent fear of hawks in baby chickens—part of our genetic heritage from a species that was both prey and predator—always hunting, seeking refuge—as it evolved over the millennia. Like that fear of hawks, and always inside the configurations of our particular culture, our emotional reactions to any particular place seem to emerge from sources equally secure in our genes, as the rather predictable responses to attachment and loss which structure the endlessly complex ways we deal with love and the threat of death inside that archetypal romance which is the family.

Psychologists are beginning to study the most obvious forms of genetically conditioned bonding responses in animals and infants, and risk projecting the results onto adults. It's the old problem of freedom, which I resolve by envisioning our genetic heritage as a set of flexible templates, archetypes in this sense being perfectly actual, which form our responses to the quite literally unimaginable complexity of those interpenetrating systems of energy which we now understand as real.

Anyway . . . although I was years from knowing that wilderness is an idea and nothing real, I surely did not understand our desert out there in southeastern Oregon as any sort of featureless, iconographic place. During my late boyhood I had summered with our chuck wagon branding crews on that desert, and I knew the country well enough to envision it as we see cities, with neighborhoods, some sacred, some demonic, some habitable, some not, which is like the sea, I'm told, as understood by fishermen.

There in 1958 I was mostly interested in beginning my real life as an agricultural manager, a job that can be thought of as craftsmanship, both artistic and mechanical. The goal of our work was to create order according to an ideal of beauty that is based on efficiency: manipulating the forces of water, soil, season, and seed; and people-power and equipment laying out functional patterns for irrigation and cultivation on the surface of our valley.

It was an effort that began in Warner in the late 1930s when my father built a seventeen-mile diversion canal to carry the spring floodwaters around the east side of the valley—our entry into the beguiling mechanics of agribusiness, a way of mind I began learning, I suppose, while playing those long-ago childhood games of war with my cousins, brother, sister, and dog Victory. I was interested in completing the transformation of that childhood homeland into a perfected agricultural dream.

And, in a way I have learned to personify as demonic, it worked. We drained and leveled the peat-ground tule swamps, we ditched and pumped, and for a long while our crops were all any of us could have asked for. There were over five thousand water-control devices. We had constructed a perfect place. And it was art, it was a vision embodied, and sacred, so it seemed, for a while.

As we grow older we begin to recognize emblematic moments of childhood, or perhaps such memories simply surface more readily as we find ways to accept them into the fiction of ourselves, the story of who we are. One of my earliest, from a time before I ever went to school, is of studying the worn, oiled, softwood flooring in the Warner Valley store where my mother took me when she picked up the mail three times a week. I have no idea how many years that floor had been tromped on and dirtied and swept, but by the time I recall it the floor was worn into a topography of swales and buttes, traffic patterns and hard knots, much like the land, if you will, under the wear of a glacier. For a child, as his mother gossiped with the postmistress in her endless way, it was a place with high ground and valleys, prospects and sanctuaries, and I in my boredom could invent stories about it and find a coherency I loved. The owners tore it up somewhere around the time I started school, and I grieved.

The coherency I found there was mirrored a few years later, just before the war began, when I was seven or eight, in the summertime play of my brother and sister and cousins and myself, as we laid out roads to drive and rectangular fields for ourselves to work with our toy trucks in the dirt under the huge, old box elder which also functioned as a swing tree near the kitchen door to our house. It was a little play-world we made for ourselves, and it was, we believed, just like the vast world beyond. In it we imitated the kind of ordering we watched each spring while our father laid out the garden with such measured precision, and the kind of planning we could not help but sense while riding with him along the levee banks in his dusty, Chevrolet pickup truck. All the world we knew was visible from the front porch of our house, inside the valley, and all the work he did was directed toward making it orderly, functional, and productive—of course, it seemed like sacred work.

Such play ended, believe this story or not, when a small rattlesnake showed up in our midst. A young woman who cooked for my mother killed the snake in a matter of fact way with a shovel. But the next spring my mother insisted, and my father hauled in topsoil, and planted the packed dirt where we played at our toylike world of fields into a lawn where rattlesnakes would never come. We hated him for it.

These stories—and again I emphasize that they form a narrative I have constructed into an autobiography for myself in relationship to the place where I mostly lived until the age of thirty-five—began to suggest reasons why, during childhood winters through the Second World War, such an important segment of my imagination lived amid maps of Europe and the Pacific. Maps delineated the dimensions of that dream which was the war for me, maps and traced drawings of aircraft camouflaged for combat. I collected them like peacetime city-boys collect baseball cards.

So you can begin to understand my excitement there on the rim, by our community TV translator, in 1958. The valley where I had always seen myself living was open before me like another map and playground, and this time I was an adult, and high up in the War Department.

Imagine the slow history of that country in the far reaches of southeastern Oregon, a backlands enclave even in the American West, the first settlers not arriving until nearly a decade after the end of the Civil War. All of the work was done by hand or with horses until my father brought in the first Caterpillar tractors in the mid-1930s. It's justifiable to think of myself growing up at the tail end of an ancient, sacred way of life, in which people and animals lived in everyday proximity on land they knew more precisely than the patterns in the palms of their hands. The real end came right at the end of World War II when all the work, the size of fields and feedlot expectations, began to be scaled to an industrial model imposed by machinery. Right there our sacred oasis went mechanical, and (in the latter-day, make-believe story of my relationship with that place) distant and correct and demonic, dead, inert, literally uninhabited.

This time our small remnant of magic died.

In that same story it takes us a long while to realize what has happened. Not until the early 1960s were we willing to acknowledge that something had gone terribly wrong, and then we blamed it on ourselves, on our inability to manage enough. But the fault wasn't ours, beyond the fact that we had all been educated to believe in a grand, bad, factory-land notion of excellence. For a long time it was our only model.

We had imposed our drastically single-minded, Corps of Engineers idea of order on a living place. We had ditched and drained and leveled, baited the coyotes with 1080, sprayed weeds and insects with chemicals such as 2-4-D Ethyle and Malathion and Parathion, and our rich peat soils were going saline, field mice free of natural predators were destroying thousands of acres of alfalfa, and the beloved migratory rafts of water birds were mostly gone with their swampland habitat. The list of woe goes on. In a quite actual way we had come to final victory in our artistic, playground warfare against all that was naturally alive in our native home. We had reinvented our landscape according to the most persuasive ideal given to us by our culture, and it had gone alien on us.

We felt enormously betrayed. For so many years, through endless efforts, we had proceeded in good faith, living a sacred narrative of our own invention, in which we worked to create a great good place on the earth, and it turned out we had wrecked that which we had not left untouched. Our living oasis had been turned into a machine scaled to agribusiness.

In the end it became evident we had always been playing another game, called Economics. Finally we took our real estate profits, sold out, and escaped to other lives. All that is part of the longer story I tell while I try to know who I am, which always begins with play and singing and mock warfare in a valley that is still naturally sacred and magically inhabited in my imagination.

But childhood, William Gass says somewhere, is a lie of poetry. When I was maybe eight years old, in the fall of the year, I would have to go out in the garden after school with damp burlap sacks, and cover the long rows of cucumber and tomato plants, so they wouldn't freeze.

It was a hated, cold-handed job which had to be done every evening. I daydreamed along in a half-hearted, distracted way, flopping the sacks onto the plants and feeling sorry for myself and angry because I was alone at my boring work. No doubt my younger brother and sister were in the house and warm, eating cookies.

And then—those are the storyteller's words, *And Then*—the action began; something happened. A great strutting bird—its black tail-feathers flaring; its monstrous, yellow-orange air sac pulsating out from its white breast; its throat croaking with popping sounds like rust in a joint—appeared out of the dry remnants of our corn. The bird looked to be stalking me with grave, slow intensity, coming after me out of a place I could not understand as real. And yet it was quite recognizable, the sort of terrifying creature that would sometimes spawn in the incoherent world of my night-dreams. In my story now, I say it looked like death, come to say hello. Then, it was simply an apparition.

The moment demanded as much courage as any I will ever experience, but I stood my ground, flopping one of those wet sacks, and the bird flapped its wings in an angry way, raising a little commonplace dust. It was the dust, I think, that did it, convincing me this could not be a dream. My fear collapsed, and I felt foolish as I understood this was a creature I had heard my father talk about: a courting sage-grouse, which we called a prairie chicken. This was only a bird, and not much interested in me at all. But for an instant it had been both phantom and real, the thing I deserved, come to punish me for my anger.

For that childhood flash I believed in an inhabited world not of my own making, which was absolutely other and utterly sacred, which was fearfully demonic and completely natural: another ancient version of the place I am calling "Home." No wonder we turn to storytelling or make-believe, and the arts of war and agriculture, to engrave our signs on the earth.

LESLIE MARMON SILKO was born in 1948 in Albuquerque, New Mexico, and was raised on the Laguna Pueblo reservation in New Mexico. She received a B.A. in English from the University of New Mexico (Phi Beta Kappa), and studied in the American Indian Law Program at the University of New Mexico School of Law. She received a Woodrow Wilson Fellowship in 1968, a National Endowment for the Arts "Discovery Grant" for fiction in 1970, won *Chicago Review*'s 1974 Poetry Award, won a National Endowment for the Arts Writers Fellowship for Fiction in 1974, won the Pushcart Prize for Poetry in 1977, received film production grants in 1978 and 1980 from the National Endowment for the Humanities, and from 1981 to 1986 was a MacArthur Foundation Fellow. Her books include *Laguna Woman: Poems by Leslie Marmon Silko* (Greenfield Review Press, 1974), *Ceremony* (Viking, 1977; Signet, 1978), *Storyteller* (Grove, 1981), and *Almanac of the Dead* (Simon and Schuster, 1991). Ms. Silko lives on a ranch in the mountains outside Tucson, Arizona.

Leslie Marmon Silko

# Interior and Exterior Landscapes: The Pueblo Migration Stories

*From a High Arid Plateau in New Mexico*

You see that, after a thing is dead, it dries up. It might take weeks or years, but eventually, if you touch the thing, it crumbles under your fingers. It goes back to dust. The soul of the thing has long since departed. With the plants and wild game the soul may have already been born back into bones and blood or thick green stalks and leaves. Nothing is wasted. What cannot be eaten by people or in some way used must then be left where other living creatures may benefit. What domestic animals or wild scavengers can't eat will be fed to the plants. The plants feed on the dust of these few remains.

The ancient Pueblo people buried the dead in vacant rooms or in partially collapsed rooms adjacent to the main living quarters. Sand and clay used to construct the roof make layers many inches deep once the roof has collapsed. The layers of sand and clay make for easy grave-digging. The vacant room fills with cast-off objects and debris. When a vacant room has filled deep enough, a shallow but adequate grave can be scooped in a far corner. Archaeologists have remarked over formal burials complete with elaborate funerary objects excavated in trash middens of abandoned rooms. But the rocks and adobe mortar of collapsed walls were valued by the ancient people. Because each rock had been carefully selected for size and shape, then chiseled to an even face. Even the pink clay adobe melting with each rainstorm had to be prayed over, then dug and carried some distance. Corncobs and husks, the rinds and stalks and animal bones were not regarded by the ancient people as filth or garbage. The remains were merely resting at a midpoint in their journey back to dust. Human remains are not so different. They should rest with the bones and rinds where they all may benefit living creatures—small rodents and insects—until their return is completed. The remains of things—animals and plants, the clay and stones—were treated with respect, because for the ancient people all these things had spirit and being.[1]

EDITOR'S NOTE: This essay was written while Ms. Silko was on a five-year MacArthur Fellowship. Although the essay was commissioned and written for inclusion in this book, another version also appears in Daniel Halpern's edited collection, *On Nature: Nature, Landscape, and Natural History* (San Francisco: North Point Press, 1987), pages 83–94.

1. By "ancient Pueblo people" I mean the last generation or two, which included my great-grandmother, just barely. Their worldview was still uniquely Pueblo.

The antelope merely consents to return home with the hunter. All phases of the hunt are conducted with love: the love the hunter and the people have for the Antelope People, and the love of the antelope who agree to give up their meat and blood so that human beings will not starve. Waste of meat or even the thoughtless handling of bones cooked bare will offend the antelope spirits. Next year the hunters will vainly search the dry plains for antelope. Thus, it is necessary to return carefully the bones and hair, and the stalks and leaves to the earth who first created them. The spirits remain close by. They do not leave us.

The dead become dust, and in this becoming they are once more joined with the Mother. The ancient Pueblo people called the earth the Mother Creator of all things in this world. Her sister, the Corn Mother, occasionally merges with her because all succulent green life rises out of the depths of the earth.

Rocks and clay are part of the Mother. They emerge in various forms, but at some time before they were smaller particles of great boulders. At a later time they may again become what they once were: dust.

A rock shares this fate with us and with animals and plants as well. A rock has being or spirit, although we may not understand it. The spirit may differ from the spirit we know in animals or plants or in ourselves. In the end we all originate from the depths of the earth. Perhaps this is how all beings share in the spirit of the Creator. We do not know.

## From the Emergence Place

Pueblo potters, the creators of petroglyphs and oral narratives, never conceived of removing themselves from the earth and sky. So long as the human consciousness remains *within* the hills, canyons, cliffs, and the plants, clouds, and sky, the term *landscape,* as it has entered the English language, is misleading. "A portion of territory the eye can comprehend in a single view" does not correctly describe the relationship between the human being and his or her surroundings. This assumes the viewer is somehow *outside* or *separate from* the territory she or he surveys. Viewers are as much a part of the landscape as the boulders they stand on.

There is no high mesa edge or mountain peak where one can stand and not immediately be part of all that surrounds. Human identity is linked with all the elements of Creation through the clan; you might belong to the Sun Clan or the Lizard Clan or the Corn Clan or the Clay Clan.[2] Standing deep within the natural world, the ancient Pueblo understood the thing as it was—the squash blossom, grasshopper, or rabbit itself could never be created by the human hand. Ancient Pueblos took the modest view

2. A *clan* is a social unit that is composed of families who share common ancestors and trace their lineage back to the Emergence where their ancestors allied themselves with certain plants, animals, or elements.

that the thing itself (the landscape) could not be improved upon. The ancients did not presume to tamper with what had already been created. Thus, *realism,* as we now recognize it in painting and sculpture, did not catch the imaginations of Pueblo people until recently.

The squash blossom itself is *one thing:* itself. So the ancient Pueblo potter abstracts what she saw to be the key elements of the squash blossom—the four symmetrical petals, with four symmetrical stamens in the center. These key elements, while suggesting the squash flower, also link it with the four cardinal directions. By representing only its intrinsic form, the squash flower is released from a limited meaning or restricted identity. Even in the most sophisticated abstract form, a squash flower or a cloud or a lightning bolt became intricately connected with a complex system of relationships which the ancient Pueblo people maintained with each other, and with the populous natural world they lived within. A bolt of lightning is itself, but at the same time it may mean much more. It may be a messenger of good fortune when summer rains are needed. It may deliver death, perhaps the result of manipulations by the Gunnadeyahs, destructive necromancers. Lightning may strike down an evildoer, or lightning may strike a person of good will. If the person survives, lightning endows him or her with heightened power.

Pictographs and petroglyphs of constellations or elk or antelope draw their magic in part from the process wherein the focus of all prayer and concentration is upon the thing itself, which, in its turn, guides the hunter's hand. Connection with the spirit dimensions requires a figure or form that is all-inclusive. A "lifelike" rendering of an elk is too restrictive. Only the elk *is* itself. A *realistic* rendering of an elk would be only one particular elk anyway. The purpose of the hunt rituals and magic is to make contact with *all* the spirits of the Elk.

The land, the sky, and all that is within them—the landscape—includes human beings. Interrelationships in the Pueblo landscape are complex and fragile. The unpredictability of the weather, the aridity and harshness of much of the terrain in the high plateau country explain in large part the relentless attention the ancient Pueblo people gave to the sky and the earth around them. Survival depended upon harmony and cooperation not only among human beings, but also among all things—the animate and the less animate, since rocks and mountains were known on occasion to move.

The ancient Pueblos believed the Earth and the Sky were sisters (or sister and brother in the post-Christian version). As long as food-family relations are maintained, then the Sky will continue to bless her sister, the Earth, with rain, and the Earth's children will continue to survive. But the old stories recall incidents in which troublesome spirits or beings threaten the earth. In one story, a malicious *ka'tsina,* called the Gambler, seizes the Shiwana, or Rainclouds, the Sun's beloved children.[3] The Shiwana are snared in magical power late one afternoon on a high mountaintop. The Gambler takes the Rainclouds to his mountain stronghold where he locks them in the north room of his house. What was his idea? The Shiwana were beyond value. They brought life to all things on earth. The Gambler wanted a big stake to wager in his games of chance. But such greed, even on the part of only one being, had the effect of threatening the survival of all life on earth. Sun Youth, aided by old Grandmother Spider, outsmarts the Gambler and the rigged game, and the Rainclouds are set free. The drought ends, and once more life thrives on earth.

### Through the Stories We Hear Who We Are

All summer the people watch the west horizon, scanning the sky from south to north for rain clouds. Corn must have moisture at the time the tassels form. Otherwise pollination will be incomplete, and the ears will be stunted and shriveled. An inadequate harvest may bring disaster. Stories told at Hopi, Zuñi, and at Acoma and Laguna describe drought and starvation as recently as 1900. Precipitation in west-central New Mexico averages fourteen inches annually. The western pueblos are located at altitudes over five thousand six hundred feet above sea level, where winter temperatures at night fall below freezing. Yet evidence of their presence in the high desert and plateau country goes back ten thousand years. The ancient Pueblo not only survived in this environment, but for many years they also thrived. In A.D. 1100 the people at Chaco Canyon had built cities with apartment buildings of stone five stories high.[4] Their sophistication as sky-watchers was surpassed only by Mayan and Inca astronomers. Yet this vast complex of knowledge and belief, amassed for thousands of years, was never recorded in writing.

Instead, the ancient Pueblo people depended upon collective memory through successive generations to maintain and transmit an entire culture, a worldview complete with proven strategies for survival. The oral narrative, or "story," became the medium through which the complex of Pueblo knowledge and belief was maintained. Whatever the event or the subject, the ancient people perceived the world and themselves within that world as part of an ancient, continuous story composed of innumerable bundles of other stories.

3. *Ka'tsinas* are spirit beings who roam the earth and inhabit kachina masks worn in Pueblo ceremonial dances.

4. Chaco Culture National Historical Park is located in northwest New Mexico, about twenty-four rough road miles southwest of Nageezi on Highway 57.

The ancient Pueblo vision of the world was inclusive. The impulse was to leave nothing out. Pueblo oral tradition necessarily embraced all levels of human experience. Otherwise, the collective knowledge and beliefs comprising ancient Pueblo culture would have been incomplete. Thus, stories about the Creation and Emergence of human beings and animals into this world continue to be retold each year for four days and four nights during the winter solstice. The "humma-hah" stories related events from the time long ago when human beings were still able to communicate with animals and other living things.[5] But beyond these two preceding categories, the Pueblo oral tradition knew no boundaries. Accounts of the appearance of the first Europeans (Spanish) in Pueblo country or of the tragic encounters between Pueblo people and Apache raiders were no more and no less important than stories about the biggest mule deer ever taken or adulterous couples surprised in cornfields and chicken coops. Whatever happened, the ancient people instinctively sorted events and details into a loose narrative structure. Everything became a story.

Traditionally everyone, from the youngest child to the oldest person, was expected to listen and be able to recall or tell a portion of, if only a small detail from, a narrative account or story. Thus, the remembering and the retelling were a communal process. Even if a key figure, an elder who knew much more than others, were to die unexpectedly, the system would remain intact. Through the efforts of a great many people, the community was able to piece together valuable accounts and crucial information that might otherwise have died with an individual.

Communal storytelling was a self-correcting process in which listeners were encouraged to speak up if they noted an important fact or detail omitted. The people were happy to listen to two or three different versions of the same event of the same "hummahah" story. Even conflicting versions of an incident were welcomed for the entertainment they provided. Defenders of each version might joke and tease one another, but seldom were there any direct confrontations. Implicit in the Pueblo oral tradition was the awareness that loyalties, grudges, and kinship must always influence the narrator's choices as she emphasizes to listeners that this is the way *she* has always heard the story told. The ancient Pueblo people sought a communal truth, not an absolute truth. For them this truth lived somewhere within the web of differing versions, disputes over minor points, and outright contradictions tangling with old feuds and village rivalries.

A dinner-table conversation, recalling a deer hunt forty years ago when the largest mule deer ever was taken, inevitably

5. The term "humma-hah" refers to a traditional genre of storytelling at Laguna Pueblo.

stimulates similar memories in listeners. But hunting stories were not merely after-dinner entertainment. These accounts contained information of critical importance about the behavior and migration patterns of mule deer, and they carefully described key landmarks and locations of fresh water. Thus, a deer-hunt story might also serve as a "map." Lost travelers, and lost piñon-nut gatherers, have been saved by sighting a rock formation they recognize only because they once heard a hunting story describing it.

The importance of cliff formations and water holes does not end with hunting stories. As offspring of the Mother Earth, the ancient Pueblo people could not conceive of themselves within a specific landscape, but location, or "place," nearly always plays a central role in the Pueblo oral narratives. Indeed, stories are most frequently recalled as people are passing by a specific geographical feature or the exact location where a story took place. The precise date of the incident often is less important than the place or location of the happening. "Long, long ago," "a long time ago," "not too long ago," and "recently" are usually how stories are classified in terms of time. But the places where the stories occur are precisely located, and prominent geographical details recalled, even if the landscape is well known to listeners, often because the turning point in the narrative involved a peculiarity of the special quality of a rock or tree or plant found only at that place. Thus, in the case of many of the Pueblo narratives, it is impossible to determine which came first, the incident or the geographical feature which begs to be brought alive in a story that features some unusual aspect of this location.

There is a giant sandstone boulder about a mile north of Old Laguna, on the road to Paguate. It is ten feet tall and twenty feet in circumference. When I was a child, and we would pass this boulder driving to Paguate village, someone usually made reference to the story about Kochininako, Yellow Woman, and the Estrucuyo, a monstrous giant who nearly ate her. The Twin Hero Brothers saved Kochininako, who had been out hunting rabbits to take home to feed her mother and sisters. The Hero Brothers had heard her cries just in time. The Estrucuyo had cornered her in a cave too small to fit its monstrous head. Kochininako had already thrown to the Estrucuyo all her rabbits, as well as her moccasins, and most of her clothing. Still the creature had not been satisfied. After killing the Estrucuyo with her bows and arrows, the Twin Hero Brothers slit open the Estrucuyo and cut out its heart. They threw the heart as far as they could. The monster's heart landed there, beside the old trail to Paguate village, where the sandstone boulder rests now.

It may be argued that the existence of the boulder precipitated the creation of a story to explain it. But sandstone boulders and sandstone formations of strange shapes abound in the Laguna Pueblo area. Yet, most of them do not have stories. Often the crucial element in a narrative is the terrain—some specific detail of the setting.

A high, dark mesa rises dramatically from a grassy plain, fifteen miles southeast of Laguna, in an area known as Swanee. On the grassy plain one hundred forty years ago, my great-grandmother's uncle and his brother-in-law were grazing their herd of sheep. Because visibility on the plain extends for over twenty miles, it wasn't until the two sheepherders came near the high, dark mesa that the Apaches were able to stalk them. Using the mesa to obscure their approach, the raiders swept around from both ends of the mesa. My great-grandmother's relatives were killed, and the herd was lost. The high, dark mesa played a critical role: the mesa had compromised the safety which the openness of the plains had seemed to assure.

Pueblo and Apache alike relied upon the terrain, the very earth herself, to give them protection and aid. Human activities or needs were maneuvered to fit the existing surroundings and conditions. I imagine the last afternoon of my distant ancestors as warm and sunny for late September. They might have been traveling slowly, bringing the sheep closer to Laguna in preparation for the approach of colder weather. The grass was tall and only beginning to change from green to a yellow that matched the late afternoon sun shining off it. There might have been comfort in the warmth and the sight of the sheep fattening on good pasture which lulled my ancestors into their fatal inattention. They might have had a rifle whereas the Apaches had only bows and arrows. But there would have been four or five Apache raiders, and the surprise attack would have canceled any advantage the rifles gave them.

Survival in any landscape comes down to making the best use of all available resources. On that particular September afternoon, the raiders made better use of the Swanee terrain than my poor ancestors did. Thus, the high, dark mesa and the story of the two lost Laguna herders became inextricably linked. The memory of them and their story resides in part with the high, dark mesa. For as long as the mesa stands, people within the family and clan will be reminded of the story of that afternoon long ago. Thus, the continuity and accuracy of the oral narratives are reinforced by the landscape—and the Pueblo interpretation of that landscape is *maintained*.

*The Migration Story: An Interior Journey*

The Laguna Pueblo migration stories refer to specific places—mesas, springs, or cottonwood trees—not only locations that can be visited still, but also locations that lie directly on the state highway route linking Paguate village with Laguna village.[6] In traveling this road as a child with older Laguna people I first heard a few of the stories from that much larger body of stories linked with the Emergence and Migration.[7] It may be coincidental that Laguna people continue to follow the same route which, according to the Migration story, the ancestors followed south from the Emergence Place. It may be that the route is merely the shortest and best route for car, horse, or foot traffic between Laguna and Paguate villages. But if the stories about boulders, springs, and hills are actually remnants from a ritual that retraces the creation and emergence of the Laguna Pueblo people as a culture, as the people they became, then continued use of that route creates a unique relationship between the ritual-mythic world and the actual, everyday world. A journey from Paguate to Laguna down the long decline of Paguate Hill retraces the original journey from the Emergence Place, which is located slightly north of the Paguate village. Thus, the landscape between Paguate and Laguna takes on a deeper significance: the landscape resonates the spiritual or mythic dimension of the Pueblo world even today.

Although each Pueblo culture designates its Emergence Place, usually a small natural spring edged with mossy sandstone and full of cattails and wild watercress, it is clear the Pueblo people do not view any single location or natural springs as the one and only true Emergence Place. Each Pueblo group recounts stories connected with Creation, Emergence, and Migration, although it is believed that all human beings, with all the animals and plants, emerged at the same place and at the same time.[8]

Natural springs are crucial sources of water for all life in the high desert and plateau country. So the small spring near Paguate village is literally the source and continuance of life for the people in the area. The spring also functions on a spiritual level, recalling the original Emergence Place and linking the people and the spring water to all other people and to that moment when the Pueblo people became aware of themselves as they are even now. The Emergence was an emergence into a precise cultural identity. Thus, the Pueblo stories about the Emergence and Migration are not to be taken as literally as the anthropologists might wish. Prominent geographical features and landmarks that are mentioned in the narratives exist for ritual purposes, not because the Laguna people actually journeyed south for hundreds of years

6. Laguna and Paguate are located about forty miles west of Albuquerque in the Laguna Indian Reservation. Highway 279 links the two villages.

7. *The Emergence:* all of the human beings, animals, and life that had been created emerged from the four worlds below, when the earth was habitable. *The Migration:* the Pueblo people emerged into the Fifth World, but they had already been warned they would have to travel and search to find the place where they were meant to live. The *Fifth World* is the world we live in today. There are four previous worlds below this world.

8. *Creation: Tse'itsi'nako,* Thought Woman, the Spider, thought about it, and everything she thought came into being. First she thought of three sisters for herself, and they helped her to think of the rest of the Universe, including the Fifth World and the four worlds below.

from Chaco Canyon or Mesa Verde, as the archaeologists say, or eight miles from the site of the natural springs at Paguate to the sandstone hilltop at Laguna.[9]

The eight miles, marked with boulders, mesas, springs, and river crossings, are actually a ritual circuit or path that marks the interior journey the Laguna people made: a journey of awareness and imagination in which they emerged from being within the earth and all-included in the earth to the culture and people they became, differentiating themselves for the first time from all that had surrounded them, always aware that interior distances cannot be reckoned in physical miles or in calendar years.

The narratives linked with prominent features of the landscape between Paguate and Laguna delineate the complexities of the relationship that human beings must maintain with the surrounding natural world if they hope to survive in this place. Thus, the journey was an interior process of the imagination, a growing awareness that being human is somehow different from all other life—animal, plant, and inanimate. Yet, we are all from the same source: awareness never deteriorated into Cartesian duality, cutting off the human from the natural world.

9. The narratives indicate that the Migration from the north took many years. But the Emergence Place north of Paguate village is only eight miles from Laguna village, the place where the people finally settled. What can it mean that hundreds of years and hundreds of narratives later the Laguna people had traveled but eight miles? Anthropologists attempt to interpret the Emergence and Migration stories literally, with the Pueblo people leaving Chaco Canyon and Mesa Verde (now a national park near Cortez, in extreme southwestern Colorado) to go south to the Río Grande Valley and the mountains around Zuñi (south of Gallup, New Mexico, on the Arizona border). And anthropologists still maintain that all human groups in the Western hemisphere originated elsewhere, probably in Asia. Yet, new methods of dating the very ancient cave campsites of paleo-Indians continue to push back the arrival dates of people in the Western hemisphere. Is it possible that evidence will eventually be found to place human beings in the Western hemisphere from the beginning?

The people found the opening into the Fifth World too small to allow them or any of the small animals to escape. They had sent a fly out through the small hole to tell them if it was the world the Mother Creator had promised. It was, but there was the problem of getting out. The antelope tried to butt the opening to enlarge it, but the antelope enlarged it only a little. It was necessary for the badger with her long claws to assist the antelope, and at last the opening was enlarged enough so that all the people and animals were able to emerge up into the Fifth World. The human beings could not have emerged without the aid of antelope and badger. The human beings depended upon the aid and charity of the animals. Only through interdependence could the human beings survive. Families belonged to clans, and it was by clan that the human being joined with the animal and plant world. Life on the high, arid plateau became viable when the human beings were able to imagine themselves as sisters and brothers to the badger, antelope, clay, yucca, and sun. Not until they could find a viable relationship to the terrain—the physical landscape they found themselves in—could they *emerge*. Only at the moment that the requisite balance between human and *other* was realized could the Pueblo people become a culture, a distinct group whose population and survival remained stable despite the vicissitudes of the climate and terrain.

Landscape thus has similarities with dreams. Both have the

power to seize terrifying feelings and deep instincts and translate them into images—visual, aural, tactile—and into the concrete where human beings may more readily confront and channel the terrifying instincts or powerful emotions into rituals and narratives which reassure the individual while reaffirming cherished values of the group. The identity of the individual as a part of the group and the greater Whole is strengthened, and the terror of facing the world alone is extinguished.

Even now, the people at Laguna Pueblo spend the greater portion of social occasions recounting recent incidents or events that have occurred in the Laguna area. Nearly always, the discussion will precipitate the retelling of older stories about similar incidents or other stories connected with a specific place. The stories often contain disturbing or provocative material, but are nonetheless told in the presence of children and women. The effect of these interfamily or interclan exchanges is the reassurance for each person that she or he will never be separated or apart from the clan, no matter what might happen. Neither the worst blunders or disasters nor the greatest financial prosperity and joy will ever be permitted to isolate anyone from the rest of the group. In the ancient times cohesiveness was all that stood between extinction and survival, and, while the individual certainly was recognized, it was always as an individual simultaneously bonded to family and clan by a complex bundle of custom and ritual. You are never the first to suffer a grave loss or profound humiliation. You are never the first, and you understand that you will probably not be the last to commit, or be victimized by, a repugnant act. Your family and clan are able to go on at length about others now passed on, and others older or more experienced than you who suffered similar losses.

The wide, deep arroyo near the Kings Bar (located across the reservation's borderline) has over the years claimed many vehicles. A few years ago, when a Viet Nam veteran's new red Volkswagen rolled backwards into the arroyo while he was inside buying a six-pack of beer, the story of his loss joined the lively and large collection of stories already connected with that big arroyo. I do not know whether the Viet Nam veteran was consoled when he was told the stories about the other cars claimed by the ravenous arroyo. All his savings of combat pay had gone to buy the red Volkswagen. But this man could not have felt any worse than the man who, some years before, had left his children and mother-in-law in his station-wagon with the engine running. When he came out of the liquor store his station-wagon was gone. He found it and its passengers upside down in the big arroyo: broken bones, cuts, and bruises, and a total wreck of the car.

The big arroyo has a wide mouth. Its existence needs no explanation. People in the area regard the arroyo much as they might regard a living being, which has a certain character and personality. I seldom drive past that wide, deep arroyo without feeling a familiarity and even a strange affection for it. Because as treacherous as it may be, the arroyo maintains a strong connection between human beings and the earth. The arroyo demands from us the caution and attention that constitute respect. It is this sort of respect the old believers have in mind when they tell us we must respect and love the earth.

Hopi Pueblo elders said that the austere and, to some eyes, barren plains and hills surrounding their mesa-top villages (in northeast Arizona) actually help to nurture the spirituality of the Hopi *way*. The Hopi elders say the Hopi people might have settled in locations far more lush where daily life would not have been so grueling. But there on the high, silent, sandstone mesas that overlook the sandy, arid expanses stretching to all horizons, the Hopi elders say the Hopi people must "live by their prayers" if they are to survive. The Hopi way cherishes the intangible: the riches realized from interaction and interrelationships with all beings above all else. Great abundances of material things, even food, the Hopi elders believe, tend to lure human attention away from what is most valuable and important. The views of the Hopi elders are not much different from those elders in all the Pueblos.

The bare vastness of the Hopi landscape emphasizes the visual impact of every plant, every rock, every arroyo. Nothing is overlooked or taken for granted. Each ant, each lizard, each lark is imbued with great value simply because the creature is there, simply because the creature is alive in a place where any life at all is precious. Stand on the mesa's edge at Walpi and look southwest over the bare distances toward the pale blue outlines of the San Francisco Peaks (north of Flagstaff) where the *ka'tsina* spirits reside. So little lies between you and the sky. So little lies between you and the earth. One look and you know that simply to survive is a great triumph, that every possible resource is needed, every possible ally—even the most humble insect or reptile. You realize you will be speaking with all of them if you intend to last out the year. Thus it is that the Hopi elders are grateful to the landscape for aiding them in their quest as spiritual people.

## Out Under the Sky

My earliest memories are of being outside, under the sky. I remember climbing the fence when I was three years old, and heading for the plaza in the center of Laguna village because other children passing by had told me there were *ka'tsinas* there dancing with pieces of wood in their mouths. A neighbor, a woman, re-trieved me before I ever saw the wood-swallowing *ka'tsinas,* but from an early age I knew I wanted to be outside: outside walls and fences.

My father had wandered over all the hills and mesas around Laguna when he was a child, because the Indian School and the taunts of the other children did not sit well with him. It had been difficult in those days to be part Laguna and part white, or *ame-dicana.* It was still difficult when I attended the Indian School at Laguna. Our full-blooded relatives and clanspeople assured us we were theirs and that we belonged there because we had been born and reared there. But the racism of the wider world we call America had begun to make itself felt years before. My father's response was to head for the mesas and hills with his older brother, their dog, and .22 rifles. They retreated to the sandstone cliffs and juniper forests. Out in the hills they were not lonely because they had all the living creatures of the hills around them, and, whatever the ambiguities of racial heritage, my father and my uncle understood what the old folks had taught them: The earth loves all of us regardless, because we are her children.

I started roaming those same mesas and hills when I was nine years old. At eleven I rode away on my horse, and explored places my father and uncle could not have reached on foot. I was never afraid or lonely—though I was high in the hills, many miles from home—because I carried with me the feeling I'd acquired from listening to the old stories, that the land all around me was teeming with creatures that were related to human beings and to me. The stories had also left me with a feeling of familiarity and warmth for the mesas, hills, and boulders where the incidents or action in the stories had taken place. I felt as if I had actually been to those places, although I had only heard stories about them. Somehow the stories had given a kind of being to the mesas and hills, just as the stories had left me with the sense of having spent time with the people in the stories, though they had long since passed on.

It is remarkable to sense the presence of those long passed at the locations where their adventures took place. Spirits range without boundaries of any sort, and spirits may be called back in any number of ways. The method used in the calling also deter-mines how the spirit manifests itself. I think a spirit may or may not choose to remain at the site of its passing or death. I think they might be in a number of places at the same time. Storytelling can procure fleeting moments to experience who they were and how life felt long ago. What I enjoyed most as a child was stand-ing at the site of an incident recounted in one of the ancient stories that old Aunt Susie had told us as girls. What excited me was listening to her tell us an old-time story and then realizing that I was familiar with a certain mesa or cave that figured as the central location of the story she was telling. That was when the stories worked best, because then I could sit there listening and be able to visualize myself as being located *within* the story being told, within the landscape. Because the storytellers did not just tell the stories, they would in their way act them out. The storyteller would imitate voices for vast dialogues between the various figures in the story. So we sometimes say the moment is alive again within us, within our imaginations and our memory, as we listen.

Aunt Susie once told me how it had been when she was a child and her grandmother agreed to tell the children stories. The old woman would always ask the youngest child in the room to go open the door. "Go open the door," her grandmother would say. "Go open the door so our esteemed ancestors may bring us the precious gift of their stories." Two points seem clear: the spirits could be present and the stories were valuable because they taught us how we were the people we believed we were. The myth, the web of memories and ideas that create an identity, is a part of oneself. This sense of identity was intimately linked with the surrounding terrain, to the landscape that has often played a significant role in a story or in the outcome of a conflict.

The landscape sits in the center of Pueblo belief and identity. Any narratives about the Pueblo people necessarily give a great deal of attention and detail to all aspects of a landscape. For this reason, the Pueblo people have always been extremely reluctant to relinquish their land for dams or highways. For this reason, Taos Pueblo fought from 1906 until 1973 to win back its sacred Blue Lake, which was illegally taken by the creation of Taos National Forest. For this reason, the decision in the early 1950s to begin open-pit mining of the huge uranium deposits north of Laguna, near Paguate village, has had a powerful psychological impact upon the Laguna people. Already a large body of stories has grown up around the subject of what happens to people who disturb or destroy the earth. I was a child when the mining began and the apocalyptic warning stories were being told. And I have lived long enough to begin hearing the stories that verify the earlier warnings.

All that remains of the gardens and orchards that used to grow in the sandy flats southeast of Paguate village are the stories of the lovely big peaches and apricots the people used to grow. The Jackpile Mine is an open pit that has been blasted out of the many hundreds of acres where the orchards and melon patches once grew. The Laguna people have not witnessed changes to the land without strong reactions. Descriptions of the landscape *before* the mine are as vivid as any description of the present-day destruction by the open-pit mining. By its very ugliness and by the violence it does to the land, the Jackpile Mine insures that, from now on, it, too, will be included in the vast body of narratives that makes up the history of the Laguna people and the Pueblo landscape. And the description of what that landscape looked like *before* the uranium mining began will always carry considerable impact.

## Landscape as a Character in Fiction

When I began writing I found that the plots of my short stories very often featured the presence of elements out of the landscape, elements that directly influenced the outcome of events. Nowhere is landscape more crucial to the outcome than in my short story, "Storyteller." The site is southwest Alaska in the Yukon Delta National Wildlife Refuge, near the village of Bethel, on the Kuskokwim River. Tundra country. Here the winter landscape can suddenly metamorphose into a seamless, blank white so solid that pilots in aircraft without electronic instruments lose their bearings and crash their planes into the frozen tundra, believing "down" to be "up." Here on the Alaskan tundra, in mid-February, not all the space-age fabrics, electronics, or engines can ransom human beings from the restless, shifting forces of the winter sky and winter earth.

The young Yupik Eskimo woman works out an elaborate yet subconscious plan to avenge the deaths of her parents. After months of baiting the trap, she lures the murderer onto the river's ice where he falls through to his death. The murderer is a white man who operated the village trading post. For years the murderer has existed like a parasite, exploiting not only the fur-bearing animals and the fish, but also the Yupik people themselves. When the Yupik woman kills him, the white trader has just finished cashing in on the influx of workers who have suddenly come to the tiny village for the petroleum exploration and pipeline.

For the Yupik people, souls deserving punishment spend varying lengths of time in a place of freezing. The Yupik see the world's end coming with ice, not fire. Although the white trader possessed every possible garment, insulation, heating fuel, and gadget ever devised to protect him from the frozen tundra environment, he still dies, drowning under the freezing river-ice, because the white man had not reckoned with the true power of that landscape, especially not the power which the Yupik woman understood instinctively and which she used so swiftly and efficiently. The white man had reckoned with the young woman and determined he could overpower her. But the white man failed to account for the conjunction of the landscape with the woman. The Yupik woman had never seen herself as anything but a part of that sky, that frozen river, that tundra. The river's ice and the blinding white are her accomplices, and yet the Yupik woman never for a moment misunderstands her own relationship with that landscape.

After the white trader has crashed through the river's ice, the young woman finds herself a great distance from either shore of the treacherous, frozen river. She can see nothing but the whiteness of the sky swallowing the earth. But far away in the distance, on the side of her log and tundra-sod cabin, she is able to see a spot of bright red: a bright red marker she had nailed up weeks earlier because she was intrigued by the contrast between all that white and the spot of brilliant red. The Yupik woman knows the appetite of the frozen river. She realizes that the ice and the fog, the tundra and the snow seek constantly to be re-united with the living beings which skitter across it. The Yupik woman knows that inevitably she and all things will one day lie in those depths. But the woman is young and her instinct is to live. The Yupik woman knows how to do this.

Inside the small cabin of logs and tundra sod, the old Story-teller is mumbling the last story he will ever tell. It is the story of the hunter stalking a giant polar bear the color of blue glacier-ice. It is a story that the old Storyteller has been telling since the young Yupik woman began to arrange the white trader's death:

*A sudden storm develops. The hunter finds himself on an ice floe offshore. Visibility is zero, and the scream of the wind blots out all sound. Quickly the hunter realizes he is being stalked, hunted by all the forces, by all the elements of the sky and earth around him. When at last the hunter's own muscles spasm and cause the jade knife to fall and shatter the ice, the hunter's death in the embrace of the giant, ice-blue bear is the foretelling of the world's end.*

When humans have blasted and burned the last bit of life from the earth, an immeasurable freezing will descend with a darkness that obliterates the sun.

The cemetery at Blanco, a small town located on the Blanco River in the heart of the Texas Hill Country, is the setting for one of Thomas Rabbitt's poems. Illustration by Susan Trammell, 1994, based on a color photograph by novelist Allen Wier.

**Thomas Rabbitt**

# A Flat Rock:
# Poetry, Perception,
# and Landscape

THOMAS RABBITT was born in 1943 in Boston, Massachusetts, and was raised there. He was educated at the Boston Latin School, received an A.B. in English from Harvard College, and completed an M.A. in English (The Writing Seminars) at Johns Hopkins University and an M.F.A. in creative writing at the University of Iowa. His poems have appeared in *Antaeus, The Black Warrior Review, Esquire, Ploughshares, Poem, Poetry, The Poetry Miscellany,* and *Shenandoah,* among other journals and reviews. His four books of poetry are *Exile* (Pittsburgh, 1975), for which he won the U.S. Award of the International Poetry Forum (The Pitt Prize), *The Booth Interstate* (Knopf, 1981), *The Abandoned Country* (Carnegie Mellon, 1988), and *Enemies of the State* (Godine, 1994). In 1980 Professor Rabbitt was a winner of one of the first University of Alabama Outstanding Scholar Awards. He is a professor of English and creative writing at the University of Alabama, and he lives on Horse Creek Farm in Elrod, Alabama, where he raises horses.

I ONCE HEARD Paul Harvey in one of his noonday radio homilies tell the story of a farmer who for years plowed around a large, flat rock in his cornfield. Before the parable was well begun, we listeners knew that Old MacDonald was remiss, if not damned, if he let that rock impede his plowing one more day. Paul Harvey, we also knew, did not go in for contour farming. Paul Harvey stood for the straight and narrow, efficiency, economy, and simplicity, which is why I have to fill in the details of the story. Mr. Harvey had time for no more than the bones and the moral, enough only for the convinced.

Early the morning after Mr. Harvey's sermon, the rooster crowed from the henyard and Old MacDonald, already up and dressed, waited at his kitchen table for his cup of Postum to cool and his wife to serve him his bacon. He was brooding.

"Malcolm," she said to him, for surely she didn't call him "Old," "Malcolm, are you still thinking about that great rock?"

Of course he was. "I should try to move it," he said.

"After all these years?"

"I should try."

"Just don't strain your heart," she said.

Malcolm drove his tractor down into the bowl of the pasture toward the creek. The logging chain rattled on the hitch; the crowbar and pickax rattled. The tractor rolled over the light frost, flattened the yellow grass, and the tires glistened. Across the creek the pasture rose out of its small, wet valley to the high ground of the cornfield, acres of frosted stalks aglow in the sunlight and rising out of them the perfect, blue November sky. Malcolm took a deep, cold breath. The world was very nice, his world, his neat house, stout barns, straight fences, full corncrib, fat Herefords. Even the crows cawing out of the woods by the river fit his world.

Malcolm let the tractor idle by the rock. He lay his tools atop it and unwound the chain. Then he sat down by his tools. The rock, he had once decided, was probably the flat top of a buried mountain. He could dig and dig and get nowhere. Or worse, he could dig enough and cart off enough and end up with a bare mesa standing where his cornfield once lay. Maybe that wouldn't be worse; maybe it would be the beginning of his own Mount Rushmore, another life's work, something new to look at from his kitchen window. He shook his head, stood, and, taking up the crowbar, wedged the curved end between the rock and the dirt. Then he pushed. The bar slid under the rock. He pried. The great flat rock lifted a hand's breadth. He used the pickax for a fulcrum and pried again, lifting the rock still higher before letting it drop with a thud.

He sat down again and listened to the tractor idle and his heart pound. So that was it, he thought. This great flat rock he had been plowing around for all these years was nothing more than a petrified pancake. Big and heavy, yes. But not so big or so heavy that it could not be easily moved. He stood up again, turned off the tractor, and rolled a cigarette. After all these years, he thought. And wait until Paul Harvey hears about this, he thought.

Of course he should have tried moving the rock years ago, but that no longer seemed to Malcolm to be the point. For all these years the rock had been a part of his cornfield, a part of his life. Every summer he would stand at the end of the field and look down the file of rows to where they curved around the rock. He imagined that, to the crows, the cornfield looked like a green river eddying in circles around the rock, the outcropping of the mountain which upheld his farm. But the crows whose caws always sounded like laughter had known: not a river, but a pond; not an upthrusting mountain crag, but the dropping of a passing glacier.

Malcolm sat for a long time. He watched a ridge of clouds begin to build in the northwest. He heard the dry corn shucks rustle and saw a female pheasant, drab and mindless, peck her way across the rows. He lofted a clump of dirt at her and was annoyed that the whirr of her takeoff unnerved him. Then his tractor wouldn't start, and then, when he finally got it cranked, he was tempted to let it roll on without him, let it tear down the fences that no longer looked so straight, let it pitch into the creek and sink to its axles in cold mud.

"No, I didn't move it," Malcolm told his wife.

"Too big?" she asked.

"Too big for a flagstone; too small for a runway." Then he laughed, a small, bitter laugh. His wife was perplexed and Malcolm knew that sooner or later he'd have to explain, but for the moment he said, "I'm going to leave it where it is till I figure where to put it."

"I could've told you that," she said.

Malcolm glared at her, then went out to work on his tractor, which is not at all what Paul Harvey had in mind. The sin was procrastination; the ironic lesson was as simple as the moral of any fable should be.

Nor was it lost on MacDonald. The trouble for him was that he'd found more than he'd bargained for: he was forced to begin to grapple with his relationship to his land, his landscape, and to do that he had to define it. Simple. The landscape was himself.

Not so simple, of course. The philosophical questions of Malcolm's relationship to nature—*in but not of, of but not in*—lurk behind our notions of landscape, and those questions are themselves a mess in constant need of definition and clarification. What Malcolm knew was that he had a problem: he didn't know what to do about the rock, because he didn't know how he felt about the rock; or, more precisely, he wanted to do several things with the rock, because he felt several ways about it and about his life. The rock wasn't his life. It wasn't that big. But it wasn't just a symbol either. It was a real rock with a place of its own, a place right in the middle of Malcolm's life. But was it the correct place? Move it or leave it? Either could bring better or worse or nothing at all. Malcolm wasn't logical enough to try philosophy. He was confused enough for poetry.

On a broadcast of National Public Radio's "Morning Edition" the poet James Galvin said that, in his own poems, content and context are not the same. By context I believe he meant landscape. By content he probably meant the intellectual and emotional complex any poem seeks to create for its audience, what Richard Hugo, in *The Triggering Town: Lectures and Essays on Poetry and Writing,* called the generated subject of a poem. I guess it's fair to say that a mountain is not grief or joy, but it's just as fair to say that perception is creative and fair to repeat the hackneyed critical notion that, at least since the Romantics, internal and external landscapes have in poetry worked as mirrors of one another.[1]

Suppose Malcolm is driving into town to buy a new battery for his balky tractor. Suppose he hasn't yet begun to worry about the rock. His harvest's in and corn futures are record high. He feels great. The sun's shining, the breeze is crisp, his pickup radio is playing his favorite Eddie Rabbitt song. Then he sees, a quarter of a mile down the road, on a section of pavement shaded by tall pines, something about the size of a large pumpkin, but paler, more squash-shaped. Sure, he decides as he gets closer, it's a bank bag, it's money, a bag of money dropped by escaping bank rob-

1. The broadcast on National Public Radio occurred on 7 September 1984. In the contemporary (postmodern) American landscape, *landscape* often means "whatever's handy." In poetry, one does not *see* a landscape as one does in representational art; the reader must imagine from a few details; and each reader's mind's eye will see something different. To most poets, this notion of landscape is obvious.

bers or fallen from the bumped open door of a speeding Brink's truck.

But suppose Malcolm has already encountered his rock and now he has to drive all the way into town and spend some of his hard-earned money on a new battery, the third one this year. The bright sun irritates his eyes. He can't roll up his window and the cold air is giving him a stiff neck. And he can't figure what Eddie Rabbitt or anyone else for that matter could find in a rainy night worth singing about. To top it off, there right ahead, smack dab

---

Traveling through the Dark

Traveling through the dark I found a deer
dead on the edge of the Wilson River road.
It is usually best to roll them into the canyon:
that road is narrow; to swerve might make more dead.

By glow of the tail-light I stumbled back of the car
and stood by the heap, a doe, a recent killing;
she had stiffened already, almost cold.
I dragged her off: she was large in the belly.

My fingers touching her side brought me the reason—
her side was warm; her fawn lay there waiting,
alive, still, never to be born.
Beside that mountain road I hesitated.

The car aimed ahead its lowered parking lights;
under the hood purred the steady engine.
I stood in the glare of the warm exhaust turning red;
around our group I could hear the wilderness listen.

I thought hard for us all—my only swerving—,
then pushed her over the edge into the river.

—William Stafford (1914–1993)

---

This poem originally appeared in William Stafford's book of poems, *Traveling through the Dark* (Harper & Row, 1962). It is presented here as an illustration. Reprinted courtesy of Dorothy F. Stafford.

in the middle of the road, is a damn rock as big as a cow. If he doesn't stop and roll it to the shoulder, someone is going to have a wreck. Probably him, on his way home.

What Malcolm has seen, what most of us have seen, is an old grocery sack. As soon as he gets close enough to make it out, he says, "Hell, it's just an old grocery sack. Could've fooled me. Looked like a dead cow." And since it is such a fine day, in spite of everything—the bright sun, the cold air, Eddie Rabbitt—Malcolm laughs at the idea of a dead cow. He feels so good he figures that on his way home he'll stop and pick the litter from the road. Who knows? There might be something in the sack.

So, if perception is creative and if the internal and external worlds often mirror one another, then landscape is not merely context, the backdrop of our lives or, in a poem, the inert setting, however bleak or charming, for whatever intellectual or emotional experience the poet seeks to create and convey. In poems—at least in my own poetry and in much of the poetry I admire—landscape is reflexive and dynamic, simultaneously a catalyst for, and a function of, moods and ideas.

Like farmer MacDonald I have a piece of land and on it I try to raise things: horses, goats, chickens and ducks, a few cattle, a vegetable garden, a small orchard, some marigolds, myself. And like MacDonald I have sought to alter my landscape, both in fact and through imagination. One year Southern pine beetles infested my woods. The trees couldn't be saved. I didn't much like the idea of cutting them down, but I had no choice. Besides, I needed the money. I had bills, plans, and, it later turned out, a woodlot full of guilt.

### TIMBER SALES

*The trees are in their autumn beauty, dry*
*Although it's winter, nearly spring, and fire*
*Rises from my neighbor's hills like plague.*
*All night wild birds and tiny insects sing:*
*This is no war to bring a lover to.*
*Yellow skidders, like life from the moon, falling*
*All night through space, are landed now; steel teeth*
*Are eating trees. The knuckle-boom hoists money*
*Onto trucks. Those who can, run off and scream.*

*I must decide to live without the trees,*
*Their other lives and old geographies.*
*The lake goes here. The gullies will be smoothed*
*To grassy fields where Charolais stand and dream.*
*The dam goes here. The road across to fields*
*Lapped by the perfect lake, stumps left for bass,*
*For where my neighbor's children have to drown*
*In August because the day swims in heat*
*And I haven't any children of my own.*

*At breakfast all my horses stand and look*
*One way—from the barn, off into the trees.*
*The horses accuse me and will not eat.*
*The noise from the woods is noise from the woods,*
*Not ghosts, not dying birds, not my self-respect.*
*These horses will not eat. Not while the trees*
*Are falling in long screams, while at my feet*
*The deer collapse whose lives have been corrected*
*In this, no place to bring a lover to.*[2]

I suppose the perfect lake represents the idyllic landscape to be achieved by selling the trees and using the money to change the topography. At least that was the dream. Instead, the whine of chainsaws, the roar of log skidders, and the crash of felled pines yield a vision of children drowning in that lake. The planned paradise becomes a clear-cut wasteland, and the speaker's punishment for his selfishness and self-indulgence is continued isolation and loneliness. The only correction for his life is ironic. His image of himself is that of a perverse St. Francis, a mirror of the destruction he's caused.

A landscape can stretch through forests and across pastures and lakes to the farthest horizon. It can and will include whatever the poet sees and chooses to use: barns, fences, high wires, a gully full of wrecked cars. It can be a *sea*scape or a *city*scape, inasmuch as one can "*land*scape" a seascape by building a jetty. And it can be limited, evoked by a few details, the merest brushstrokes, and reduced in scope to include only the foreground, perhaps just the ground at the poet's feet, if that ground provides the material for the poem.

2. "Timber Sales" appears in Thomas Rabbitt's third book of poems, *The Abandoned Country* (Carnegie Mellon, 1988), page 46.

A PROSPECT OF DIAMONDS OUT BACK

A small trek from the house to barn occupies
My morning like a cardiac arrest.
I'd avoid this; I can't. So I enjoy
As the onanist enjoys his daily death.
My farm is a salesman's dream,
Monkey paw or wild ass's skin, grown
But for trash a measure smaller each time
It's sold, each day it suffers rain.
I know that I must drink too much.
Erosion satisfies me, slowly, from within.

Would you wonder that a barn might loom
At fifty feet? Hog briar and cracked shale loom.
The night's dropped rain can loom.
The red clay, slick as a lover's tongue,
And the barn, a symphony in rust, these loom.
Everything I own reminds me that it must
Be fed or else will die on my hands.
In one pocket one hand looms
To accomplish nothing. One hand totes a pail,
One hand feels the air against my face,
One hand pulls my hair. All hands fail.

I buy this farm in order to be saved.
Payments haven't worked that way.
Horses, goats, dogs, chickens, the debits
Of a grossly other life. Subtract one day
After another from that life, till one knows why
This land is never held, is never sold,
Is simply left like a child's tooth
To be redeemed from the wrinkled sheets
And sweat by a dream of any day's success.
Each night it rains. Clay and sand wash off
The rough edges of a predecessor's trash.
Each dawn lights the light of their success.

And so I pass it. On the way from house
To barn. And though I see it shine
I know it can be nothing more than glass,

*A bright lozenge turned up from a mine*
*Of all the scattered, mortgaged trash*
*Onanists have used to seed the land.*
*Take pride. Take pleasure. Please. Stay undeceived.*
*The livestock love you. Yes, the horses do.*
*The rising sun nibbles daylight from your hand.*

*On the path back to the house the lozenge*
*Eats at your eyes. It was never glass.*
*I think you too should settle for the truth:*
*For the dark blue stone cut like clear cobalt,*
*For the gold cord disguised as baling twine.*
*You will sit like me, digging with a Cree axhead*
*At a half-buried square of whitest ivory.*
*All failure is remote. You will be glad,*
*Like me, to stay here, carefully, forever.*
*You will give up prospects, your job, your wife.*
*Half-buried, important ivory, color, shape,*
*This bathroom tile from other people's lives.*
*We will have to help each other, we must decide.*[3]

Poets do like to fool around a lot. At least I do. And I hope the play adds to the effect. In this poem the title's "out back" means behind the house, the area between backyard and barnyard. But it's also supposed to carry with it a hint of the alien, of Australia maybe, some distant place where finding diamonds is not so impossible.

The speaker recognizes—perhaps wryly, perhaps self-deprecatingly—the relationship between himself and the land in the references to Onan and erosion. Maybe irony keeps the poem's aesthetic in check. Whatever the case, the poem is after all a close-up of that relationship. The speaker becomes a kind of archaeologist, self-indulgent and shortsighted, who sees himself as one more in a long line of littering occupants, Indian to white trash. Creative perception is not meant to be self-delusion so much as a way of changing quotidian disappointment into delight and, through the shifting address, a way of convincing the self and maybe even the reader that the real deception is to insist on the commonplace, the judgmental, some futile notion of just how the land is to be used or valued.

3. "A Prospect of Diamonds Out Back" appears in *The Abandoned Country*, pages 44–45.

What I have to say about landscape is bound to annoy some poets, those for whom setting is merely context, be it highway or kitchen, and those whose poems are not necessarily anchored to the furniture of this world. My notions might strike them as prescriptive or, worse, hopelessly agrarian. My poems, too. Too bad. For better or worse, I am a poet whose life and work are at the mercy of my neighborhood. If I lived in the suburbs, then my poems would have nice lawns and neat hedges plagued by gophers, moles, and aphids. Right now I happen to live on a farm in west-central Alabama. There isn't an enormous slag heap across the road, but if there were you could bet it would occupy my thoughts and probably a poem or two. The fact that there wasn't a slag heap there when I got up this morning does not mean I won't have imported one by bedtime.

Right now I'm typing. If, from where I sit, I look out the window to my left, I see a small pond, the water brown, its level low because this is the dry season. Some black and white ducks are huddled under the weeds that grow down from the dam. If I look out the window in front of me, I see beyond my front fence and the road the edge of a forest, mostly pine, sweetgum, and oak. The woods climb a hill you can't see from my house, Dixie Hill, the highest in this part of Tuscaloosa County. I've ridden to the top. From there you can see strip mines and slag heaps. They're not that far from my house. I could see one move closer. For, while all landscapes are real, some landscapes are imagined. If necessity demands them, they'll be found.

This is the essence of Malcolm's landscape, and it gets me to the obvious point that landscapes are to be found everywhere. So what makes one place at one time more compelling than another? One summer long ago some friends of mine and I drove across the country from Massachusetts to California. I didn't know how to drive then so I was just a passenger. Just after sunset one day we stopped for gas at a station somewhere in Kansas. It seems to me now that we were miles from the nearest town. On the far side of a field across the two-lane highway from the station a man was baling hay. The countryside rolled gently to the horizon, the air was beginning to cool, the colors were growing darker and richer, and the only sounds were the buzzing of insects in the station's lights and, carried on the breeze, the clatter and thunk of the tractor and baler. The scent of fresh hay was intoxicating. I stepped away from the station and its lights. I stood in the gathering dark, watched and listened and inhaled as if this were the finest air I would ever get to breathe. And I thought, "I could stay here forever."

I was almost paralyzed by the idea. Corny? Sure. I was tired from the trip and reluctant to face the cramped miles we had to travel before Denver. I knew that, if we had stopped at noon or if I managed to come back the next day at noon, the heat alone would have been enough to change the place and my mind. But those few minutes after sunset were perfect. Maybe *harmony* was the momentary result of fatigue, but for its moment it was wonderful and I couldn't get enough of it. Wanting the time to last forever and knowing it couldn't were functions of one another, of me, and of the landscape. That landscape no longer exists, not because the topography is changed, though it may be, but because I am not a part of it.

I recognize that this position must seem as egocentric and anthropocentric as that of the person who believes that a tree falling in the forest makes no sound unless there is someone there to hear it. In fact I sometimes think one can separate the Romantic and the Neoclassicist by the answer each gives to that old conundrum. It's easy enough to admit my own Romantic heritage; still, I recognize that process occurs, and the world is, with or without me. The centrality I ascribe to myself or any poet involves the agency of the poem's processes: perceptual, intellectual, emotional, and compositional. And I believe that a poet for whom content and context are inextricable also recognizes that, besides being caught between the mirrors of inner and outer worlds, the poet is simultaneously and paradoxically inside and outside his or her landscapes. No matter the persona of the poem or the attitude of the speaker, the poet generating the poem is working on the energy provided by the tension of that paradox, an energy perhaps like that of the subatomic particle whose tensions compose our world.

### THE CEMETERY AT BLANCO

*He tends his graves. I walk with his wife*
*To a dim brown corner of the graveyard where*
*We wonder why the nineteenth-century Hungarians*
*Decorated their dead with scallop shells.*
Watch out, *he yells,* for rattlers. Does he mean me?
*I can tell her nearly nothing, what I can guess*
*From the stones, what she can see: twin infant girls*
*And then their mother, dead in days; the second wife,*

*Her husband's sons; her and him; the long slow*
*Dying out of generations. No rattlesnakes.*
*No plagues or Texas cattle wars. Just scallop shells.*

*The wife has her ideas, the husband his*
*Of what we've come to find among these dead.*
*Around us Blanco County's dull gold hills roll off*
*Into fictions. He drags a garden hose*
*Like a green snake across the parched boneyard.*
*A sapling. His daddy's grave. His wife. And me.*
*These improbabilities cannot connect.*
*The center of the universe has frightened me.*
*The air is full of soft Comanche cries, scrub oak,*
*The view toward town, a family whose funerals I missed.*
*Here lies your wife and son. This grave is yours.*

*Here, where all the world is held in place*
*On stone by dates, the dead are saying, Comfort.*
*The highway is silent. In the hills, cattle ease*
*From dusty meal to meal. Beneath the mesquite*
*A thousand years wait with the rattlesnakes—*
*Out there, or here, watching my friends and me.*
*There are a few flowers, a redtail hawk, some shrubs.*
*The graveyard slopes—I shouldn't tell—like a bed,*
*From pillow to foot, downhill, gentle, orderly,*
*Across the highway and into the dried up river bed.*

*He is done with his daddy as he is.*
*She and I watch him coil the hose too carefully.*
*Drought makes the matter-of-fact seem less so.*
*I understand. The dead have broken through their shells*
*And are crying, Water! Water! But he moves on*
*To his pickup. Then his wife moves with him.*
*I am standing in the center of distance. Of dust.*
*The wampum-covered graves are dusty, like the hills,*
*The cattle, the highway, the town and the river,*
*White with the dust the living stir as they leave.*
*This is the easy end where what I want to say is:*
*Leave me. Take yourselves and your hose away,*
*Your oaks and your hills into kinder weather.*
*I understand and I am not afraid. Leave me.*[4]

4. "The Cemetery at Blanco" appears in *The Abandoned Country,* pages 10–11.

This poem tries to resolve a few tensions: from the incongruity of scallop shells in the dry Texas hills to the deceptive comfort of death. Once again I was along for the ride. I saw myself as simultaneously in the picture and out of it. In the middle of a landscape as beautiful and alien as any I have ever seen and with friends who belonged to one another in a way I could not, I felt isolated, rootless, and absolutely inconsequential. The frightening center of the universe was both myself and, as in E. M. Forster's *A Passage to India,* the great nothingness inside a hollow rock. Perhaps this recognition of personal inconsequence combined with the panoramic placidity of those dry hills to dissipate the terror. Whatever the case, I wanted to be left where I was forever in a moment as sure and calm as any I have ever felt and which, of course, I knew could never last.

Maybe what we value most about landscapes is our own insubstantiality. Maybe it's like falling in love on a two-week vacation in Tahiti; we invest everything because we know it cannot last. Maybe that's why, if we were Malcolm, we, too, would be bollixed by that great flat rock. Last I knew he was talking of setting it up on edge, letting it sit in his cornfield like a monument, a granite sun, a kind of art.

John R. Stilgoe

# Boyhood Landscape
# and Repetition

JOHN R. STILGOE, born in 1949, is a native of Norwell, Massachusetts. A Fellow of the Society of American Historians, he is the author of *Common Landscape of America, 1580 to 1845* (Yale, 1982), for which he won the Francis Parkman Medal, *Metropolitan Corridor: Railroads and the American Scene* (Yale, 1983), *Borderland: Origins of the American Suburb, 1820 to 1939* (Yale, 1988), *Shallow-Water Dictionary: A Grounding in Estuary English* (Exact Change, 1990), and *Alongshore* (Yale, 1994). He lives on Brookside Farm in Norwell, and is the Robert & Lois Orchard Professor in the History of Landscape at Harvard University.

EDITOR'S NOTE: This essay was commissioned and written for inclusion in this book. Another version also appears in *Places*, Volume 4, Number 2 (June 1987), pages 64–74.

THE BOG, The Pit, Mrs. Norris's Woods, The Swamp, Fuller's Dam, and The Landing all linger as landmarks in a landscape of childhood. Adults in the 1950s and 1960s knew the places treasured by boys growing up in a small, New England coastal town, but used other designations, if they applied designations at all, to a collection of semi-used or long abandoned spaces. Only one bog deserved "the" as title; perhaps fifteen acres in extent, it produced few cranberries, but innumerable wild ducks, frogs, herons, and the big snakes eventually identified from junior high school nature guides as the common northern water snake, *Natrix sipedon sipedon*. Beaver now and then dammed the brooks flowing through the worn dike built in the early part of the century; if the beaver stayed "up bog," boys rolled fieldstone into the breaches, insuring a tiny pond all summer and—with luck—a larger skating pond by Christmas. Three miles away, south by southeast, endured The Landing, a ragged gash in a salt marsh opening into the estuary. From the 1650s to the 1920s boat-builders, fishermen, and farmers used it, making it common land; its steep slope and slick mud defeated cars and trucks, however, and as the age of the horse passed bayberry and sumac crowded the lane. Officially, if occasionally, visited by the Highway Surveyor, used by fishermen seeking striped bass and by rare, summer-person canoeists, it remained the possession of boys bored with the well-kept gravel and asphalt of the densely populated town landing slightly seaward. Hidden by second-growth forest, defended by twisting, muddy paths and rotted bridges, The Bog, The Landing, and the other constituent elements of the intricate landscape of childhood thrived within an equally complex landscape of adults.

Now and then intersection of interest shattered peaceful co-existence. Forest fire signaled the arrival of the volunteer firemen, adult onlookers, and the boys, breathless on bicycles. Always the fire chief barked the same question: "Boys, what's the best way in?" Then followed the frantic flinging down of Indian pumps—four-gallon, Army surplus hand-pumps worn on the back—to the boys, the filling of the pump tanks by a fireman nearly knocked down by boys with pumps and too-small boys screaming for the honor of a pump, then the dragging of the hose along the trail known only to boys thrilled to be guiding the townsmen and squirting tiny streams on smouldering white pines or smouldering canvas hoses. Day after day, however, after school, in the frigid winter vacations, the landscape of boys remained almost untrodden by adults. Separate, protected, and regularly modified by its stewards, it passed eventually to younger boys when the wonders of driving family automobiles in distinctly adult space deflected sixteen-year-olds from marshes, swamps, and the forgotten plantation of balsam fir designated "Christmas Tree Land."

Of course, men return now and then, even a landscape historian weary of typewriting and determined to improve the last of a November afternoon by following the old route to The Bog. Windfalls and poison ivy have deflected the path a bit, but the long vista across the now grown-over sand pit remains. And in the gray light, at the crest of the drumlin, the historian descries a man walking as he walked a quarter century earlier. In the hollow thick now with chokecherry the old friends meet, the historian asking the lawyer dressed for court what brings him onto the path to The Bog. "She just told me. She wants a divorce. Somehow I just wound up out here."

Discreteness distinguishes a landscape from *landscape*. A landscape typically acquires discreteness from natural or artificial boundaries or as it evolves peculiar spatial and structural characteristics. The landscape of Nantucket Island or Sombrero Key extends to the low-tide mark and is easily bounded by any observer on foot or equipped with a map or chart. Even the landscape of Missouri or Montana can be delineated by political boundaries. But more often geographers and other dedicated observers of the built environment identify a landscape not only by tracing its edges, but also by defining its distinguishing characteristics. Bank barns, double-pen cabins, adobe-wall construction, and a thousand other characteristics serve to define landscapes. In the past two decades landscape identification and definition have grown sophisticated. Edges and details, cherished by discoverers, dovetail with frameworks evolved by philosophers, economists, and mathematicians.

Landscape is not *a* landscape. As I define it in *Common Landscape of America, 1580 to 1845*, landscape is not cityscape, but essentially rural, essentially the product of tradition.[1] To discern and define *a* landscape means knowing what landscape is in general, then devising some system of noting the important edges

1. (New Haven: Yale University Press, 1982), pages 3–7, 339–346, and passim.

One last turn, and the overgrown path opens onto *The Bog* in Norwell, Massachusetts. Photograph by John R. Stilgoe, 1984.

*The Landing* in Norwell and the view beyond startle strangers wandering down the tree-choked dirt road. Photograph by John R. Stilgoe, 1984.

and other features of the place under study, be it a suburb, a valley devoted to cattle ranching, or a Great Lakes resort island. Scholars have lately devised such systems; many prove immediately useful, others suggest improvements or adaptations to specific landscapes.[2] Implicit in most are prisms, however, prisms that subtly distort the usefulness of the systems in the work of others.

Consider scale. What is a long vista across a grown-over sand pit? To a native of Moab in Utah, perhaps two or even three miles; bright sunlight, clear air, and unobstructed views combine in Utah to produce attitudes toward distance alien to West Virginians. In Norwell, Massachusetts, it means about two hundred yards, a figure not immediately surprising for a heavily wooded town. But what, then, is the impact of the town's coastal location?

2. See, for example, Yi-Fu Tuan, *Topophilia: A Study of Environmental Perception, Attitudes, and Values* (Englewood Cliffs, NJ: Prentice-Hall, 1974); D. W. Meinig, ed., *The Interpretation of Ordinary Landscapes: Geographical Essays* (New York: Oxford University Press, 1979), especially Peirce F. Lewis, "Axioms for Reading the Landscape: Some Guides to the American Scene," pages 11–32; Annette Kolodny, *The Land Before Her: Fantasy and Experience of the American Frontiers, 1630–1860* (Chapel Hill: University of North Carolina Press, 1984); and Tadahiko Higuchi, *The Visual and Spatial Structure of Landscapes* [1975] (Cambridge, MA: The MIT Press, 1983).

*The Landing,* an inlet graced with two planks and long-frayed manila line, opens on an estuary leading to Massachusetts Bay and shores beyond schoolroom maps. Photograph by John R. Stilgoe, 1984.

What influence has the sea, stretching away flatter than any eastern Wyoming wheatfield? Such are the issues that perplex the reader of undergraduate and graduate term papers. What local values, unrecognized by their bearers, distort visions of landscape? The question lies at the heart of landscape analysis. "In certain of its fundamental features, our rural landscape," asserts the French historian Marc Bloch in *The Historian's Craft,* "dates from a very remote epoch." But to examine the rural landscape of the past, "in order to ask the right questions, even in order to know what we were talking about, it was necessary to fulfill a primary condition: that of observing and analyzing our present landscape." Bloch says little about the actual observation and analysis; he does, however, liken the task of the historian to that of someone examining a roll of photographic film. "In the film which he is examining, only the last picture remains quite clear. In order to reconstruct the faded features of the others, it behooves him first to unwind the spool in the opposite direction from that in which the pictures were taken."[3] The state of the last negative, therefore, determines the whole study of the prior ones. And as any surveyor or navigator knows, the slightest error at the start of a long course produces increasingly serious errors as the course is run.

J. R. R. Tolkien, the British folklorist who produced *The Hobbitt* and *The Lord of the Rings* for fun and in so doing created one of the richest of fantasy landscapes, wondered about the start of landscape perception, about the very frame that worried Bloch least. "If a story says 'he climbed a hill and saw a river in the valley below,' the illustrator may catch, or nearly catch, his own vision of such a scene," Tolkien argues in *Tree and Leaf,* "but every hearer of the words will have his own picture, and it will be made out of all the hills and rivers and dales he has ever seen but specially out of The Hill, The River, The Valley which were for him the first embodiment of the word."[4] If Tolkien is correct, then the landscape of childhood has immense meaning for the student and interpreter of landscapes, for that first landscape remains—despite training, system, and years of fieldwork—a prism through which actual landscapes are viewed and through which long-vanished landscapes are reconstructed using the written documents favored by Bloch and other historians. And, as all prisms do, the prism distorts, perhaps dangerously.

Innocence suffuses the landscape—or cityscape—of childhood. To the child yet unaware of thermonuclear fire, landscape is permanent. It is no accident that landscape history is largely a postwar phenomenon; the work of Maurice Beresford and W. G. Hoskins in Britain and J. B. Jackson in the United States evolved out of wartime experience and technique.[5] The devastated landscape of continental Europe advertised the fragility of built form, spurring interest among people ever less certain of permanence.[6] "The city has never been so uncomfortable, so crowded, so tense," wrote E. B. White of New York in 1949. "The subtlest change in New York is something people don't speak much about but that is in everyone's mind. The city, for the first time in its long history, is destructible. A single flight of planes no bigger than a wedge of geese can quickly end this island fantasy, burn the towers, crumble the bridges, turn the underground passages into lethal chambers, cremate the millions."[7] World War II destruction and the subsequent threat of atomic warfare did not create the field of landscape history and the profession of historic preservation, but they urged them onward. If Tolkien is correct, if the last frame of

3. Translation by Peter Putnam (1953; reprint New York: Random House, 1964), pages 46–47.

4. (Boston: Houghton Mifflin, 1965), page 80.

5. Jackson is especially eloquent about the role of war; see "Landscape as Seen by the Military" in his *Discovering the Vernacular Landscape* (New Haven: Yale University Press, 1984), pages 133–137.

6. World War I had, perhaps, a similar effect, at least on Edith Wharton; see her *A Backward Glance* (New York: Appleton-Century, 1934), pages 362–363.

7. "Here is New York" [1949], *Perspectives USA* 4 (Summer 1953), page 44.

Bloch's film is seen through the prism of childhood, it may be simply because the landscape of childhood is the last safe place, the refuge to which adults can never return.

A landscape, therefore, can certainly be what geographers or landscape historians so frequently say it is—a discrete area. It may also be something else, something defying photography. It may be a prism, or a pipe dream.

*prism*

In autobiography lies the shadow of the prism, if not the prism itself. Often writers of autobiography stare backward at some well-remembered space, the details of which remain crisply clear. "In the foreground lay a marvelous confusion of steel rails, and in the midst of them, on a vast cinder-covered plain, the great brick roundhouse with its doors agape, revealing the snouts of locomotives undergoing surgery within," writes Russell Baker in *Growing Up*. "Between the mountains that cradled the yard there seemed to be thousands of freight cars stretching back so far toward Harpers Ferry that you could never see the end of them." Baker recalls the long approach up the Potomac River to Brunswick, "as distant and romantic a place as I ever expected to see," the toll bridge with its loose boards, the "incredible spectacle" of an express passenger train "highballing toward glory," a department store, movie house, and drugstore. For the boy from the farm, Brunswick is a "great smoking conurbation," a "metropolis."[8] But for the town-bred boy, the country is equally exciting.

"I realized at once that we had been transported into a different world, far from the dust and heat we had left behind," muses Gerald Warner Brace in *Days That Were*. "It is always in my memory a pure summer morning with white glinting across the eastward bay, the waters all calm except for the long heave of the ground swell that reared and creamed along the rocky shores of the islands on our port hand, and the air is faintly redolent with the fragrance of fir and spruce." For Brace, entering Rockland Harbor aboard the *Bangor* or another coastal steamer proves as memorable as arriving in Brunswick by flivver proves for Baker. Brace recalls every vacation as "rediscovering" the town's "perfect harmony of function, where everything seemed to fit into a natural design," but clearly Baker savors the memory of the industrial order of the railroad town so unlike his own.[9]

Memories of Brunswick and Rockland Harbor endure so strongly simply because they originate in what the novelist-philosopher Walker Percy calls a "rotation," a successful escape from daily routine, something different. For students and other observers of landscape, however, it is the concept of repetition,

8. (New York: Congdon & Weed, 1982), pages 50–53.

9. (New York: Norton, 1976), pages 66–67.

not rotation, that proves of more lasting value in defining one sort of landscape. "A repetition," argues Percy in *The Moviegoer,* "is the re-enactment of past experience toward the end of isolating the time segment which has lapsed in order that it, the lapsed time, can be savored of itself and without the usual adulteration of events that clog time like peanuts in brittle." The narrator of the novel provides an example: In glancing at a newspaper he sees an advertisement identical to one he saw twenty years ago in a magazine on his father's desk. For a moment, "the events of the intervening twenty years were neutralized," and "there remained only time itself, like a yard of smooth peanut brittle."[10] The concept of repetition explicates the prismatic function of a remembered childhood landscape.

Baker recalls his boyhood in the agricultural town of Morrisonville, "a poor place to prepare for a struggle with the twentieth century, but a delightful place to spend a childhood." He describes it almost in shorthand. "It was summer days drenched with sunlight, fields yellow with buttercups, and barn lofts sweet with hay. Clusters of purple grapes dangled from backyard arbors, lavender wisteria blossoms perfumed the air from the great vine enclosing the end of my grandmother's porch, and wild roses covered the fences."[11] Such memory remains strong because it is grounded in sensory experience, a range of sensory experience extending well beyond sight. Baker recalls sounds, smells, and textures, the heat of the sun on his skin. As Edith Cobb, in *The Ecology of Imagination in Childhood,* and other researchers have noted, children experience space through all senses, achieving, for a few years at least, a powerful intimacy.[12] Smell acquires an importance in childhood that it quickly loses, perhaps with the discovery of reading, and the consequent emphasis on vision. Just as Brace recalls the fragrance of Maine-coast conifers, Baker savors the lingering aroma of newly stacked hay and the perfume of wisteria. As sensitive adults know, smells trigger repetition more quickly, more directly than visual stimuli. The traveler alights from an airliner, smells the odor of the floor wax used in his kindergarten room, and is momentarily transported across time with awesome immediacy. Children—or some children, at least—know a landscape as they know the back of their hands, not only through sight, but through the other senses as well.

Certainly rural and small-town children have the "back-of-the-hand" knowledge; so much autobiography springs from such roots. About urban children, the young inhabitants of cityscape, not landscape, the evidence is much less clear. City life may be qualitatively different for children; researchers have only begun to examine it.[13] In deciphering the mysteries of landscape, how-

10. (1960; reprint New York: Avon, 1980), page 68.

11. Page 42.

12. *The Ecology of Imagination in Childhood* (New York: Columbia University Press, 1977).

13. See, for example, Kevin Lynch, *Growing Up in Cities* (Cambridge, MA: The MIT Press, 1977); Irwin Altman and Joachim F. Wohlwill, *Children and the Environment* (New York: Plenum, 1978); George Butterworth, *The Child's Representation of the World* (New York: Plenum, 1977); and Charles Zerner, "The Street Hearth of Play: Children in the City," *Landscape* 22 (Autumn 1977), pages 19–30.

ever, the role of childhood space in rural and small-town America may acquire importance in proportion to the degree of repetition it engenders. The landscape of childhood can function exactly as Tolkien suggests, by becoming a prism; it can also evoke repetition.

Many scholars—and artists—agree on the importance of memory in the intellectual life of creative adults. Indeed Cobb suggests that powerful memories of childhood may be the roots of genius. Powerful memories, vibrant enough to stimulate repetition frequently, often involve landscape or interior space. "Memories are motionless, and the more securely they are fixed in space, the sounder they are," muses Gaston Bachelard in *The Poetics of Space*. "Each one of us, then, should speak of his roads, his crossroads, his roadside benches," he continues after describing how powerfully his memories of a childhood attic inform his thinking, "each one of us should make a surveyor's map of his lost fields and meadows." Bachelard argues that such remembered space, whether attic or "familiar hill paths," is somehow "creative," that to visit it in dreams or daydreams is to partake again of its energy.[14]

Artists rarely deal explicitly with this issue. Even Wordsworth's "The Prelude; Or, Growth of a Poet's Mind" or Whitman's "There Was a Child Went Forth" are many-layered constructions, not simple autobiographical statements.[15] From time to time, of course, artists do write explicitly about the significance of memory of childhood landscape, however, and their work bears the scrutiny of landscape students and interpreters, for some artists understand the prism.

Eudora Welty perhaps understands the prism better than most writers of fiction. In *Place in Fiction*, Welty suggests that place can focus the eye of genius, and so concentrate its energy. "Place absorbs our earliest notice and attention, it bestows on us our original awareness; and our critical powers spring up from the study of it and the growth of experience inside it," she asserts after insisting that place is the fundamental component of successful fiction. "Imagine *Swann's Way* laid in London, or *The Magic Mountain* in Spain, or *Green Mansions* in the Black Forest."[16] Throughout this slim book, she insists on the absolute importance of place in ordering all else in fiction—character, plot, period.

In *One Writer's Beginnings*, published twenty-seven years after *Place in Fiction*, Welty sharpens her argument, focusing on her own childhood. The book's first sentence introduces the striking of clocks; the first paragraphs introduce the "elegant rush and click" of her brother's electric train, the rocking chair that "ticked

14. Translation by Maria Jolas (1958; reprint Boston: Beacon, 1962), pages 10–12.

15. *Complete Poetical Works* (Boston: Houghton Mifflin, 1904), pages 124–222; *Leaves of Grass* (New York: Random House, 1950), page 287. One critic has discerned the role of childhood space in the poetry of Hart Crane; see Sherman Paul, *Hart's Bridge* (Urbana: University of Illinois Press, 1972).

16. (New York: House of Books, 1957), unpaginated.

in rhythm" to the stories read aloud by her mother, the appearance of illustrations in her first storybooks. Early in *One Writer's Beginnings,* Welty suggests that "childhood's learning is made up of moments," and offers a catalogue of hers, beginning with sitting in a kindergarten circle of chairs and drawing three daffodils just picked in the schoolyard. The middle third of the book, "Learning to See," lovingly describes a series of discrete landscapes, the landscapes that eventually appear, sometimes in altered shape, in her fiction.

By "a landscape," therefore, the artist may designate a concatenation of images remembered in the creative moment, indeed somehow merging with the creative moment, perhaps in a near-magical repetition. "But it was not until I began to write, as I seriously did only when I reached my twenties, that I found the world out there revealing," writes Welty near the close of her book, because "*memory* had become attached to seeing, love had added itself to discovery."[17] Welty italicizes the word *memory* because memory sparks the creative process; love receives no such emphasis.

Baker and Brace, Cobb, Bachelard, and Welty assert or imply the importance of remembered childhood landscapes in the creative process. For them, landscape can be a prism through which they look at present experience and space. But landscape may also be a pipe dream, not a prism, and the distinction is subtle.

## pipe dream

Urbanization in the years following the Civil War prompted many Americans to savor the memory of rural childhood, of childhood in landscape abandoned for the city, or at least for the built environment of towns and villages. The last decades of the nineteenth century consequently witnessed the appearance—and acceptance—of nostalgic works concerning rural childhood. *Being a Boy,* an 1878 volume by Charles Dudley Warner, not only represents the *genre,* but hints at the *genre* that replaced it.

*Being a Boy* describes a farm boyhood to readers intimately familiar with such experience. Haying, weeding, woodchuck baiting, toting firewood, and all the experiences of farm boys Warner sites in an environment focused on house and barn, and encompassing fields, dirt roads, and woodlots. And Warner is aware of repetition, of the immediacy with which an urbanite may be momentarily transported to another time and place. "But that which lives most vividly in his memory and most strongly draws him back to the New England hills is the aromatic sweet-fern; he likes to eat its spicy seeds, and to crush in his hands its fragrant leaves;

17. (Cambridge, MA: Harvard University Press, 1984), pages 3–7, 10, 76, and passim.

their odor is the unique essence of New England."[18] No description of grown-over, half-wildered pasture or shaggy roadside prefaces the sweet-fern sentence; Warner assumed an audience familiar with the habitat of the shrub.

Twenty years later no writer could so easily assume a once-rural audience; indeed the turn-of-the-century era witnessed a new scorning of farmers, a scorning evident in words such as *hay-seed* or *clod-hopper*.[19] No longer did farm boys grow up to prosper in professions other than farming; the new generation of male urbanites recalled a boyhood spent on the fringes of farming, in villages or small towns. Between 1880 and 1930, American authors turned out a staggering literature focused on small-town life; for many writers, the small town represented the best of all possible worlds, a place free of the new evils of corporate industrialism and massive urbanization, but for others it exemplified a sterile, conformist, dull existence useful only as a starting point for urban splendor.[20] Social and literary historians continue to examine the wonderfully rich, markedly divided literature ordered about small-town life, and they reach only rare accords.[21]

One window on late nineteenth-century small-town life remains oddly unstudied. The small-town weekly newspaper, for all its biases and inaccuracies, endures as the voice of the moment. Consider, for example, the 8 May 1880 issue of the *Saturday Evening Journal* of Crawfordsville, Indiana. By 1880, the *Journal* had published for thirty-three years, apparently always weekly. The left-hand column of its front page consists entirely of advertisements for pianos, groceries (including nine varieties of coffee), ornamental poultry, and patent medicines. Five additional columns of fine type report stories involving the circus stranded by debt, changes of railroad schedules, the organizational meetings of an equal-suffrage society and a baseball club, the twenty-five-dollar fine levied on a man convicted of attempted murder, an Illinois rapist reported to have given Crawfordsville as his address, and a drunk rescued from a railroad track. Beyond the front page lies more news, similar in content and tone; only a few advertisements in the back pages for McCormick reapers and other field machinery aim at farmers. Clearly the *Saturday Evening Journal* is a town paper.

More than a century after its appearance, the 8 May issue fuels both interpretations of small-town life. On the one hand, it is evidence of a closely knit, friendly community; most articles emphasize names—everyone organizing the baseball club, for example—and demonstrate the essential quietude of Crawfordsville. Trouble comes from outside, and internal difficulty is immediately confronted, if not by bystanders, then by the town

18. (Boston: Osgood, 1878), page 177.

19. Eric F. Goldman, *Rendezvous with Destiny: A History of Modern American Reform* (New York: Vintage, 1956), pages 30–31; see also Warner Berthoff, *The Ferment of Realism: American Literature, 1884–1919* (New York: Free Press, 1965). The place of farm boyhood in the American spatial and cultural imagination deserves separate, detailed study.

20. For an introduction to the arguments still swirling about small-town life, see Carl Van Doren, *The American Novel* (New York: Macmillan, 1920), pages 294–302 and *Contemporary American Novelists, 1900–1920* (New York: Macmillan, 1922), pages 146–171; Richard Lingeman, *Small Town America: A Narrative History, 1620 to the Present* (Boston: Houghton Mifflin, 1980); Anthony Channell Hilfer, *The Revolt from the Village, 1915 to 1930* (Chapel Hill: University of North Carolina Press, 1969); and John R. Stilgoe, *Metropolitan Corridor: Railroads and the American Scene* (New Haven: Yale University Press, 1983), pages 191–220. One of the most thought-provoking studies is John A. Jakle, *The American Small Town: Twentieth-Century Place Images* (Hamden, CT: Shoe String, 1981).

21. Since very few farm children grew up to be writers, there is a consequent dearth of written evidence explicating the farm child's view of the town—something frequently overlooked by literary historians.

judge. On the other hand, the articles make easy the argument that the town is stuffy, nosy, and determined to maintain close scrutiny of all activity. For the landscape historian concerned with landscape perception and the role of childhood landscape perception in particular, however, the newspaper proves at first glance less than useful.

The *Saturday Evening Journal* reports almost nothing of landscape, indeed of space. To name a person or business is sufficient; scarcely one address intrudes in news stories or advertisements. Just as Warner assumes an audience familiar with the habitat of sweet-fern, so the newspaper editor assumes a readership familiar with the town's landscape. And with the exception of a brief story concerning school enrollment and another describing the abandonment of a baby by a city woman who arrived in Crawfordsville for that purpose, stories involving children are lacking, too. Landscape and children deserve no notice by the editor because they are simply part of the scene.

What the *Saturday Evening Journal* provides so exquisitely is the official, adult view of things in Crawfordsville on 8 May 1880. To discover the other view, one need only examine the memories recorded decades later by boys who recalled the landscape and the escapades it hosted.

More than many writers, the cartoonist Clare Briggs scrutinized the childhood small-town landscape left behind by city residents. Throughout the first decades of the twentieth century, Briggs's sketches delighted readers of the *New York Tribune;* after his death appeared a multivolume memorial edition of his drawings.[22] Briggs recalled all the spatial details so lacking in small-town newspapers, and he knew exactly the thousand and one familiar places so vitally important in the lives of children. His sketches depict boys playing on railroad tracks, playing follow-the-leader through an orchard, playing in lumber yards, old barns, half-finished houses, on rooftops, and in a hundred other places. Now and then the boys tolerate the company of girls, but in the many sketches focused on swimming holes, girls—and women—are conspicuously absent. Briggs's drawings of boys running past haunted houses, dreaming of hopping freight trains, and taking a thousand shortcuts now and then include urban backdrops, but chiefly they memorialize the small-town landscape out of which so many New York City men had come, a landscape of boyhood, a landscape of innocence. In actuality they memorialize the landscape of Reedsburg, Wisconsin, the late nineteenth-century boyhood home of Briggs himself.[23]

Autobiography savors the landscape of small-town boyhood; the most cursory survey of American autobiographical

22. *When a Feller Needs a Friend* (New York: Wise, 1930); *That Guiltiest Feeling* (New York: Wise, 1930); *The Days of Real Sport* (New York: Wise, 1930); et alia.

23. *National Encyclopedia of American Biography,* XXIII, page 317.

"Fun on the Railroad Track" (1925) and "Down in the Lumber Yard" (1923), from *That Guiltiest Feeling* (Wise, 1930). Cartoons by Clare Briggs. © New York Tribune, Inc.

"The Barn" (1921) and "The Haunted House" (1924), from *The Days of Real Sport* (Wise, 1930). Cartoons by Clare Briggs. © New York Tribune, Inc.

writing uncovers hundreds of twentieth-century books extolling the intricate world unreported by the *Saturday Evening Journal*. Now and then, as in Edmund G. Love's *The Situation in Flushing* and Loren Reid's *Hurry Home Wednesday: Growing Up in a Small Missouri Town, 1905 to 1921,* most or all of the book focuses on the boyhood environment, but more often, only the first chapter records the timeless details of intimately known small-town space.[24]

"The golden age of childhood can be quite accurately fixed in time and place," begins a typical autobiography, Dean Acheson's 1965 *Morning and Noon*. "It reached its apex in the last decade of the nineteenth century and the first few years of the twentieth, before the plunge into a motor age and city life swept away the freedom of children and dogs, put them both on leashes and made them the organized prisoners of an adult world." Morning for Acheson is life in Middletown, Connecticut, in the 1890s, a place where "nothing presented a visible hazard to children," where "no one was run over," where only his mother fleetingly worried when she saw him hooking a ride on the ice wagon. As do so many other male authors, Acheson catalogues structures and spaces, some certainly noticed by local newspaper reporters, but many a part of the invisible landscape of boys: "an open field of perhaps three acres" where the boys refought the Boer and Spanish-American wars, the dentist's "large, round bed of luxuriant canna plants" in which baseballs vanished, "the maze of backyards and alleys." Acheson recalls the importance of naming spots like the pond "too muddy and choked for bathing and appropriately called by 'Polliwog Pool'" and shaping and reshaping places like the three-acre field and the caves in the wooded hills just west of town. Acheson concludes that "life in the golden age was the very distillation of that place and time," a distillation whose essence, at least, lingered with him through the decades.[25] Safety, spatial freedom, the power of naming, the power of shaping and reshaping space, such are the attributes so frequently catalogued in male autobiography of the mid-twentieth century.

Only rarely does an intrepid observer long departed from his boyhood small-town landscape return and scrutinize contemporary space. Eric Sevareid's long, incredibly detailed 1956 *Collier's* account of his own return to a small, North Dakota town illustrates so forcibly the shock of confrontation and the meaning of memories strong enough to provoke repetition.

Sevareid catalogues smells, sounds, and a wealth of boyhood spaces remembered clearly enough, and describes the strain of finding some smells and sounds absent, and many once-familiar, once-cherished spaces changed beyond recognition by the building of a small office building or the demolition of the

24. (New York: Harper, 1965); (Columbia: University of Missouri Press, 1978). Also, to the best of my knowledge, there is no parallel development of autobiographies by women who grew up in small towns. Women's autobiographies stress interior places, such as kitchens. And, in preparing this essay, the women of my home town recall not the semi-wild places my male friends recall with ease, but interior places, backyards, and stores.

25. (Boston: Houghton Mifflin, 1965), pages 1–24.

town's water tank. At first profoundly disappointed—*disenchanted* perhaps designates better his melancholy shock—he gradually discovers some boyhood elements still unchanged—a faded lumberyard fence, for example—and recognizes in the movements of boys the existence of an equally rich space. Eventually, Sevareid uses a photographic metaphor to explain his new perception. "I could run through the film exposed this day of 1955 and see it all, the hills, the rapids, the bridge and the house and the streets, all of it as it *is,* in black and white, exact, life-size, no more, no less," he muses. "Then I could run off the old, eternal negative, larger than life, in its full color and glory—the same scenes and trees and faces—and there was no fading or blur of double exposure." He emphasizes the photographic nature of memory. "I had both reels now, sealed in separate cans, and I knew I could keep both, as long as I lived."

What then of Marc Bloch's notion of the historian unwinding the film backward in order to study the rural landscape of time past? Sevareid answers the question, albeit obliquely: "In stark clarity I remember running away from home at the age of four, crossing the Soo Line tracks, trudging up South Hill and then, suddenly confronting the sky and the plains: I was lost, alone, in the eternity of nothingness."

In the era of his boyhood, towns had definite edges, edges of genuine significance to the people who lived "in town" and to those farmers or ranchers who lived "outside." In walking back from "outside," the adult Sevareid recalls the one terrifying incident of brutality of his childhood, the senseless, deliberate shooting by a farmhand of his friend's dog. As he remembers burying the dog in a weed patch, "across from our island," Sevareid enters the town, and his essay immediately changes subject and tone. With the prairie at his back, the adult Sevareid "felt for a moment, faintly, the joy this passage had brought me at each re-entry into the oasis with its familiar shapes and smells and sounds, its thousand secret delights, cool water and shade, and home and safety." And suddenly, he pierces the veil of mystery that shrouds so many first chapters of autobiography: "I understood then why I had loved it so and loved its memory always; it was, simply, *home—* and *all* of it home, not just the house, but all the town. That is why childhood in the small towns is different from childhood in the city. Everything is home." Walking the old path across the edge of town, turning his back on the place where he had witnessed evil, he perceives the childhood reality of town as oasis, as refuge, as home.

"We are all alike, we graying American men who were boys in the small towns of our country," he muses. "We have a kind of inverted snobbery or recollection and we are sometimes bores about it, but that's the way it is."[26] Of course, for Sevareid, for Acheson, for Baker, the way was not permanent residence—the way led to the corners of the earth, to success not only in great cities, but also in national and international arenas. For such men, the landscape of small-town boyhood is, in Robert Frost's "Take Something Like A Star," a fixing point, a place in which later life is moored, however long the mooring line.[27]

For others, for many according to the most recent United States census, the landscape of small-town boyhood is a contemporary, accessible place. In *Return to Main Street: A Journey to Another America,* Nancy Eberle chronicles and analyzes her family's move from a Chicago suburb to a rural small town. Before its appearance in 1982, portions of the text appeared as a long article in *McCall's Magazine* in which Eberle argues that small-town life redirected her two sons toward richer, simpler living. *McCall's,* and many so-called women's magazines focused on middle-class audiences, have lately emphasized child-rearing issues. Eberle, in her article and subsequent book, argues explicitly that small-town physical and social environments strengthen both individual and family character. "It's never wondering if storekeepers think you're a shoplifter and never being asked to produce your driver's license," she asserts in her final chapter. "It's a swimming hole, a haunted house, a Halloween Parade, and a nickname."[28] *Return to Main Street* emphasizes not only the physical and social setting so casually presented in the 8 May 1880 *Saturday Evening Journal,* but also that of the cartoons of Clare Briggs. Eberle delicately balances the adult view of small-town life—and space—with that of her sons, the stewards of shortcuts and swimming holes.

In her first chapter, entitled "Main Street," Eberle begins her balancing with a command: "Picture a primitive." She then describes the buildings and spaces along Main Street, the residential streets adjacent to them, the farms at the edge of town. For Eberle, it *is* primitive, and as her argument evolves, one learns it is Edenic. Galena, Illinois, in 1982 is pre-lapsarian America, the Republic before the fall, the U.S.A. before urbanization, industrialization, Viet Nam, drug abuse, divorce, even before the nuclear bomb. In her last chapter, the balance kept poised, Eberle asserts that "quality of life" is increasingly important to thoughtful men and women, often more important than social status, salary, professional advancement. And Eberle grounds her argument, her balancing of adult and child views, in space, in the landscape of small-town America.

Eberle is no lonesome soothsayer. As she correctly points out, periodicals such as *Mother Earth News* now boast circulations

26. 137 (11 May 1956), pages 38–68.

27. "Take Something Like a Star," *Poetry* (New York: Holt, Rinehart, and Winston, 1969), page 403.

28. (New York: Norton, 1982), pages 214–224, 19–23, and passim; portions of the book appeared as "A Good Place to Live," *McCall's* 109 (October 1981), pages 127–131. When Eberle finished the book, her daughter was only three years old, and not roaming the small-town landscape, pages 206–207.

over one million, suggesting that even many urban and suburban families feel a tug toward rural living and small-town residence. The tug is more than emotional. Harley E. Johansen and Glenn V. Fuguitt demonstrate in their 1984 study, *The Changing Rural Village in America: Demographic and Economic Trends Since 1950,* that the growth rate of the small town in the countryside has surpassed that of suburbs and metropolitan regions.[29] As the 1960 census hinted, as the 1980 census proved, and as the 1990 census reconfirms, something important, something massive now looms in the American psychological horizon. A geographic shift of staggering implications is underway. As Sevareid suggested in the middle 1950s, the small town remains the American home, the cultural cradle. And if the statistics indicate anything, they indicate many Americans are going *home.*

## bog

Perhaps people seek a home landscape for the reasons Eberle, Johansen, and Fuguitt catalogue—fear of urban crime, distrust of new forms of community, and disgust with unhealthful air, water, and food. Perhaps they go for such reasons, and for many more. Perhaps they also go for a more elemental reason. Perhaps they search for the landscape of childhood.

If they go to rediscover the full-color photograph Sevareid describes, to experience not only fleeting repetition, but also permanent repetition, to restore themselves with the energy of place about which Welty orders her fiction and autobiography, to experience a place known in the years before they recognized that the atomic bomb destroys all, then indeed they are in search of the landscape described not in the *Saturday Evening Journal,* but in the nostalgias of the heart. One popular prime-time television series, *The Waltons,* drew energy from this concatenation of thought and feeling, each show concluding with an epigraph extolling not only childhood security, but also the importance of childhood space enduring into adulthood: "Forty years have passed, but that house still stands, and the solace and love that we knew there as children still sustain us." Solace and love, important as they are, gather strength from the *still-existing house,* the physical manifestation of family life.

What underlies the power of boyhood landscape, what attracts so many men—and women—to the small town today, is not only the memory so strong it engenders repetition. It is also the recapturing of the right, the freedom to shape space. The small-town childhood landscape is not simply enjoyed by boys. It is maintained and changed by boys. As Clare Briggs depicted in so many of his sketches, as so many graying men remember in

29. (Cambridge, MA: Ballinger, 1984).

their autobiographies, the small-town landscape permitted and re-warded shaping. Boys felled trees to make rafts, cut saplings to lace together as huts or duck-blinds, begged slabs from the saw-mill to make tree houses so high in the white pines that even the lighthouse could be seen through field glasses borrowed from father's dresser drawer. No one, not even the highway surveyor, considered the fieldstones rolled into the bog dam spillway an act of vandalism; no one, not even the Coast Guard crew chugging seaward, looked askance at the boys laboriously pounding a newly cut cedar tree into the salt marsh to make a mooring bollard at The Landing. Men who had long ago shaped the boyhood places expected new generations of boys to shape them, and so long as real estate developers stayed clear of the abandoned, half-forgotten acreage, the boys did shape space, and do so still.

And as long as bits and pieces of the boyhood landscape endure, grown men can visit them, sometimes in the panting rush of the volunteer fire department, grunting under the weight of hoses—"Used to come here when I was a kid, huge tangle of barbed wire under those wild grapevines, stay left"—sometimes alone, seeking the solace of innocence. For that landscape is, as Sevareid so accurately saw, *home*, all of it is home, for it flows into backyards and barnyards, to backsteps and screen doors. And home, as Frost discerned in 1914 in a poem entitled "The Death of the Hired Man," is indeed special. As one of the poem's narrators says:

> *Home is the place where, when you have to go there,*
> *They have to take you in.*[30]

The landscape of childhood, if it endures in an age of sub-urbanization, exurbanization, condominium development, and shopping malls, is perceived by many grown men as Sevareid perceived it, as being somehow obligated to give solace, rest, and repetition. And even when modernization has obliterated it, it can survive as a prism, or even as a pipe dream, changing the perceptions of grown men or luring others, with their families, back to small towns.

Understanding landscape must, I think, involve coming to terms with the power of boyhood landscape. Tolkien is correct. Words like *river, hill, wooded valley,* and *salt marsh* mean in part the visual images adults first associated with them. Consider the word *steam shovel*. Now used by nearly everyone to designate diesel-powered equipment, it carries special meaning in my little coastal town. For decades, boys old enough to explore the abandoned sand pits bordering the cranberry bogs—not The Bog—

30. *Poetry,* page 38.

have found The Steamshovel, a derelict diesel-engined vestige of
long-vanished activity, a derelict still standing watch over sand
pits growing up in chokecherry and now green with sweet-fern.
For many Norwell men in their early forties, now graying and
wondering about their own children, *steam shovel* evokes memories of The Steamshovel—of races ending at it, of precarious balancing on its outstretched boom, of shaping the abandoned sand
pits and bogs around it—and of living in an innocent summer
afternoon free of The Bomb, of living at *home*.

Season after season, the aging *Steamshovel* keeps watch over sand pits and
cranberry bogs in Norwell, Massachusetts. Photograph by John R. Stilgoe, 1984.

# PART IV

# Landscape as Art

*In descriptive language, the detail
becomes wearisome long before its
quantity is sufficient, but as it
appears in pictures, the detail is
less an inventory that needs translation
and more directly the idiom of experience.*

—PAUL VANDERBILT

# Second Growth: Changing Views in New England

Janet Hulings Bleicken

JANET HULINGS BLEICKEN was born in
Erie, Pennsylvania, in 1943 and was
raised in Harborcreek, Pennsylvania. She
studied at the Rhode Island School of
Design, and received a B.A. in fine arts
(printmaking) from The Pennsylvania
State University. She is an exceptionally
fine painter who has been working on
the subject of human relationships to
nature for many years. Reproductions
of her work have appeared in *The New
England Naturalist's Journal, Bostonia
Magazine*, and *Landscape Architecture*,
and she has had numerous one-person
and group exhibitions throughout New
England. Of her major retrospective in
1988 at the Currier Gallery of Art in
Manchester, New Hampshire, Marilyn
Myers Slade of the *Boston Globe* wrote:
"A haunting rhythm pervades Bleicken's
painting, a marking of time past and
time now. Through this historical assem-
bly of myth and reality the artist raises
the question, 'Will modern man live in
harmony with nature or will he once
more destroy the mountain?' . . . Bleick-
en's series presents a compelling and
dramatic story that draws viewers directly into nature's beauty . . ." Ms.
Bleicken, once a resident of Hancock,
New Hampshire, now lives in the sea-
coast region of the Granite State.

A FRIEND of ours, who is a storyteller and a sophisticated observer of rural life in New Hampshire, once told my husband and
me that, when he was a young man, "You could see Harrisville
from the top of City Hill. Matter of fact, I have a photograph,"
and he hurried off to the other end of the room to search for it
among the piles of paper on his desk.

We stayed at our end of the large living room, held there by
Newt's view. The Tolmans' house sits near the top of a steep slope
that has been carefully cleared over the years to perfect the view.
From where we stood we could see Spoonwood Pond, a quarter
of a mile below and to the east, and Beaver Briggs's Island, which
now belongs to Keene State College. Beyond that uninhabited
island we could see another pond called Nubanusit and the green,
wooded hills that roll up to and beyond our region's only real
mountain: Monadnock, elevation three thousand one hundred
sixty-five feet.

"Here," he said, as he returned to our end of the room and
handed us a snapshot. It showed the young Tolman brothers,
Newt and Fran, on skis next to a couple dressed in alpine cos-
tumes. They stood on a snow-covered knoll with a grainy landscape of snow-covered hills spreading out behind them. "It could
be Vermont" or "a hilly spot in upper New York State," I thought,
but, according to Newt, the photograph was taken "right here on
City Hill" looking south toward Harrisville.

We were amazed. We didn't doubt him, but it was beyond
our imagination to "see" it. "Seeing it" requires time, the time to
let the changes that had taken fifty years to occur to appear again
in our mind's eye. Over those fifty years, millions of trees had
grown up through those snow-covered hills. Trees that were noticed first as whipits, with a couple of comically large leaves, had
spread out over those slopes in the first year to become a crop the
height of tall grass. A season later they were saplings whose root
systems were so strong they could no longer be pulled out like
weeds. The farmers, who had worked so hard to keep those fields

open, were gone. They had moved on to the valleys of Ohio for reasons of their own, and left behind a legacy for the trees.

Their fathers and older brothers had returned from the Civil War restless and anxious to forget. Some went to the mills in Manchester and Leominster to try a different kind of work. Others, needing to put even more space between their past and their future, moved out west. Over the next forty years the population statistics for the town of Nelson, New Hampshire, plummeted just as they did over all of rural New England. The war and the hard pan and the economy defeated the farmers who had settled those hills. The trees that had covered them before the settlers arrived were standing by and were anxious to return. The landscape created by these settlers, the one that allowed a man and his wife to stand in their field with their feet on solid earth, their heads tilted to the sky, seeing Harrisville, was lost. Two years after human abandonment, this changing landscape had trees taller than you and me. In another fifty years, the trees were seventy feet tall. Today we stand seventy feet *below* the "surface" (the treetops, the canopy) of those green-flocked hills, and we no longer "see" anything. Reality has changed. There is no view. Though most of what the settlers called Harrisville remains—the red brick buildings of the Colony's mill and the doll-like houses that line the edges of the two ponds—one has to go there if one wants to "see" Harrisville.

The landscape of Nelson has been redesigned and completely redefined by nature's reclaiming the abandoned landscape. The City Hill that had earned its curious name before our American Revolution (the hill which at two thousand two hundred thirty-three feet was the third highest elevation in southern New Hampshire; the hill whose prospect offered a view not only of nearby Harrisville, but also south into Massachusetts, west into the Green Hills of Vermont, and north to the White Mountains of northern New Hampshire; the hill that had been a major focal point in the landscape of southern New Hampshire) had disappeared. It can no longer be seen. It remains the third-highest elevation in southern New Hampshire, but it plays no role in the minds of women and men. It no longer can be seen. Subsequently it was removed from the maps of Nelson.

In 1768 Breed Batchelder and his committee of settlers surveyed the eastern slope of the hill that would soon be called City Hill. "They were in the east part of the town, on or near the 'Island' one Saturday afternoon, and being about to quit . . ." Samuel Maguire had taken his gun down to the shore of Spoonwood Pond to see if he could get a duck for supper. After a short time, the surveyors heard his shot. When some time later he did not return they began to search for him. "The next day they raised a large party in Keene. Fires were built on the hills, horns sounded, guns fired and everything done that could rescue him, but he was never heard of afterwords." [1]

It is possible, of course, that Mr. Maguire accidentally shot himself, but repeated searches of the vicinity of the shot did not turn up a body. The area wasn't particularly dangerous. The Indians had been "drawn off" during the French and Indian War. Wild animals were numerous, but threatened the livestock more than the farmers. During that time, when there were no local grain mills to supply flour for bread and no well-established gardens, the animals were viewed more as a resource than as a threat. The exception was the wolf, who wore heavily on the minds of the settlers: "wolves often kept up such a howling as to make a night hideous." So during the next fifty years, those settlers built two enormous fires and burned thousands of acres of southern New Hampshire for the express purpose of driving off the wolves. But the conventional wisdom of today—that there is no recorded incident of a wolf attacking a person during that period of American history—allows us to dismiss that as the fate of Samuel Maguire.

I think the clue to his mysterious disappearance lies in a description of the day Mr. Maguire vanished: "The whole country was covered with a dense forest, there were no roads or paths through the wilderness except to go by marked trees, and in some cases the nearest neighbor was miles away." And although "the pioneers in these settlements were of powerful frames, strong constitutions and wonderful endurance," and "many a one of them would chop down his acre of heavy timber in a day, and drink a quart of rum," it is my considered opinion that Samuel Maguire became lost and stayed that way.

Another surveying committee at that time submitted a written layout for a road that proposed to connect the town of Nelson with the town of Keene, fifteen miles to the southwest. It reads: "Bounded as follows, begins at a small Beach and stones, East of the Meeting House at the east line of the public land and runs south easterly to a Hemlock (tree marked), then to a spruce, then to a Beach, to a Birch, then to a Beach—then Birch, then to a Beach . . . then to a Large Red Oak . . ."

Most of us would base our image of that "virgin" forest on experiences we have had in state or national parks. We see large and nicely spaced trees fanning out in all directions with a smooth and spongy layer of pine needles underfoot, a condition that is

1. All of the historical quotes are taken from Nelson's town history, *Nelson and the Flag,* published in 1917 by the Nelson Picnic Association.

maintainable if the predominant tree is pine, and if an army of forestry workers picks up the deadfall and trims the eye-poking lower limbs from the trees.

The forest encountered by the pioneers contained few pine trees, to the dismay of the king's ship-builders. The predominant trees on these slopes were hardwoods. The boggy places were hopelessly constricted by hemlock and hornbeam. Walking through these woods was often very hard work. Saplings grew up through a tangle of deadfall, and hobblebush filled in the scattered sunny places. A walker did not often look to the sky for direction because of the canopy of leaves. A walker could not see into the woods for more than a few feet in any direction because of the leafed-out, young trees, and could not on many occasions see her or his feet for the ferns and fallen tree branches. Rocks, holes, and the mistaken belief that the common snakes were poisonous made progress through these woods slow indeed.

The "idea" of escaping into this eighteenth-century New Hampshire frontier must have seemed a blessed opportunity to those expatriated from overcrowded Europe. Their first view of the landscape that actually awaited them must have been daunting. They set about to shape it to their own vision of Eden and were highly successful. It was a noble effort that was quickly abandoned, however, when word reached them of the fertile grasslands discovered in the West.

The landscape awaiting us today on City Hill, now returned to the maps of southern New Hampshire as Osgood Hill, is in some ways much like the landscape that awaited the settlers. The trees that capture the high ground are today most likely the pines. The hemlocks maintain their control of the boggy soils, and the mixed hardwoods have reclaimed the slopes. But there are new hazards for the walker in the form of low-bush and high-bush blueberries and thorny, berry vines to tear clothes and flesh. There are a dozen or more abandoned cellar holes and an equal number of wells to discover as one falls into them. There are a couple of deeply rutted logging roads that start up the hill and vanish.

In another way there are fewer hazards for the walker today because the pioneers and their children managed to eradicate the wolves, the mountain lions, and most of the bears. There is, however, little reward for hikers who climb City Hill today. Oh, if one goes quietly and doesn't bring along a dog, then one is likely to get a good, long look at a red fox on top of a stone wall or hear a deer or two crash through the undergrowth. If one goes in autumn, one can fill a backpack with mysterious apples that look like Macs and taste like Delicious. But that is little return for all the work of getting up there.

Fran Tolman's wife, Florence, once rescued me by driving me around the base of that hill back to where my car was parked. She said, "Everyone of any substance has been lost on City Hill at least once." There are no trails worth a damn, and, worse, there are no good views. There is no place in the region now where one looks out through the trees and says, "What's that hill over there called? Is that City Hill?" The reason is simple: we cannot place it in our world visually because there is no place that affords us a view of anything significant to our lives. City Hill is not part of the landscape of southern New Hampshire.

Our perception of a landscape is filtered too often through an unfocused screen called "usefulness to me." Our concept of the New England landscape is frozen by human experience, proving that nature is far more flexible than the minds of women and men. It is easier to rely on a cultural memory and an old definition of how the world works than to keep our definition of landscape current with the actual events occurring on the land. And when our observations disagree with our definitions, we can always remove a landscape from a map. After all, the map is the only accepted tool with which we record what we already know about a landscape, and the landscape can never be more than what one can "see." Right?

I return to City Hill as often as I can these days. I almost always get lost. I invariably end up miles from my car when I think I know exactly where I am. I almost always get chased by deer flies, and my dog usually leaves the woods in a flat run. One time I saw a rockfall (as in "waterfall") that was home to many porcupines and possibly a bobcat. I've tried to find it since and failed. One time I saw a lot of bear scat. (The bear had been eating fruit.) I've seen foxes and grouse and Carolina hornbeam and a bathtub that had been chipped out of the rock next to a waterfall. I'm told there is a lead mine up there, but I've never seen it, only another lead mine on the other side of town and it's truly beautiful. The old mine has filled with water and the pool's color is a most amazing emerald green.

I climb City Hill to see the cellar holes. One or two apple trees mark the location of every hole. The apple trees are easy to spot, if one stays near the old roads, which are sort-of-easy to stay on, as long as one walks between two stone walls. It is rare to find a cellar hole with straight sides. Most of them have caved-in walls and appear as grass-lined depressions. Some, however, were obviously built to last. There is one I look forward to seeing that is in very good shape. It's been suggested that the owners were the last to leave, but the ash tree growing up through it is quite old. It has wonderfully straight sides and the front door's stepping stone is in place. There are a few tiny bricks scattered around that seem crude by today's standards. There is lady's-bed-straw and tansy growing along the south-facing wall. I imagine what life was like for the people who lived in that house in 1790, or in 1890, knowing all along it was either heaven or hell to live there, depending on the attitudes behind the eyes of the beholder. There were the wars and countless fluctuations in the weather and one family's luck; but if one were an optimist, then it was probably a pretty wonderful place to call "home."

Ten years have passed since I made my last visit to Newt Tolman's house on City Hill, when I had stopped by to hear how he was doing and to get a good look at his new Rolls Royce. We sat on the porch for a while, and I couldn't help but notice: Newt's view was growing in.

Newt and his wife, Janet, led long, prolific, and very colorful lives. Janet was an artist, hunting guide, and state legislator, a job she shared with brother-in-law Fran by taking turns running for the office. And everyone in the Tolman family wrote books, it seems. Fran wrote and illustrated one called *Mosquitobush.* His wife, Floppy Blackwell Tolman, recounted her early years with her mother-in-law in *More Spit than Polish,* and she is still writing "just for her grandchildren." But Newt—the fisherman, musician, and world traveler—was *the* writer in the family. Every morning he sat at his desk at the end of that big room and wrote.

The house was a saltbox-shaped affair with an unfinished interior I think of as the Adirondack style. Most of the surfaces were made of wood, and there was a big stone fireplace and hearth which served as the stage and backdrop for every variety of theory, argument, theology, and philosophy that the family and their many friends wanted to share. (Perhaps "share" is too mild a word.) From this place came Newt's *North of Monadnock, Our Loons Are Always Laughing,* and a musical collection called *Quick Tunes and Good Times.* Newt was fun, often outrageous, and a heavy drinker. I adored him and was thrilled when he asked me to make a drawing for the cover of his book, *The Blue-Tailed Skink.*

A few days after my last visit with Newt, his nephew Barry cajoled him into getting into the Rolls and drove him to the nursing home in Peterborough. He stayed there a short time making "masterpieces" by cutting paper with round-tipped scissors, and then he died. But, happily for Newt, he had the entire region in a complete uproar at the time when Gabriel blew his horn. His Rolls Royce, you see, had been a gift—or, should I say, a "Faustian bargain"—for City Hill.

Janet had died a few months earlier and, without her pragmatic hand, he had decided to sell his land to a logger—a logger-developer of the worst sort who had driven up the hill and found Newt alone. Understand that Newt "alone" was like a vortex without a context, so the deal was struck: City Hill and all its trees in exchange for a gold-colored Rolls Royce.

But relax, dear reader. (I've always wanted to say that.) Shortly after Newt's death, his family went to court and had the transaction overturned. The judge realized that Newt had suffered from dementia and, as we knew at the time, had "lost it." The judge also knew that the trees on City Hill were worth more than forty Rolls Royces!

Today, the car is gone and the developer is gone. The land was purchased by the Harris Center for Conservation Education. Newt's glorious Spoonwood Pond is preserved, forever accessible only by portage from Nubanusit Lake. Nelson, New Hampshire, is quiet once more. No one cuts trees on City Hill except, perhaps, for Barry and Tom getting in some firewood.

But this story won't die. All over the state today loggers are whining up their chainsaws because the Far East is buying logs from New Hampshire and has run the price way up. Everyone, including yours truly, has had a price estimate done on stumpage.

When I drive into Portsmouth each day along the Piscataqua River, I see logs pile up and get hosed down waiting for the next boat to the Orient. Around and around we dance with the land. We use it, abuse it, and then abandon it. Fortunately for the New Hampshire landscape, our economy is too thin, our population too small, and our effort too weak to leave more than isolated examples of permanent damage.

All of my "walking in the wilderness" that I describe in this essay was, in the end, a search for the paintings that follow. I was, at the time, reading everything I could find that described settlement, occupation, and eventual abandonment of the first farms in our region. I spent hours pawing through old photographs and, over the span of a few years, I wrung the local storytellers dry.

Then a friend at Harvard suggested that I should try to find the *memory* of the place. Much to my amazement, it was everywhere—not just the things that the settlers had left behind, such as the bathtub cut in the rock, but also the actual *emotion* of the time and the *memory* of the events.

By this time, you may think that I have "lost it." But, please, take a look at the art that came out of my experience with that New Hampshire landscape, and out of my look at second growth and the changing views in New England.

# MONADNOCK BURNING

EDITOR'S NOTE: The following text is from Robert M. Doty's introduction to a catalog, *Monadnock Burning*, published by the Currier Gallery of Art in Manchester, New Hampshire, which sponsored a major retrospective of Ms. Bleicken's work in 1988. Courtesy of the Currier Gallery of Art.

The mountain known as "Grand Monadnock" is an obsession for Janet Hulings Bleicken, but it seldom appears in her drawings. Instead, her images document the life that has come and gone on the slopes of the peak in southwestern New Hampshire. She is recorder and narrator. Together, her pictures become a panorama of local history. Individually, they are visual evidence of perceptions and impressions gleaned from years of personal experience.

Mount Monadnock is the most prominent geological feature in southern New Hampshire and central New England. It is the most visible landmark in the area and the name has been adopted by geologists to describe "an isolated hill." The first surveys of the mountain were done in the late nineteenth century, but it attracted attention long before that time. Several writers, including Ralph Waldo Emerson, John Greenleaf Whittier, and Edwin Arlington Robinson saw the mountain as a manifestation of strength and solidity, rising, as should the best of people, above the forest and lesser hills. Henry David Thoreau made several trips to the summit between 1844 and 1860, and his experience fills many pages of his *Journal*. In 1857 he wrote to his friend Harrison Blake, "You must ascend a mountain to learn your relation to matter. . . ." Janet Bleicken has done this in an attempt to learn something of a person's relationship with nature. Because this mountain has been the subject for so many writers and philosophers, and is now the focus of so many picture-windows, Bleicken has chosen it as a symbol of the wilderness. She has gone wandering through history to see how people have treated this mountain.

Though most nineteenth-century painters passed Monadnock by on their way to higher elevations in Vermont's White Mountains, a few artists at the turn of the century were attracted to so "important" a mountain close to Boston and New York City. To them, the mountain was truly an inspiration. Painters such as William Preston Phelps, Abbott Handerson Thayer, and John White Allen Scott have rendered its image so often and have inspired so many more painters that it is sometimes said that Monadnock rivals Fujiyama for the most often painted mountain.

In 1922 Abbott Thayer led the campaign to protect Monadnock from the growing onslaught of tourists, much as Thomas Cole had spoken out seventy-five years earlier to defend the wilderness along the Hudson River. If Thayer, like the Transcendentalists, could look on the mountain with an awe bordering on reverence, farmers showed none when they set the mountain on fire, twice, to eradicate the wolves.

Thayer sought to render the physical quality of light and the land. Bleicken searches for memories of prior inhabitants which become the basis for images evoking the conflict between the actions of people and the forces of nature. Her goal is to show the passage of an idea through time, particularly a person's changing attitude toward nature. Her benchmarks in history are the painters John James Audubon and Thomas Cole. Their works define their time by telling us what they valued, where their curiosity sent them, and where their prejudices left them. The subjects of her drawings comprise a wide range and combination of myth and history. Images within an image are used often and interchangeably, effecting new connotations and associations. There is a tragic sense in her pictures, a plea for compassion with the promise that, by understanding the discord between people and nature, there is a way to make a better future.

Bleicken's way is to move through the wilderness and to take away only the memories and impressions that constitute the spirit of the place. And her art suggests that we shall learn from the past or we will live to repeat the same mistakes. Between desecration and preservation there is a middle ground, and the potential for a successful choice is available to all who carefully consider a landscape such as Monadnock and its past.

On my walks in the mountains near my previous home in Hancock, New Hampshire, I look for cellar holes abandoned by settlers over a century ago. In one cellar hole in Alstead Center near the Vermont border, Dr. Benjamin Allison started a fern garden more than forty years ago. He collected rare ferns and ferns common to southern New England. Today fifty-four varieties thrive and winter in this protected environment. "The Fern Garden," by Janet Hulings Bleicken, 1982. Fresco secco on a four-panel folding screen, 6.5 feet by 8 feet. Collection of the artist.

The return to wilderness on the New Hampshire landscape is a gentle play filled with good and bad memories for both people and nature. Artists have always reflected the attitudes of their time, place, and culture. While the nineteenth-century European painters idealized pastoral life, Bierstadt was putting the Grand Canyon, the Rocky Mountains, and Yosemite on the map. The reflections in this painting are by Monet, Kensett, and O'Keeffe. "Art and Nature," by Janet Hulings Bleicken, 1980. Fresco secco on three wooden panels, 6 feet by 6 feet. Collection of Rick and Duffy Monahon, Harrisville, New Hampshire.

The woods at night can be a malevolent place for the unknowing. The
wind forces the leaves to rustle. Something weightier causes twigs to snap.
The pioneers who settled this region in New England managed to eradicate most of the devils supplied by nature, but made little headway against
the devils supplied by their uncertain minds. "The Green Man," by Janet
Hulings Bleicken, 1981. Fresco secco on three wooden panels, 6 feet by
6 feet. Collection of the Chubb Life Insurance Company, Concord, New
Hampshire.

In this painting a pink ribbon is tied to a white birch and demarcates the division between wild nature and private ownership. Too often the symbols of our order seem ludicrous in landscapes we know to be wilderness. "The Corner of the Land," by Janet Hulings Bleicken, 1985. Acrylic on canvas, 6 feet by 6 feet. Collection of the artist.

The battles between our blind conceits and good intentions will continue to shape the landscape. Memories of times past can also collect in hollow places. "Little Birches with Audubon," by Janet Hulings Bleicken, 1985. Acrylic on canvas, 6 feet by 6 feet. Collection of the Currier Gallery of Art, Manchester, New Hampshire.

During the eighteenth century on New England's frontier, animals were viewed as resources, not threats, except for the wolf, who wore heavily on the minds of the settlers. "Wildman and the Wolf," by Janet Hulings Bleicken, 1987. Acrylic on canvas, 8 feet by 8 feet. Collection of the artist.

A mountain that was once humble in a shroud of trees is now majestic and snow-covered because farmers in New Hampshire burned it over to wipe out the wolves, twice. "Monadnock Burning," by Janet Hulings Bleicken, 1986. Acrylic on canvas, 10.5 feet by 8 feet. Collection of the Thorne Art Gallery, Keene State College, Keene, New Hampshire.

At times the relationships between wild and domestic animals and
frightened and restless people on small farms are too entangled for easy
understanding. "Chickens with Audubon," by Janet Hulings Bleicken, 1984.
Fresco secco on three aluminum panels, 4 feet by 7 feet. Collection of Ann
Roe-Hafer, Washington, D.C.

**Alan Gussow**

# Beauty in the Landscape: An Ecological Viewpoint

ALAN GUSSOW, whom the *New York Times* once described as "Artist in Residence for Mother Nature," was born in 1931 in Bronx, New York; he was raised largely on the south shore of Long Island. As a pioneer in the art and ecology movement, Mr. Gussow has always made reference to nature in his work, whether it be as a shaman on site-specific ceremonial art, as expert witness on scenic beauty, as an essayist on the sense of place, or as a policy formulator for national environmental organizations. He received an A.B. in American literature from Middlebury College, attended Cooper Union Art School in New York City, and was a Fellow at the American Academy in Rome, Italy, on a Prix de Rome in painting from 1953 to 1955. He conceived of and directed the Artist in Residence Program in the National Parks beginning in 1968, and was an editorial board member of *Landscape Journal* from 1982 to 1987. He has taught at the University of California at Santa Cruz numerous times, serving for both the art and environmental studies boards and, in 1990, as Regents Professor. As an artist, he has had over forty solo exhibitions, and his work is represented in fifteen museums and public collections in Italy and the United States. He is the author of *A Sense of Place: The Artist and the American Land* (Saturday Review Press and Friends of the Earth, 1971) and *The Artist as Native: Reinventing Regionalism* (Pomegranate Artbooks, 1993). He lives in Congers, New York, in the lower Hudson River valley.

FOR MANY YEARS I was a landscape painter. I thought little about the meaning of the word "landscape." For artists there is a well-defined tradition of landscape painting, particularly in North American art where the Hudson River school of painters celebrated the natural beauty of their valley by depicting the glades and vistas, the waterfalls and forest interiors in that region north of New York City. As a landscape painter my job was clear: seek out natural places and paint what I see. The role of the landscape painter was that of mediator. The scene was in front of me, my art history was behind me. I located myself along that continuum, sometimes moving closer to the scene, and on other occasions falling back, seeking distance, and finding reassurance in the way nineteenth-century landscape painters had regarded vistas. The meaning of landscape was not an issue. Landscape was my subject matter.

In the late 1960s, two events occurred which, though seemingly unrelated, shifted the way I perceive a landscape. An unexpected commonality in both events caused me to redefine my relationship to the landscape both as an artist and as an expert witness, testifying in behalf of natural and scenic beauty.

For a number of years I had attempted to persuade the National Park Service that artists should be allowed to live in residence in national parks. My intention was to give contemporary artists, many of whom were living in urban areas, an opportunity to confront nature at its most glorious. My hope at the time was that artists would respond to natural beauty by making landscape paintings. The artists' role, as I then saw it, would be to serve as "spiritual caretakers," working in tandem with others whose job it was to care for the game, the trails, and the public facilities. Initially, my idea was met with great skepticism by authorities in the Department of the Interior. Only when I began to suggest that artists might complement and enhance the interpretive programs of the National Park Service—by showing work made on location in the local visitors' centers, by leading sketching trips, by presenting slide shows—did I find signs of possible support. In 1968, aided by a modest grant from the America the Beautiful Fund, I was invited to test the idea of an artist-in-residence program in a national park by living and working on the Cape Cod National Seashore.

My two months on Cape Cod eventually led to a residence program which placed artists in national parks from Hawaii Volcanoes to Big Bend in Texas, culminating in the establishment of an artist community in the Delaware Water Gap National Recreation Area. What is relevant here, however, is a personal experience on Cape Cod, not a review of the history of the artist-in-residence program in national parks. One morning during my tenure on Cape Cod, I went out to the beach near Truro and found the shore washed clean by a night's high tide. The shore was new and unmarked. The sun shone brilliantly. The wind from the beach blew spindrift high in the air. It was a glorious morning. I was moved to make what I determined would be the world's largest drawing.

Picking up a bleached stick, I rapidly began to make markings in the unmarked sand. Every time I saw a gull turn or spindrift rise, or when a wave was spent and the flow returned to the sea, I made a marking, a kind of sand calligraphy. This action continued until I had covered more than one hundred fifty feet of shoreline with my drawing. Cape Cod's outer beach consists of three parts: a very high dune, a low middle plateau, and, two or three feet lower, a slope of sand that leads to the surf. I climbed the middle plateau and, without looking at my enormous drawing, walked head down until I was approximately at the center of my work. I then looked up and out to see what I had made.

I was horrified at what I saw. Mixed in with my beautiful markings were all my footprints! I had not realized I was walking in and through my drawing. My mental image had been that I was suspended above the work, making only art. All the while, I now saw, my body had been there, leaving its own imprint. What I understood at that moment—and what has remained with me—is the idea that we are never merely spectators to the landscape. We are *in* the scene. The landscape is not simply "out there," a place to be viewed in a glance. My conventional definition of landscape as subject matter, a view or vista which I might paint, now seemed inaccurate and incomplete. To sense myself in the scene, to understand that I was in the landscape, required a new perception. My presence altered the place. As an artist, I had to communicate something more than a view. I had to depict a relationship. Although my artwork did not immediately reflect this new perception, within a brief period I found myself shifting from making paintings of what I saw to making paintings of what I did, paintings which attempted to convey a range of sensory responses to the landscape. Instead of placing the landscape in front of me and my art history behind me, I understood that I had stepped into the landscape. I was inescapably a part of the place.

The second event that contributed to my redefinition of landscape came when David Sive, an attorney representing the Sierra Club and village of Tarrytown, New York, asked if I would be willing to testify in Federal District Court, as an expert witness, in proceedings on the proposed Hudson Riverway Project. Sive's hope was that I would offer some legally defensible definitions of natural and scenic beauty. The proposed project required the modification of the Hudson shoreline with a 1,000-foot riprap landfill. Operative legislation stated that consideration be given to any potential adverse effect the project would have on natural and scenic beauty. Sive wanted me to define the terms "natural" and "scenic" and to indicate what effect, if any, the proposed project would have on those qualities in the landscape.

With considerable misgivings about my expertise, I consented to Sive's request. In retrospect, the move into this new role was logical. If I believed that the landscape is more than a view and saw myself as a participant in the landscape, then it was necessary to take responsibility for the quality of the landscape. I had come to believe that the landscape is everything outdoors that surrounds us and that landscape gives shape to our character. If the events of life occur somewhere, then it was reasonable to assume that location exerts an effect on the perception of such events. Our landscape is more than a passive backdrop to human events—it is a stage on which we move. The objects and forms on that stage shape our actions, guide our choices, restrict or enhance our freedom, and in mysterious ways even predict our future.

I was convinced that the structure and quality of the physical space surrounding us influences our sense of well-being and contributes to our body image. Our view of ourselves, our sense of potency, our sense of self-worth—these images of self—are profoundly affected by the physical (natural) and cultural (human-made) landscapes in which we move. The struggle to maintain diversity and quality in both the natural and the human-made landscape is more than an aesthetic struggle. As I saw it, it was a battle to preserve a body image, each of us unique, yet functioning harmoniously in a coherent landscape.

The joining of my roles as artist and expert witness on natural beauty emerged vividly during an exchange with a New York

State attorney during a cross-examination in the Hudson River-way case. At one point the lawyer for the state abruptly shifted his line of questioning by asking, "Are you one of those aesthetic few who are artists?" His question implied that what I value in the landscape is different from qualities the general public appreciates. In my reply I expanded on the idea that everyone enjoys natural beauty, that all kinds of people respond to scenic landscapes. The only difference between artists and the rest of the population, I speculated, is that the artist is trained to give form to pleasurable experiences in nature, experiences which are common to us all. The artist might paint a picture, write a poem, choreograph a dance, compose a song, make a photograph, or design a landscape. The difference between the artist and the layperson is not in the depth of experience; the difference lies in the artist's ability to make something of the experience which will permit the pleasure to be communicated.

J. B. Jackson, in a now-familiar quote from his book, *Discovering the Vernacular Landscape,* has defined landscape as "a concrete, three-dimensional, shared reality." Both as an artist and as an advocate of natural beauty, I had set out to depict and to defend that "shared reality." In attempting to formulate legally defensible definitions of natural and scenic beauty, I have continued to regard the landscape as more than a setting. In the largest sense, the landscape is a resource, something we may draw upon, be nourished by, something available for use and for misuse. Increasingly I have focused on the landscape as a scenic resource, defining scenery as an aggregate of physical and cultural features that give character to a landscape. Yet when we use the word "scenic," we invoke more than an aggregate; we are prompted to think of a place or a view as possessing pleasing and natural qualities.

What exactly is a scenic resource and how may we preserve and protect it? Conventional wisdom suggests that a scenic resource is simply a beautiful view and that we protect it first by locating it, deciding on its physical limits, inventorying its components, and then devising means whereby we prevent anything bad from occurring in it. Following this logic we preserve our scenic resources by restricting what happens to them (or in them) and by setting up an enforcement process which guarantees that, over time, present wishes are carried out.

Conventional wisdom, however, does not deal with difficult questions: Who decides what is a scenic resource? From what view is a judgment made? What do we mean when we say a landscape is beautiful? With what criteria do we assess the impact of proposed changes in a scene? Can we assume that any value judgment made today should, or could, prevail forever? The largest question concerns motivation: Why is it important to protect and preserve scenic resources? Of what possible value is a scenic resource, assuming we can agree on a definition of terms?

If confronted with the term "scenic resource" many people will focus on the word "scenic," quickly noting that we all know at some intuitive level what is scenic and what is not and that, in general, a landscape is scenic when it appears to be beautiful and picturesque. It is the word "natural" which comes to mind when we think of scenic qualities. The word "scenic" suggests a view, a vista, or a prospect. A scene is like a distant background. We look at a scene. Yet we must remind ourselves that we live in a landscape that has character—and its character is derived from its natural and cultural history.

Even if we agree with what I would term a proscenium theory of scenery—that is, a scene is a view from a fixed point, a view that is selected, limited, and controlled—how can we agree on the selection of vantage points? Is it desirable to preselect a series of vista points from which the public can enjoy a scenic landscape? Who will decide what views are the most scenic, and what criteria will they use? Are we as citizens to be restricted in our relationship to pleasing landscapes by being told to enjoy the views only from predetermined vantage points? Don't preferences change?

To think of scenic resources in such static terms is to blunt the value and underestimate the contribution scenic resources make to our lives. A scenic resource is first and foremost a resource, something capable of use. That any resource may be degraded, exploited, or poorly used there can be little doubt. This is as true of scenic resources as of mineral or water resources. In order to make some judgment about the highest and "best" use of any resource, we should always consider a range of possible uses. The question then is: What purpose or purposes might be served by a scenic resource?

We must first set aside the idea that a scenic resource is merely a view or even a series of views. A scenic resource is the landscape we see, and all of it, not merely some predigested, preselected, arbitrarily focused view. A scene is more than a backdrop to action. We are in the scene. We are not spectators at a performance, but active participants in events that take place in a landscape. The objects and forms in the landscape that surrounds us shape our lives, influence our attitudes, and may even determine the quality of human relationships. The sights and smells, the sounds and textures, the shapes and proportions of the physical world we inhabit shape our character. If we define scenic landscapes only in terms of satisfying views, we risk neglecting an appreciation of the profound attachments we have to the landscape we inhabit.

René Dubos once noted, in "Symbiosis Between Earth and Humankind," that there are two different kinds of satisfactory landscapes: "wilderness still undisturbed by human intervention" and "various humanized environments created to fit the physiological, aesthetic and emotional needs of modern, human life." Arguing that we need both kinds of landscapes, and for different reasons, Dubos suggested that wilderness, apart from maintaining essential ecosystems, also satisfies a human need for primeval nature "to establish contact now and then with . . . biological origins, a sense of community with the past and with the rest of creation." Ever the realist, Dubos was also aware that most people spend most of their lives in what he called "humanized nature," "landscapes that have been transformed in such a way that there exists a harmonious interplay between human nature and environmental forces, resulting in adaptive fitness."

One way to view the scenic landscape, then, is as an arena of adaptation. The landscape is alive and changing, characterized by a constant interpenetration, each modification transforming the environment which in turn influences the forms and behavior of everything that resides within the environment. There is no separate existence. When we tamper with the physical landscape, we change the world we inhabit, and that changed world, for better or worse, changes us.

Yet, by defining the scenic landscape so broadly, we risk losing the meaning of "scenic" altogether, for it is important to retain a sense of quality. If the landscape is not merely a background, as I asserted earlier, but a stage on which our lives are played out, then the quality of objects on that stage—the richness of detail, scale, variety, and proportions—the intrinsic qualities of the form with which we are surrounded, affect us profoundly. It is here that the notion of aesthetics must be considered, since aesthetics deals with what is beautiful in art and in nature. When I use the term "aesthetics" I refer to satisfactions gained through the senses—what we touch, taste, smell, hear, and see. The quality of the physical landscape can be measured by the degree to which our senses are pleasurably engaged. I doubt there is any scientific way we can determine ultimately whether a landscape is aesthetically satisfying to experience, though social scientists will no doubt continue to try. Except in those instances when professional architects and landscape architects are engaged to design elements within a landscape, most actions in the physical world are unintentionally taken to improve aesthetic qualities. Yet some places and some scenes are more satisfying than others.

What qualities in the landscape contribute to "appreciative perception?" In the past I have argued that the essential quality is wholeness, a sense of integrity. An object has integrity if it possesses soundness. A landscape expresses integrity by the way its various constituents fit together. Value judgments are inevitably involved. When the visual landscape loses its integrity, it is impaired. Impairment should not be confused with variety, however. All landscapes are, to some extent, resilient. As expressions of human and natural order, landscapes usually present a diverse scene. We should welcome the sensual stimulation of varied forms and textures. The fitness of any landscape does not require monotony. To impair the landscape is to diminish its ability to enrich human experience.

On what basis do we decide that something is fit or unfit for a landscape? Can we declare with certainty that a specific addition to the landscape will impair its potential as a scenic resource? Aldo Leopold once wrote, in his classic book, *A Sand County Almanac,* that "a thing is right when it tends to preserve the integrity, stability and beauty of the biotic community. It is wrong when it does otherwise." What fits into the visual landscape is anything that enhances coherence, renders the landscape comprehensible, contributes to a sense of order, and adds a perception of harmony. Also necessary is the preservation of life.

The landscape of integrity engages our senses and calls forth good associations. There are no quantitative criteria for identifying or producing such a landscape, only qualitative measures requiring judgment and experience. The best landscapes may be totally wild or wholly human-made; they may be physically expansive or hermetic and intimate. There are no rules. The very idea of scenery is cultural and temporal. Different people in different times thus make different choices.

Earlier I quoted J. B. Jackson when he spoke of landscapes as a "shared reality." One of the reasons I have testified on the visual landscape is my growing concern about threats to the quality of this shared reality. The landscape is simply not neutral space observed. I see the landscape as part of a feedback loop, shaping human qualities just as human events in turn shape a landscape. When a landscape changes its inhabitants are altered. While it is necessary to preserve the life-supporting qualities in the environment—the quality of air, soil, and water, for instance—we must equally provide for a landscape that enriches the human spirit. I do not regard beauty in the landscape purely as an amenity, desirable but hardly essential. Part of the difficulty we experience in defending beauty comes from defining beauty in often personal and subjective terms. Beauty should not be confused with style and fashion.

Some of us seek to be surrounded by nineteenth-century proportions. My wife and I choose to live in a Victorian, three-story wooden house, which we prefer to sleekly modern forms. Others just as ardently prefer contemporary images. There are those who opt for the typical English countryside as a model for the ideal landscape. Many Americans define landscape beauty in forms congruent with paintings by Grandma Moses. Others like the wide, flat, open textures of tall-grass prairies. No one attempting to set criteria for judging landscape quality should fall into the trap of praising one style or type of landscape as beautiful while dismissing other locations by saying they lack satisfying qualities. As a diverse people, we must understand and value the widest range of landscape qualities, perhaps preserving first those that are physically and culturally indigenous to an area or region.

In the past I have measured beauty in the landscape by evidence of wholeness and integrity, arguing that the ultimate test lay in fitness, the ability of things to work together. There are two troubling deficiencies in this argument. First, I have overestimated human values. Second, I have defined beauty more in aesthetic terms as opposed to ecological considerations. Is it fair to suggest that a landscape possesses values apart from human use? Certainly there are ecological values in sustaining a natural system, values we do not understand completely. Since the impact of people on a landscape is not fully known, we should always move with modesty, restraint, even humility in making any changes in the physical landscape.

The ultimate issue is not merely fitness for human use, but the regenerative, organic, sustainable attributes of the physical terrain and all the creatures, human and otherwise, who inhabit the place. I propose that a new criteria for measuring landscape quality be developed, one that places highest priority on an ecological viewpoint, a vision across boundaries, one that senses wide connections between the quality of the physical environment and the quality of life. This criteria would build on Aldo Leopold's standard of "integrity, stability and beauty of the biotic community," adding to it the considerations of human history and culture.

What is beautiful in the landscape is what is healthy and sustainable. Appreciation of this more subtle kind of beauty requires a shift in our perceptions. It necessitates a move away from personal tastes for certain landscapes and the cultivation of an ability to see beauty in more modest, less aggressive settings. I am all for the preservation of majestic and unique natural areas such as the "crown jewels" in the National Park system. Equally, I support moves to preserve historic settings and small towns and urban enclaves. What we must now learn to value, however, is a less visible landscape, settings in which natural processes are allowed to function without interruption. We need to praise tidal wetlands and wildlife habitats with as much enthusiasm as we exclaim for the Grand Canyon or Yellowstone or Mt. Rainier. Beauty does not mean bigger or even finer; beauty exists in sustainability. We should continue to raise questions about scale, variety, and uniqueness when major proposals for alterations to a landscape are presented. Even more, however, we must inquire about the probable effects such actions will have on the self-healing qualities of the landscape.

The most beautiful landscapes are those that convey life, that resonate with sweet smells, as does compost, that reflect slow changes, that allow nature itself to dominate and integrate. For too long we have declared that "beauty is in the eye of the beholder." We may indeed appreciate beauty when it presents itself. Beauty, however, is intrinsic to the life-supporting, life-sustaining landscape, and those qualities do not require our perception. Given the continued stress on natural, ecological beauty, we may yet be called upon to intercede and place restraints, not on nature, but on human actions in order that such beauty may continue on earth.

This is a view of a scene. "The Lake in Winter," by Alan Gussow, 1962. Oil on canvas, 50 inches by 58 inches. Permanent Collection of the Rockland Country Day School.

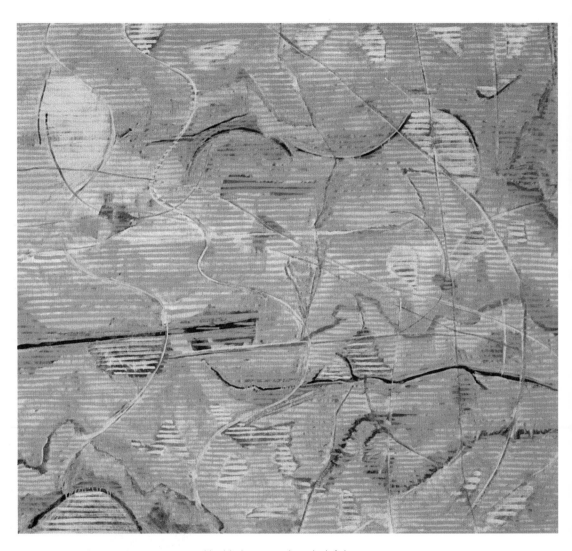

The images in this painting are prompted by blade cuts and marks left by
my wife and me after ice skating on a lake. The painting is a record of what
we did, not a picture of what we saw. "Skater's Ice," by Alan Gussow,
1976. Oil on canvas, 44 inches by 48 inches. Collection of the artist.

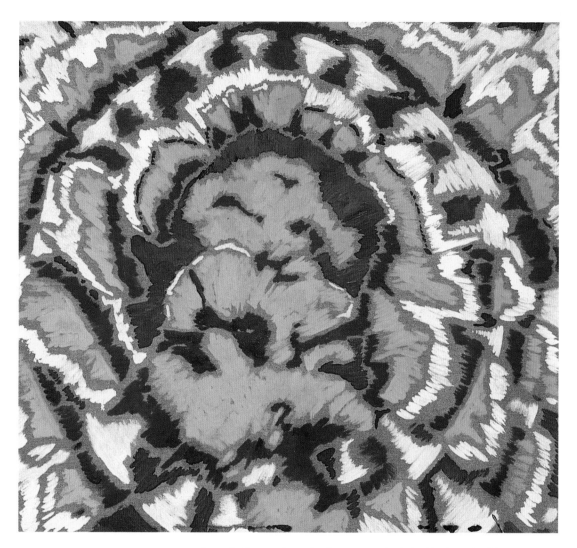

Inner feelings and exterior forms commingle in this visceral, athletic response to landscape. "Runner's High," by Alan Gussow, 1978. Oil on canvas, 27.5 inches by 30.5 inches. Collection of the artist.

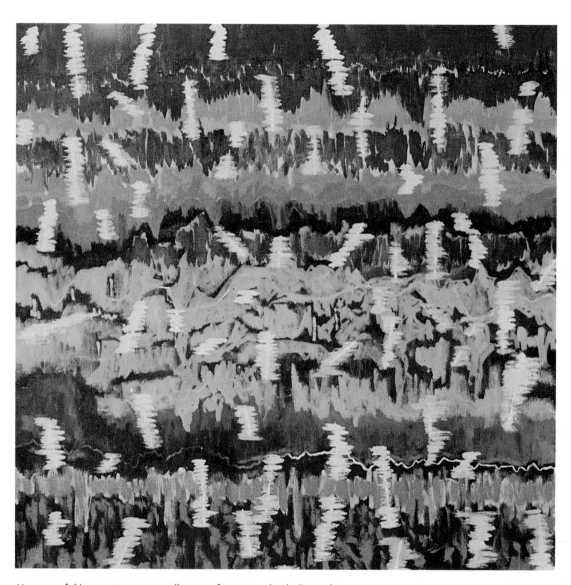

Unsuccessful in my attempts to pull carrots from a garden in December,
I imagined the cold earth was breathing frosty wisps into my face. "Rime
Time," by Alan Gussow, 1976. Oil on canvas, 30 inches by 30 inches.
Collection of the Washburn Gallery, New York City.

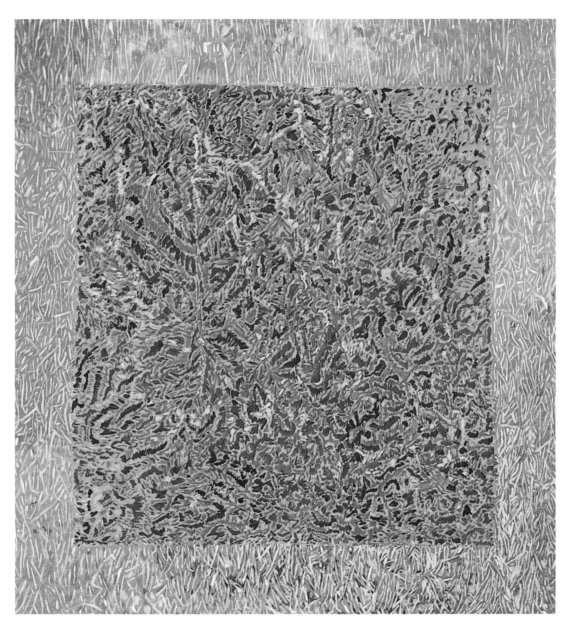

The brittle patterns of late leaves fill the center of the picture. The leaves, once gone, reveal the silvery forms of branches and tree trunks which rim the edges like a frame. The painting is my commentary on the shifts in texture from autumn to the beginning of winter. "November Leaves, November Branches," by Alan Gussow, 1977. Oil on canvas, 58 inches by 55 inches. Collection of the artist.

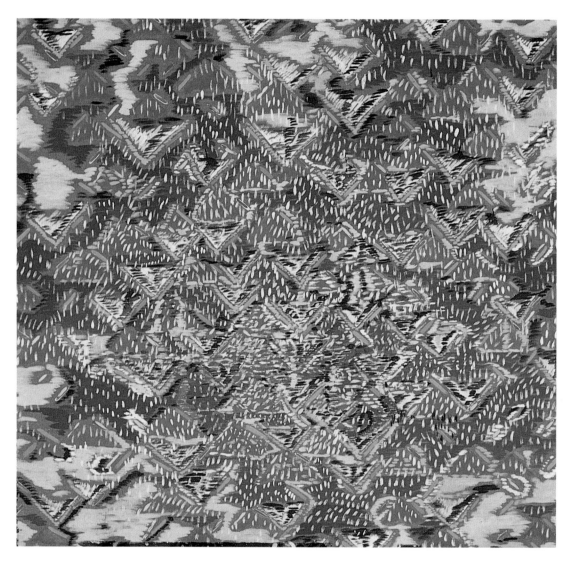

Two hundred miles north of Winnipeg, Manitoba, is a landscape filled with lakes and low trees. It is the home of the Metis, a people descended from Indian women and French and Scots fur-traders. The images in the painting derive from the extraordinary light. We never saw darkness. For us, going to sleep at 23:00 and waking at 5:30, the light was continuous in June. The entire image refers as well to a stretched animal skin and to tepees, although the Metis no longer live in them. The painting is my response to the physical and cultural landscapes of the Metis; it conveys my belief that *wholeness* is the essential quality of a landscape. "Memory of a Metis Village," by Alan Gussow, 1977. Oil on canvas, 50 inches by 58 inches. Collection of the artist.

Once I used mechanical means to dig our garden. This drawing is the culmination of the experience. Rocks, rocks, and more rocks, and the air was filled with clanging. Since that time, we have dug our French-intensive, bio-dynamic beds by hand. "The Roto-tiller," by Alan Gussow, 1974. Brush and ink on paper, 18 inches by 24 inches. Collection of the artist.

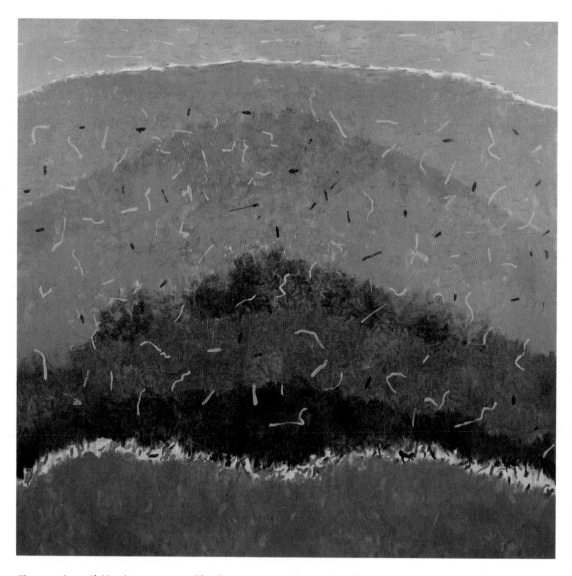

The most beautiful landscapes convey life. They resonate with sweet smells. They reflect slow changes. They allow nature to dominate and integrate. In this painting, the compost pile has turned into a landscape. "The Compost Pile," by Alan Gussow, 1977. Oil on canvas, 46.5 inches by 48.5 inches. Collection of the artist.

Lawrence Halprin

# Nature into Landscape into Art

LAWRENCE HALPRIN was born in 1916 in Brooklyn, New York, and was raised there, although he lived three years as a teenager in a kibbutz in Israel. He received a B.S. in plant science from Cornell University and an M.S. in horticulture from the University of Wisconsin-Madison, and he graduated from Harvard University's Graduate School of Design. A Fellow of the American Society of Landscape Architects and the American Institute of Interior Design, he also has received the American Institute of Architects Gold Medal for Distinguished Achievement. His design credits include the Sea Ranch on California's north coast, the Seattle Freeway Park, Levi's Plaza in San Francisco, Nicolette Mall in Minneapolis, and the Manhattan Square Park. He has made numerous contributions to our understanding of design and place as an author and filmmaker. His books include *Cities* (Reinhold, 1963; revised edition, The MIT Press, 1972), *Freeways* (Reinhold, 1966), *The RSVP Cycles* (George Braziller, 1970), and *The Sketchbooks of Lawrence Halprin* (Process Architecture Publishing, Tokyo, 1981). In 1986 the San Francisco Museum of Modern Art honored Mr. Halprin with a major retrospective of this work. He lives and works in San Francisco.

WHEN I WAS A BOY I had a secret hiding place in the woods near my parent's home. When I could I would escape to it, sometimes with my friends but more usually by myself. In that hidden landscape I felt very safe, safe from all the complexities of my life at home and the everyday problems of growing up. In that natural environment I felt whole and unthreatened. There were trees and small animals, plants and good natural smells, snakes and birds. It was a holistic universe which I could inhabit, where I could fantasize. Perhaps most importantly it felt nonjudgmental. I didn't feel I had to adapt to anyone's ideas or demands or dictates. I could be myself. I could dream. I could play games. I could make up stories and fantasies.

That place in the woods has remained with me all my life. I suppose what I have been doing as an adult is trying to find the basic meaning of my relationship to that natural place. Through that search I have hoped to discover the elements of people's inherent connections to the landscape which serves as a guide to design principles.

I have discovered among other things that nature and landscape are two different ideas; the difference between the two holds deep significance for me. In nature we perceive elemental forces. The "heavens above, the earth beneath, and the waters under the earth." The beginning is awesome, as it is reported in the Bible: "In the beginning God created the heavens and the earth. And the earth was without form and void and darkness was upon the face of the deep; and the spirit of God moved over the face of the waters."

The essence in the quality of nature is the unbridled force of its energy and power. The act of creation was a force which "primitive peoples" throughout the world celebrated with fear and invested with incredible meaning in their myths of creation. All of these myths focused on the way it happened. The process by which creation occurred was a significant event for early humans, and each culture reveals much of its unique characteristics in its creation myth. The Judeo-Christian Bible tells of a God who created the Earth from chaos in five days, fashioned "man" in His own image on the sixth day, and rested from His labors on the seventh. Among the people of the Southwest, as explained by Joseph Campbell in *The Way of the Animal Powers,* the emergence myth of the Jocarilla Apache states: "In the beginning there was nothing where the world now stands—only the Hactcin (the gods). These had the material out of which everything was to be made. The earth they made in the form of a living woman, the sky in the form of a living man. . . ."

In all creation myths it is the concept of nature as a symbol of the world *occurring*—coming into being—which is important and which describes events leading to the emergence of earth and all its creatures. The power of this happening invested the earth with both the mystery of religion and an inevitability that defied question. Nature is raw elementary power beyond human control. Nature *is,* and at the core of all religions lies a transactional search in which humans try to understand its power and then negotiate a creative and functional relationship to that power. One of the basic thrusts of religion is the human attempt to understand the forces of nature and to act in ways that will placate its power.

"Primitive people" instinctively made this relationship a vital part of their lives. They integrated themselves with nature through their whole being, both personal and communal. They interacted and identified themselves with plants and animals. They acknowledged and personalized the catastrophic forces of floods and earthquakes, fires and pestilences, and ascribed godlike characteristics to the forces that caused them. They made their art, dance, and music to serve as intermediaries between themselves and the great awesome powers of nature. They perceived themselves as tiny participants in the great continuous cycle of the universe.

Landscape is a less awesome concept than nature and has developed different implications. It implies people's intervention and the application of human values. It has more to do with scenery, with picturesque scenes, almost with nature as theater. Landscape is design of the mise-en-scène for human occupation of nature. It is nature converted into an opera invested with human passion so it becomes functionally and emotionally related to the needs and uses to which we put nature.

Landscapes are cultivated. They reflect human values. They are made or modified by human beings. In the very real sense they have become human-made artifacts. The English country landscape, for example, is almost wholly human-made: every tree has been planted, every meadow sown, and every view arranged.

Landscapes express what we think of ourselves. Like landscape paintings they are human handiworks. They use nature as a tool, as a resource, as a material for our own enjoyment. They are nature tamed and used for our own needs and pleasures.

Landscapes include farms and villages, open spaces in cities, national parks, recreational lakes, suburbs, and gardens. The Garden of Eden was the first biblical fantasy of an idealized landscape once the incredible act of a creation had been completed. Eden was a garden in which the first couple, man and woman, strolled amongst the plants and animals in a utopian landscape. Life there was pure, idealized, ecologically right, and simplistic. It had developed from nature without human involvement, and therefore it was perfect, a place without a human history, a place without death.

Nature is pure process made visible. For that reason we respond to nature as being beautiful and right. We respond to nature because we ourselves are a part of its making. We are biologically part of its creation, and therefore we empathize with the order and interrelationships in it. Like a mother's love we accept nature because we ourselves are formed by its creation.

Landscapes on the other hand are equivocal, resulting as they do from human decision making and all the issues of values and human foibles, of human acts of choice. They are open to question. We do not perceive all landscapes as being beautiful. Like the other art forms we judge them, we apply artistic criteria to them. Since we inhabit them we also have expectations of them, some of which are fulfilling, some of which are not. We perceive some landscapes as beautiful and acknowledge others as ugly. Differences of opinion exist about the beauty and/or utility of specific landscapes. As we design our landscapes, formal questions of design and artistry arise. What is valid or invalid? How do we design for a postindustrial age? What is the role of geometry, of patterning concepts, of architectural composition, of community plans, of roads and highways and cities in the landscape? What relationship does nature have to landscape?

My empathy with nature is intense, and I derive emotional and psychological nourishment from contact with it. I enjoy being in nature on many levels. I enjoy hiking in the High Sierra as a recreational activity, I botanize and watch birds, and I draw or paint the picturesque landscapes I walk whenever I can. These relationships mean a lot to me. But there is a deeper, more primitive series of interactions which are more significant to me in my search for a landscape aesthetic.

A whole range of biological and emotional human responses to nature seems to me essential as background for landscape art; they are available as source material to the designer. The sense of shelter, for example, is basic to us all: the nurturing quality of protection and privacy, of territoriality and personal space. These are achievable in myriad ways, but the essence of shelter is the real need. In the landscape we need not only a house, room, wall, and roof, but also grottoes and canopies, semicover and full cover—a primordial and prenatal need shared by all.

Another example of a basic need is water, not only for our survival as biological entities, but also as it links us to our sources (erosion, wave actions, irrigation of crops, a multitude of interactions in nature, and from our common prenatal experience of a nourishing liquid environment *in utero*). Water as part of the made landscape relates us in profound ways to the origins of our beginnings. Its sounds and shapes and feel in parks and plazas call up deep emotional responses in us.

Gateways and entrances link us back to our origins, too: how we come into the world and the dark mysterious ways in which we react to the change of day and night as well as to the seasons. Gates and entrances to houses and to the enclosures of our public and private spaces are a major resource for the landscape designer; how we step through from space to space, the transitions from outward to inward, lies at the core of deep emotion.

These needs to which we respond are not totally bound by culture, but belong to the human species. As Joseph Campbell wrote in *The Way of the Animal Powers,* they are "of nature, innate, transpersonal, pre-rational and (when altered) compulsive. In this way there became established between the earliest human communities and their landscapes a profound participation mystique."

In developing a landscape aesthetic I have attempted to base design principles on these inherently biological (archetypal, if you will) needs that are common to all of us as human beings. Although many of these needs are functional, most go beyond mere survival and reach deep into the subconscious needs and desires that form a common ground in the human psyche. The physical provision for these deep biological and emotional motivations can be delivered through designed environments whose physical form is an aesthetic creation. As a designer, I return to nature's primitive processes in order to make landscape into an art based on deep human desires and needs.

I look to nature's process as a generating force both in form-making and composition. The origin of natural form-making comes from mountain building, from erosion generated by wind or water or freezing and thawing. I call these processes the *ecology of form*. The compositional relationship of natural objects in space

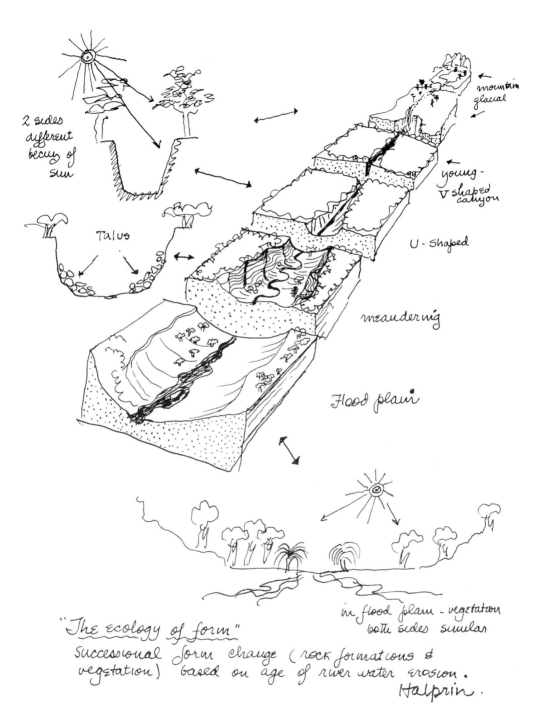

2 sides
different
becuz of
sun

Talus

mountain
glacial

young -
V-shaped
canyon

U - shaped

meandering

Flood plain

in flood plain - vegetation
both sides similar

"The ecology of form"
Successional form change (rock formations &
vegetation) based on age of river water erosion.
                        Halprin.

As a designer, I look to nature's processes for ideas in form-making and
composition. I call these processes the *ecology of form*. Drawing by
Lawrence Halprin, 1981.

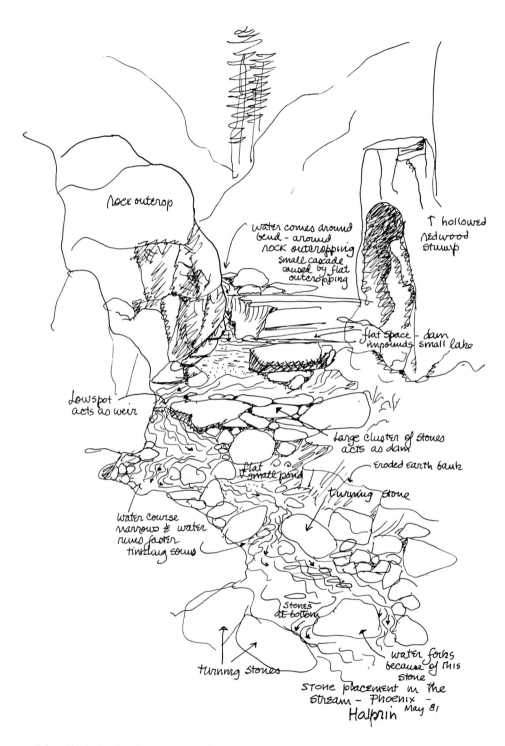

When I look at natural arrangements in space, I am amazed by how right
they are. Drawing by Lawrence Halprin, 1981.

or of plant mixtures in monocultures and diverse plant communities also comes from process—ecological processes. These can arise from glaciation, erosion, or successional change; each produces different results, but they all compose well. In the compositions that result from natural forces, nothing seems wrong, every relationship appears inevitable and perfect.

When I look at natural arrangements in space I am always amazed at how right they are, how stones in the bottom of a tidepool seem arranged just right and their relationships to each other cannot be improved upon. When I see rock forms carved by wave action they move me as great works of form-making. I empathize with the forms of trees windswept on the edge of cliffs, with meadows and their intricate interrelationships of grasses and flowers and animal burrows as evidence of the qualities of composition. In the same way patterns of wave action seem to me great role models for group choreography.

If these results of natural process always seem so inherently right to us and if nature forms natural objects, aggregations, and landscapes that we inevitably find beautiful, then in my view they can form the basic source of our aesthetic sensibilities. They are the grammar of our aesthetic language, the ultimate source to which we can refer in our search for a landscape art, perhaps the source of all art. How can we utilize these basic resources creatively and fundamentally to produce environments so right that they enhance all our lives?

The essential dilemma in the art of making landscapes is how to transmute experiences with the natural landscape into human-made environments that are fit for living. If the source of our aesthetics and our judgments of art lie in the results of nature's processes, perhaps we must turn to the experience of nature as our primary design tool.

My own way has been to design landscapes that do not imitate the *outward forms* of nature but emphasize the *results of the processes* of nature. I try to capture the essence of my own empathy with nature and evoke for others the impact that form, composition, and character in nature have had upon me. When I have discovered that impact I can then transform the natural into the human-made and deliver through that transmutation the experiential equivalency of an empathy with nature.

This act of transmuting the experience of natural landscape into human-made experience is, for me, the essence of the art of landscape design. The issue is more difficult in landscape design perhaps than in the other arts, however, because we work primarily with nature's materials and the degree to which we develop abstractions of nature is more obvious and open to question. For example, topiary work can abstract trees and shrubs into geometric or other forms to the point where they do not seem at all like natural, living material.

In all the art forms this issue of the degree of abstraction is of major aesthetic importance. In our own century we have seen a shift from realism to expressionism to cubism to abstract expressionism to minimalism and back again to realism. What emerges is this: The essential quality of art lies outside the degrees of abstraction and depends on the evocation of intense human experience. We can ask the same question about the degree of abstraction appropriate to the landscape art: Should we use nature's materials and try to copy natural landscapes in a form of landscape realism, or should we develop abstractions of pattern and geometry? As in the other arts, the motivating force of landscape design is to evoke a deep emotional response. This can be achieved in many ways so long as the primary focus of design is based on archetypal human experience.

We can use natural materials (flowers, moss, rocks, shrubs, trees, water, etc.) in our designed landscapes. There is no question that we relate easily to nature's own materials, although many trees and plants used in our yards and gardens (and city parks and streets) are now largely a result of human intervention, bred and hybridized as modes of production until they have little resemblance to their natural ancestors. Still, they carry with them the imprint of inherent naturalism. Human-made materials such as concrete and paint can also be used in producing color and shade and texture, as long as the effect of the made landscape relates to a biologically natural experience.

This is also true of another element which the designer of landscape must consider: choreographed movement through space. Design for movement can evoke similar experiential feelings, if it is on a natural trail through a woods or a pedestrian walk through a city, as long as the evocation is similar. In designing a walk through a city, for example, we should pay attention to the same effects that are achieved on a walk in nature. We can design for pace, rhythm, and textures underfoot. We can design the spaces we walk through and how they are modulated (wide and narrow, straight and jagged). In addition, there are the sentinels and objects along the way, the views we see or glimpse in the distance, and the occasional shafts of sunlight with resting places provided in the light. There are the noises and smells and perhaps the sound of water that follow us. All are important to understanding the *ecology of form through landscape*.

These wonderful qualities that we treasure in a walk in nature can be captured by intelligent design in a city. I often think

The act of converting the experience of natural landscape and the ecology of form into human-made experience is, for me, the essence of the art of landscape design. Lovejoy Fountain in Portland, Oregon, shown here in a photograph by Maude Dorr, was designed by Lawrence Halprin and Associates as part of its large landscape redevelopment plan for this great city. The fountain, dedicated in 1966, expresses the beauty and natural ecology of a mountain stream, possibly in the Cascade Range.

of how nourished I am emotionally when I spend a day in the Old City of Jerusalem, just walking. Though I may stop to buy something in the tiny caverns along David Street, the important experience is not in the buying but in the quality of my movement and the variations in the urban space: the stony walls and pavings, the smells, the sounds as well as the relatedness to the walking that has gone on for so many centuries by so many people.

It is the natural experience we seek to evoke in cities. To be in a city can be as beautiful an experience as being in a forest, as long as the city is designed with sensitivity to the natural, atavistic needs of its inhabitants.

In landscape design, as in any art form, the care and passion and talent of the designer have a major role in the resulting qualities of the artwork. The big difference that characterizes the art of landscape, however, is the need to empathize with natural processes. It is that deep understanding which subsumes function, technical knowledge, and architectural structures, basic as *they* are to the landscape art. Ultimately landscape design must connect to the earth and to primary human needs that we all share as inhabitants of the earth. Then landscape design, using all the evocative, fragile, compositional, and choreographic forces central to the other arts, can create works that link us with nature in its most evocative forms.

We can appreciate that a close rapport between people and their natural environment has always existed. It built up over millennia because of our common ancestry and our integrative physical and psychic interdependency. Now we are becoming increasingly and alarmingly isolated from nature, which remains *the* source of landscape. The human need for nature, however, deeply and subconsciously rooted as it is, is encoded in our biology and in our archetypal patterning. The core of making places for ourselves as individuals and communities thus lies in the perception that these deeply rooted, subconscious needs are the basis of design, and that finding the essential characteristics of nature is to find the vocabulary in our own design processes.

When I recall that secret place of my childhood, which influenced me so strongly, I realize how ingrained it was in my archetypal, human needs. It became, in a real sense, a design for living. It evoked the primitive mysteries of a relationship to nature, of protections and privacy, and the fantasies and dreams that tell us what we want to be. For that reason, the experience of that childhood landscape impressed in me those basic emotional and functional requirements which our landscapes, through art, can help to satisfy.

# Landscape in Motion

**John Gamble**

JOHN GAMBLE was born in 1943 in Albany, New York, and was raised in that area. He was a premedical student at Cornell University and Union College, and later studied psychology at the New School for Social Research in New York City and theater arts at American University. He cofounded and directed the Georgetown Workshop in Washington, D.C., from 1967 to 1970, at which time he was the production stage manager for the National Ballet, and later was a teacher with, and administrative director for, Anna Halprin's San Francisco Dancers' Workshop from 1972 to 1975. He was coartistic director of Zero Moving Dance Company in Philadelphia from 1975 to 1980, and founded and directed Seminole Works in Philadelphia from 1980 to 1985. He produced a film on contact improvisation, which was screened as a finalist at the American Film Institute in 1982, and is currently working on a book on dance and philosophy. From 1975 to 1985 Mr. Gamble was the chairman of the department of dance at Temple University; he has since been a professor and head of the dance department at the University of North Carolina, Greensboro.

DURING MY FIRST dance class, toward the end, after completing what at the time I thought of as the exercises—the stretching, bending, balancing, swinging, and skipping across the floor—we were asked to improvise an imaginary landscape. I was twenty-two years old, the only man in a class with twenty women, and already feeling a bit uncomfortable in my new tights and leotard. Now I was being asked to be a tree or a rock or perhaps even a flower. This request stimulated all of my prejudices about dance. How could I seriously pretend to be part of a landscape? This is for primary school children, not for adults, at least not for male adults. (At twenty-two I had not yet been cleansed of my tendency toward sexist conclusions.) I complied, since to refuse would have called attention to myself. I wanted to disappear, literally melt into the floor and be gone, so I chose to be a block of ice on the desert sands. I forced my body into as rigid a cube as possible and proceeded to soften slowly and slip into the ground. As my body went from a tight, enclosed, solid object to a loose, open, amorphous blob, I tried to imagine my fingers and toes, then my arms and legs, and finally my torso becoming liquid. I imagined this liquid seeping into sand and disappearing.

To my chagrin, the teacher decided I had solved the problem quite well and asked me to show the class, and thus I had my first dance class, my first dance performance, and had escaped being a flower all on the same day; but, it wasn't until many classes later that I understood the importance of this lesson. What I had perceived as a childish exercise was, in fact, teaching one of the most difficult and profound skills in dancing—the ability to embody, to become something with your spirit, your senses, and your imagination, and then to allow that something you have become to inhabit your body, reflecting outward so that it reads to an audience. This creates the magic in movement. Mimes do it literally and narratively, creating chairs, tables, dogs, and fire hydrants with such clarity that we almost see each object as the story is told. Dancers usually work more abstractly, but they also create images and qualities that strike archetypal chords in the viewer. Without the ability to embody, a dancer's performance would be dead.

I learned another lesson that day (which remained embedded in my subconscious, only to surface as I pondered this essay): The primary source for all my dancing and my dance-making is the landscape. Natural, human-shaped, human-made, and imaginary landscapes are the images that provide the energy and the context for my work.[1] As I stated, I didn't know this; yet I "knew" it. I believe this knowing yet not knowing may be the most unique aspect of landscape as art; more than any other form it works subliminally. When we go to the theater, listen to music, or read a good book, we expect to have an aesthetic experience. True, we may judge those experiences by their superficial entertainment quotient and absorb much of the meaning subconsciously, but we are, at least, wary that the artist may be trying to affect us. The landscape escapes such suspicions much of the time. This is not to say that I am, or we are, unaware that the landscape has an effect, but rather that we are unaware of the human thought and emotion that are inherent in the design. We tend to accept all landscapes, both natural and artificial (human-made), as inevitable. But, in fact, there are few, if any, landscapes left on earth that have not been partially shaped or affected by people, and, as a result, landscapes reflect the human condition perhaps more profoundly and certainly more immediately than (what we normally think of as) art does. We choose to see a play, or visit a gallery, or hear an orchestra; we must live in a landscape daily.

Art arises from nature. The poems of Wordsworth, the photographs of Ansel Adams, and the paintings of Paul Cézanne come to mind. The first cave paintings, the first dances, and the first music each were in response to natural surroundings; art was literally born of nature. But art arises from our human-shaped nature as well. The poetry of Allen Ginsberg, the music of Edgard Varèse, and the art of Marcel Duchamp are in response to physical and social environments created by people. I have often wondered at my negative response to crisply designed parks and suburban tracts which seem to impose themselves on their surroundings. I do not like to see a new building surrounded by trees and shrubs placed in geometric designs, everything looking planted rather than grown. It hurts my eyes and pains my soul. It is ugly. I recognize this is my prejudice against artificiality, but I am unsure whether this prejudice is the entire reason for my reaction. I think I may be responding to bad landscape art as much as to the ab-

1. By *landscape* I mean our physical surroundings, the environment through which we move and in which we live. In the most inclusive sense this includes landscape architecture and architecture, urban spaces at every scale, and the land that has been shaped by farming and other human endeavors; but more specifically landscape means, to me, the shape of the land, the earth's surface. By *nature* I mean both the process and the result of natural forces at work.

sence of the natural. I have a similar response to a play stiffly performed, or to a dance that seems more technical than felt. I think what disturbs me in all of the above is not that reality is shaped by people, but that the shaping is so one-dimensional. Perhaps the fact that so many of our landscapes have been reduced to a sprawl of concrete and billboards has led to a reduction in what we expect of beauty, a creeping nihilism in thought and one-dimensionalism in art.

We live in a curious age. Art, in the Western world, is most often the product of one artist's unique vision. Folk art is rarely accepted as current or relevant. New directions, eccentric predilections, and the sensational are revered; tradition is suspect. Of course, the single artist can and does produce multilayered art, and that art can and does reflect our culture, but the degree of layering and the depth of reflection must be limited. In our quest for individualism, we have gained uniqueness, but have lost depth, and it is depth that can tie art to the wholeness of our existence. In the not-too-distant past, art, ritual, religion, myth, and daily codes of behavior were inextricably linked. Art arose from a collective consciousness, and art looked backward as well as forward. In this sense, art was grown, not planted; its roots sunk deep in the culture and its limbs were pruned by generations of master gardeners.

Architecture and landscape design, by necessity, are forms that have retained their connection to daily life, to history, and to the folk tradition. The landscape cannot be fixed in time. It will grow and be reshaped by natural forces and generations of people. The new building with its geometric plantings will become old, other buildings will be erected around it, its gardens will be re-planted, and its trees will respond to the light, moisture, and soil. In time, it will become more "natural" because the forces of nature, which include people, will act upon it.

I now recognize that my art is affected by the landscape in two ways. First, I draw images from nature (and my not-so-natural surroundings); from these I create an imaginary landscape. This archetypal landscape is usually the basis from which a dance arises. (This I knew.) Second, I have learned to work through a process that allows a dance to grow. Through my work in theater and dance improvisation, and particularly my work with Anna and Lawrence Halprin, I have come to value the collective process in the making of art. I want a dance to be affected by the dancers, by its performance, and by my own gropings. I do not regard a dance as fixed, but as a living and evolving organism. (It is this connection to the process of the landscape that had eluded me.)

There are many sources of imagery for dance, but a landscape offers some of the most powerful. Dance is the art of motion, motion created by human shapes moving through space and time. Landscapes are, to the eye, temporally fixed representations of change and motion, each shape reflecting the continuing movement of water, ice, wind, and forces in the earth. In a landscape, the dancer can see motion crystallized. Each weathered rock gently scooped and polished, each bent tree violently pulled and twisted, and each shoreline systematically gouged and eroded presents a lesson in movement. By visualizing textures, contours, juxtapositions, tensions, shapes, and structures, the dancer can imagine and embody the forces that shape an environment.

The distinction between the word "motion" and the word "movement" is important to the dancer. Motion is the more compelling term, applied to movement that is vested with particular qualities. Motion has spiritual overtones. Motion is movement that embodies the texture, the inherent force, and the life spirit of something. On the other hand, movement, for the dancer, tends to be a clinical term meaning the physical mechanics. Motion is a process. Motion has flow. Motion evokes. Other phrases that attempt to make this same distinction are "interpretive movement," "expressive movement," "artistic movement," and, of course, the word "dance" itself. I prefer the word "motion." It doesn't carry the limiting connotations carried by "interpretive" and "expressive." These two words have come to be associated with dances that interpret a particular piece of music or express an emotion, such as love, in a literal and often simplistic way. When I hear the words "interpretive" and "expressive," I think of Jules Feiffer's skinny modern dancer in her black leotard passionately flitting about in celebration of spring. Artistic movement sounds exclusive, or effete, or it conjures an image of high-class strippers strutting their stuff. The word "dance" is fine, but usually it refers only to structured human movement associated with art, ritual, or entertainment. We don't say that a mountain range was formed by the dance of the earth's crust. We could, but we don't. Motion implies great forces at work; motion is a holistic concept.

One dictionary defines emotion as "a mental *and bodily* reaction marked by strong feeling *and physiological* responses which prepare *the body for action*" (emphasis is mine). A definition for motion is an act, a process, or an instance of changing place. Emotion is a feeling vested with action. For the dancer, motion is an action vested with feeling.

The word "emotion" encompasses more than feelings of anger, fear, love, and hate. An emotion may be a mental and bodily response to a force not normally defined in human terms. Prob-

A landscape offers some of the most powerful sources of imagery in dance, because in a landscape the dancer can see motion crystallized. By visualizing textures, contours, juxtapositions, tensions, shapes, and structures, the dancer can imagine and embody the forces that shape an environment. Here, four members of Seminole Works perform "Falls from Grace" at the Conwell Dance Theater in Philadelphia, Pennsylvania, 1984. Choreography by John Gamble, 1984. Photograph by Deng-Jeng Lee.

ably we would not describe our emotional response to a landscape as fright, compassion, pity, or sadness; more often we would use adjectives such as awesome, moving, spiritual, or inspiring. These are general terms that indicate an emotional response, but one we cannot easily describe; we have no precise terms for such feelings. Even modifiers such as agitated, bitter, frustrated, furious, laconic, melancholic, and piqued only approximate emotional responses to human situations. In reality, each emotion is more complex, more finely shaded, more physical, and *more motional* than the words convey. Dancing our feelings is, in some respects,

more accurate and more profound than language; a dance contains a physical reaction to, or an embodiment of, the emotion.
Dance appeals directly to our emotional/motional center; our
bodies have a sympathetic reaction, responding kinesthetically.
The kinetics trigger feelings, and the feelings trigger associations.

It is this link between our bodies, our emotions, and our
visual perceptions that integrates our experiences and allows us to
be moved profoundly by a landscape. When we see movement
that is vested with feeling and imagery our bodies are stimulated
physically, thereby releasing sympathetic feelings and images.
When we see details in a landscape that were created by the movement of natural forces our bodies anthropomorphize this motion,
thereby releasing human feelings in response to purely physical
phenomena. A windswept point of land, jutting into the ocean,
produces trees, grasses, rocks, and dunes all shaped by the movement of air and water. Even in a dead calm this landscape embodies the storm. Rocks are fluted to permit wind and waves to
slide by with minimal resistance. Soil is piled and rippled, filling
small, protected crevices while reflecting the whirling and fluttering pulses of the water and air. Trees and grasses grow in perpetual curves leaning away from the pushing forces. The shapes
evoke the crashing and sweeping energy that created them. The
struggle is evident. The land and the vegetation tenaciously hold
their ground, willing to adapt to remain. The wind, rain, and
water seem determined to remove them, as if in a dance called
"King of the Mountain." The physical tension is palpable. Just by
looking at these shapes, our muscles, our bones, and our flesh feel
the force of the wind and extrapolate the bodily sensation of re-
sisting it. A twisted tree suggests our own form, coiled by oppos-
ing tensions. We imagine the sensation of our limbs being wound
around the torso and pulled tight, as in a straight jacket, rendering us bound and vulnerable. The crinkled shapes of medieval
martyrs, such as Saint Sebastian, come to mind. The shape itself
projects tangible torture.

There are several techniques for using landscape imagery in dance.
Some train the performer to embrace movement fully, so that patterns of individual movement merge as a unified flow of motion.
Some demand specific images from the dancer in order to create
a particular picture on stage. Some provoke movement qualities
that might be inaccessible without the power of imagery. Some
define concepts of space, shape, or time. Some illuminate basic
physical principles about movement, thereby helping the dancer
to execute particular phrases. In all cases the images are used as a
technique to encourage the dancer to move with more conviction,

All choreography is, basically, the act of creating a landscape by crafting human motion to fill the void of the stage. The result can be described as "landscape as choreography." Here, five members of Seminole Works (Mr. Gamble is standing, far left) perform "Other Moving Parts" at the Painted Bride Arts Center in Philadelphia, Pennsylvania, 1983. Choreography by John Gamble, 1983. Photograph by Deng-Jeng Lee.

thereby making the dance more evocative. The modifier "evocative" is the key. A landscape that serves as a source for a dance is one that evokes.

"On Dry Ice" is a dance work based on an imaginary landscape. The landscape for the dance is almost a void. My image came from a dream, a holocaust nightmare, in which the surface of the earth had been denuded. What remained had been flattened and turned into a single expanse of white, much like a field of snow, but more ominous. In the dream, the entire surface of the earth had become one continuous slab of dry ice. Cold yet hot, shadowless and formless, without a single landmark upon which to fix and orient, in the dance the landscape became a metaphor for both the inner void where truth must be sought and the outer void of a world without direction. The literal image for the dancers was that they were lost on the endless surface of this void and had to find their way. The dancers had to create all forms, all energy, all direction, and all motion. The dancers gave texture, contour, shape, and meaning to the landscape. In a sense, this image was both a theme and a device. All choreography is, basically, the act of creating a landscape by crafting human motion to fill the void of the stage.[2] I merely extended this principle and heightened the drama, first by performing the piece in the round on a surface twice as large as a normal stage and by painting the surface blue-white, and second by calling attention to the void in the thematic progression of the dance.

The task this image precipitated allowed the dancers to be the landscape, to be the forces that shape the landscape, and to be the inhabitants of the landscape. In developing the movement for the piece, images of the wind and the shapes created by its whirling pressure were used to shift the space constantly and to deposit afterimages that would give momentary definition to the void. A solo figure, who represents the seeker, was at times buffeted by the force of the other dancers, and at other times was literally passed and carried from dancer to dancer as a body might bob and be carried by surf. Throughout the dance, specific landscape imagery was used to create both the shapes and the quality of the movement.

Understanding the dramatic quality of space, and shapes in space, is an essential tool of the choreographer. The mere placement of figures in a ground defines relationships, creates tensions, and often implies drama. At one point in "On Dry Ice," a second solo figure, the antagonist if you will, enters and stands at one edge of the space while the seeker performs a repetitive, ritualistic solo. With each new beginning the seeker faces a new direction. The antagonist circles to remain always behind and out of sight, but moves closer and closer with each cycle. Finally he stands directly behind the seeker, stealing her movement and reducing the energy of her performance by his proximity. It is a confrontation produced by the juxtaposition of the two figures in space and by an exchange of energy and motion. The design and the forces are enough to evoke a struggle for power. Words, emotional gestures, and facial expression are unnecessary.

This choreographic principle is inherent in the juxtaposition of elements in a landscape. The essence of a drama is evident in all spatial relationships, be it a struggle or a harmonious symbio-

2. For those readers who may be unfamiliar with dance and choreography, this statement is bold and, I think, original, and it will provoke some discussion among the profession. That is the point. The relationship between landscape and choreography deserves further attention on the part of artists, scholars, and writers. Anna and Lawrence Halprin are, of course, fully aware of the connection; so, too, is Robert Wilson.

Understanding the dramatic quality of space and the shapes within a space is an essential tool of the choreographer. Because the essence of a drama (struggle and harmony) is evident in all spatial relationships, I would think that comprehending and crafting a drama in a landscape is like crafting a dance. In these two photographs by Deng-Jeng Lee, two members of Seminole Works perform "Contact" at the Conwell Dance Theater in Philadelphia, Pennsylvania, 1980. Choreography by John Gamble, 1980.

sis. I would think that understanding and crafting this drama in a landscape is like crafting a dance.

And when I think of actually designing a landscape, a task I fortunately need not undertake, I am terrified. The only way I could, in good conscience, embark on such a project would be to acknowledge the smallness of my role in the process. Even when making dances, which is a more modest undertaking, I realize the role of the choreographer is only one small link in a chain that leads to a final production. But if I did make the attempt and actually designed a landscape, I would try to keep in mind that my role is to shape a little bit of what is there, to stimulate its growth, and to expect my design to be changed by time and the meddling hands of nature and people who, I trust, would respect the design. I would try to enhance the motion of the land and the vegetation, and I would create drama. I would judge the work with my body, feeling the power and emotion in the movement that is implied. If my design evoked a sense of unity and depth, it would be judged a beginning. If, in time, it made me want to dance, I would judge it a success. A landscape in motion.

Charles Montooth

# Landscape as an Extension of Architecture

CHARLES MONTOOTH was born in 1920 in Rushville, Illinois, and grew up there. He received a B.A. in history and music from the University of Chicago, and he studied architecture from 1945 to 1952 at the Frank Lloyd Wright School of Architecture. He was an environmental design consultant on highway design for the Vail Pass section of Interstate 70 in Colorado from 1971 to 1979, for which he won seven ACI and ASI awards for the design of bridges. His long list of credits includes services as a planner for the 825-acre Desert Highlands development in Scottsdale, Arizona, as architect for the Springs Resort at Spring Green, Wisconsin, and as architect for the Prairie School in Racine, Wisconsin. Mr. Montooth is a registered architect in Arizona, Colorado, Illinois, Kentucky, Missouri, New Mexico, Wisconsin, and Wyoming. He is an architect and planner with Taliesin Architects of the Frank Lloyd Wright Foundation in Spring Green, Wisconsin, and Scottsdale, Arizona.

LANDSCAPE nourishes us physically and spiritually. It can inspire us at the same time it provides our sustenance. Our life-support system is based on it, and we are constantly attached to it, albeit sometimes by slender, invisible threads. It is ever present, yet it must be perceived to have meaning. It can be defaced and desecrated, eroded and ruptured, fought over and bought. It can also be shared and enhanced by human design and actions. It is the glory of our universe. It is the primeval (original) architecture.

For me, growing up in a small town in rural west-central Illinois, landscape was integral to my subconscious life. I was aware of it always, and considered it not apart from climate and the changing seasons. It was there to be enjoyed without feeling the need for special reflection or understanding. Landscape was most fascinating in its natural form, especially as I encountered it along the Illinois River or up the narrow valley where the branch line of the Burlington Railroad threaded its way through thickly wooded hills and ravines. But landscape was also the grass and the giant elms in the town square and along the principal streets. Great canopies of shade cooled our lawns and walks and sheltered old houses from the summer sun. Landscape was the stiff, ordered, and neatly trimmed hedges, the flower beds, as well as the gardens of corn, peas, and asparagus. It was the seeming acres of lawn to be mowed with all manner of weeds and thistles to be extricated from it. That was my boyhood landscape.

What first gave definition to the word and caught my fancy was the appearance of a cabin set deep within the woods along the Illinois River. There, suddenly visible from our moving, flat-bottomed riverboat, was a handsome if modest house on stilts, removed from the river by a neatly trimmed lawn leading from the river's bank to the structure. The human element, indicating the touch of someone who must have considered the appearance of the grounds in addition to the cabin's location on the flood plain, added relief and excitement to the natural composition of the riverbank. Somehow it seemed right for the human imprint to be there. I did not perceive this intellectually, but emotionally.

This admiration for human constructions in natural settings later became the dominant theme in my life's work. It attracted me to the American architect, Frank Lloyd Wright, whose words about enhancing a natural site inspired me to pursue a new profession: "Architecture and acreage together are landscape." For me, landscape began to be defined as part of an architecture that is harmonious with its setting. To be sure, landscape, in the broadest sense, included the surface of the earth, but in a more manageable meaning it related to the buildings and cities and towns that housed people and their activities. A practitioner of the art of planning and building could not, after all, manage the vastness of the country, much less that of the whole world, so landscape became integrated and inseparable from building.

As a boy, before I advanced into the organized realm of space and structure, I was much affected by weather and the changing seasons. There were the daily walks to school and the weekend trips up the Illinois River in late summer, when the very anticipation of oncoming autumn kindled fires deep within. Adventure in the backwaters of the Illinois was promised, but it was not the hunting of ducks that excited me. In fact, that prospect meant little. Rather, it was the wisp of wood smoke rising from the river cabin's chimney, the far-off call of cranes, and the experience of remoteness and of being away from the architectural disorder of a small town that appealed to me. By the time serious duck hunting commenced later in the season, the thick foliage had changed to stark black and gray stalks rising to the November sky. This grimness was relieved by the gold of dried grasses and underbrush.

The world of the river was one of extended space: trees bordered by sloughs, flat, satin water as gray as the sky, a lonely landscape mostly undisturbed by people. Wilderness, to a boy. Walking along the backwater shores, poling a boat across the open water, and trudging around remote islands gave a young man time to reflect and to dream and sketch and conjure visions of shelters on the river that could be called *home*. It also meant something special to those rough-and-ready men who launched from it their daily forays into the backwaters. Could it be they were fulfilling some need to replenish their reserves with beauty? Of course they would not admit this, if it were true.

After a day in this cold, awesome, and yet inspiring setting, the cabin with its promise of warmth and hot food beckoned. The cabin was a simple structure built with boards exposed inside and out. No plaster, no fine finish. The honesty and directness of its design appealed to some deep-seated feeling within me, and the experience of shelter in the "wild" setting was exhilarating, but I did not understand why. It was during this time when I first encountered Wright's marvelous wood and brick houses of the late 1930s and early 1940s. In them I found the same direct, honest use of wood, beautifully finished and polished, fitted and joined, that I associated with the cabin. An inner beauty of the wood so much admired in its primitive state was here revealed for human enjoyment and edification.

These houses, called Usonian by their architect, were usually situated in unusual settings, often on sloping ground amid trees or along a seashore. The original profile of the ground was always allowed to come to the very walls of the structure so the building would appear as if growing organically from the land rather than being placed obtrusively on it. In this manner, architecture became one with landscape. The existing terrain was disturbed only enough to permit the placement of the house. It was a temporary disturbance. The adjacent land was then restored to its original contours. This principle was employed almost universally in Wright's work, and it was a device widely appreciated by a public growing increasingly aware of the need to treat the physical environment with respect. Highway engineers and farmers, for example, saw the practical side of such careful treatment of the land. Raw cuts with resultant erosion and damage from landslides could be avoided. (Those of us who worked with Wright absorbed this respect for terrain as one of several principles we applied in our work with him and in our practices.)

Eventually my appreciation for this kind of architecture led me to seek its originator as my teacher. I arrived at his famous Wisconsin establishment in cold, gray November. One of my first tasks as an apprentice at Taliesin was to load coal from a truck into the boiler room below the main house. Inevitably shiny, black chunks of coal were strewn about the ground alongside Taliesin's sand-colored walks. As we green, budding architects made ready to depart the scene, the architect came by for a lesson on landscape: "Clean up the excess coal, boys. Black is not in our scheme of things here." It was an obvious lesson, but one overlooked until pointed out. Appropriateness of parts to a whole (surroundings to a building and a building to a site) was to be a guiding principle for me and for several generations of American architects.

In my own career a unique opportunity presented itself in the early 1970s. At Vail Pass, Colorado, I became part of a team of consultants that designed a fourteen-mile segment of Interstate

On Interstate 70 near Vail Pass, Colorado, no attempt was made to make bridges such as this one appear rustic. Instead, plain surfaces were allowed to convey their purpose in harmony with, not in imitation of, their natural surroundings. Undated photograph by Anthony Puttnam. Courtesy of the Frank Lloyd Wright Foundation.

70 through a particularly scenic and ecologically sensitive portion of the Rocky Mountains. In a multidisciplinary effort involving architects, engineers, geologists, highway specialists, landscape architects, and zoologists, an attempt was made to integrate the roadways into the rugged terrain with a minimum of visual impact. Eastbound and westbound pairs of lanes were separated where space permitted. Each roadway was allowed to seek its own path even to the point of occasionally disappearing from the sight of the other. Cut-and-fill slopes were gentle, seeded with native grasses, and protected with green-colored mats of jute: instant "ground cover" rolled down the slopes.

In cuts through large blocks of rock in narrow canyons, a fragmented, terraced effect was implemented; the vertical faces were left to weather to a natural appearance. Steep slopes were benched to capture pockets of soil in which plants gained footholds, a technique later used on a Bureau of Reclamation dike designed by a colleague at Taliesin, landscape architect Anthony Puttnam. (In an arid landscape he used benching to provide areas for natural revegetation of native desert plants.) For the Interstate 70 project at Vail Pass, retaining-wall structures were used where roadways were confined in narrow valleys. These walls were assembled from mass-produced, precast concrete components, integrally colored to be harmonious with the adjacent terrain. The units were designed to encourage plant growth in the sheltered spaces provided behind the walls, similar to the spaces found along the natural ledges of rock cuts.

Bridges carried the roadways over ravines, through treetops, and along canyon walls. No attempt was made to make the structures appear rustic. Instead, by keeping the component elements simply designed and few in number, plain surfaces were allowed to convey their purpose in harmony with, but not in imitation of, their natural surroundings. Their forms were clean, uncluttered, linear, and expressive of their purpose. They were designed to be seen as continuations of the highway ribbon, and not as distinct and separate entities unto themselves. They were colored to blend with the terrain. We established a general rule to the effect that in order of importance came color, form, and texture. We were able to afford color and form. The result was a pleasing blend of highway and scenery, architecture integrated with landscape.

In our work on the highway we discovered that the broader the roadway (and the more "improved" the facility) the more removed passengers became from the landscape experience. In the vastness of the Rocky Mountain terrain, of course, this was not as important a concern as it might have been elsewhere. Yet, after the highway was completed, I noticed and marveled at how easily and quickly the route was traversed. What once took about thirty minutes to drive and was a rich aesthetic experience of savored views became little more than background music for the motorist.

In restoring some natural areas along a relocated streambed, a conscious effort was made to forgo the human look. A mountain creek was raised, a pond created, and the stream water allowed to cascade over a series of informal rock dams. In the work at Vail Pass, it also seemed best to follow the natural "look" when the time came to plant materials such as grasses and forbs. In less natural, more urban locations, it is often argued that a formal, tailored landscape scheme may be an appropriate design solution. Yet, even in urban situations, such as Central Park in New York City and the Riverside, Illinois, plan of Frederick Law Olmsted, the free-flowing landscape scheme is convincingly more human and natural.[1] Ordered, rigid, and formal patterns of gardens and settings for classical buildings and urban environments may have had some merit in the past, but they are neither relevant for our time nor appropriate for the kind of democratic, indigenous (regional) architecture and landscape architecture the United States deserves and its citizens should demand.

The Riverside plan, for example, arranges individual residential lots well above street level to diminish the noise of automobile traffic. Boundaries are not parallel so the houses can be situated whereby the residents can enjoy more open views than can be obtained by lining up houses side by side. Long vistas from carefully placed side-windows are made possible, and street intersections are carefully laid out to provide an unobstructed flow of urban space. Years later, in his siting of houses, Frank Lloyd Wright avoided the obvious lining up of front and back to street and compass. Orienting houses to sun and view when possible was his preference.

In the case of his own home, he wrapped Taliesin around the brow of a hill in the Wyoming Valley near Spring Green, Wisconsin, and chose to face his living room to the southeast. By developing adjacent and connected outbuildings along a northwesterly direction, he was able to provide a variety of views while taking advantage of the winter sun. Here he illustrated his principle, "of the hill, not on it." The house and gardens became part of the grounds; the rock outcroppings, steps, retaining walls, and walks looked natural as they were integrated with the site. In building after building during his long career, Wright managed to demonstrate not only how landscape and architecture are interlocked, but also how exterior space is the apparent extension of interior space. This integration of human-built structures with the

1. Central Park was codesigned by Olmsted and Calvert Vaux (pronounced Vox), who was Olmsted's partner and associate for many years. Ironically, to achieve the "natural" look in Central Park required significant alteration to the original landscape. This kind of grand reworking of the land to create a certain look has occurred throughout the world, perhaps most ostentatiously at Versailles in France.

A stream bed was raised and it created a pond during construction of Interstate 70 near Vail Pass, Colorado. In restoring the natural areas alongside the pond, a conscious effort was made to forgo the human-made look. Photographer unknown, no date. Courtesy of the Colorado Department of Transportation.

ground on which they stand struck a responsive chord in a goodly number of Americans. It was this proven ability to harmonize structure with terrain that prompted highway engineers to seek Wright-trained professionals who could aid them with their environmental design problems.

An earlier celebrated architect built his home on a site comparable to Taliesin's. At Monticello ("Little Mountain") near Charlottesville, Virginia, Thomas Jefferson built more formally than did Wright, but for practical reasons portions of his home were integrated into the side of the mountain on which the main structure stood so prominently. (Facing south, for example, was the kitchen with its related facilities.) Here the building completes

Taliesin ("Shining Brow"), the home of Frank Lloyd Wright in the Wyoming
Valley south of Spring Green, Wisconsin. Undated photograph by John
Amaranthres. Courtesy of the Frank Lloyd Wright Foundation.

the mountain top (the result of some terracing on Jefferson's part) as Monticello commands expansive views in all directions, including the one he treasured of the University of Virginia, which he founded in 1819. There on his campus a quite different situation is presented by Jefferson. Beautifully scaled pavilions and connecting covered walks flank the sides of a gradually descending expanse of lush green grass. Great trees rise along the way to provide shade. The entire composition is dominated by the dome of the Rotunda. Off to the sides and subtly out of view are charming, intimate gardens sequestered within Jefferson's famous serpentine walls of brick. This design represents an ordered, but human, landscape, appropriately scaled. The formality is not oppressive; rather it is inviting and democratic. It is *landscape:* a quiet setting, architecture in repose in the midst of a measure of modest urban chaos.

The first house I built for our family was situated on two acres of urban desert in Paradise Valley, Arizona, near Phoenix. The soil was rocky and the vegetation was sparse. A small wash ran through the property; there were some creosote, sage, and a lonely saguaro. There were mountains to the west and to the northeast across a broad valley. The site was rather barren, devoid of shade and other planting amenities. After a summer of living in a bare-bones shelter, it was clear that some kind of heat-absorbing ground cover was needed. The lot was too large to cover with a lawn, and a water-consuming, East Coast–looking lawn seemed completely out of character with the climate and grounds. Plants that thrived in the sun were added and small patches of ground adjacent to the banks of glass doors, which formed most of the walls of our house, were seeded with dichondra, a cloverlike herb related to the morning glory family. Small, desertlike trees were inserted in the rocky soil where their modest shade would help to deflect the merciless sun rays. We did indulge in banks of bougainvillaea, which in time sprawled over strategically placed trellises. A well-placed leach field did wonders for the indigenous plants nearby.

The house itself was in the form of a narrow curve with glass facing both the north and south to capture views and winter sunlight, while excluding it in the summer. The budget was small. There were no funds for the kind of extensive walls and architectural features required to wed the building to its site. In time, however, miniature lawns, trellises, and some do-it-myself stone walls were added to produce the proper effect. The neighboring houses and overhead power lines were screened from view.

The entry garden to the Montooth residence in Paradise Valley, Arizona.
Photograph by Minerva Montooth, 1960. Courtesy of the Frank Lloyd
Wright Foundation.

The need for water conservation was made apparent to me
when the water bills were delivered. The wisdom of using desert
plants was confirmed. My own work in the desert made use of
such plants which tended to conserve water themselves. At Taliesin West the lawns were also modest. The original vegetation was
all cactus; as the winter stay in Arizona was extended to late
spring, the cool shade of less sparse vegetation was found desirable.[2] Mostly water-conserving plants were introduced at Taliesin
West. The cactus, creosote, mesquite, palo verde, sage, saguaro,
and staghorn were left untouched beyond the compound walls,
but a softer, less hostile planting was used within. The plantings,
which grew profusely, were pruned periodically to permit the architecture to be revealed and the space to breathe.

2. Mr. Wright and his apprentices
migrated back and forth between
Scottsdale (Taliesin West) and Spring
Green (Taliesin), a tradition still carried on today.

The entrance court and fountain extend outward from the office at Taliesin West in Scottsdale, Arizona. Photographer unknown, no date. Courtesy of *The Arizona Republic.*

3. Nature's music was a constant companion on these walks. Melodies in literal profusion came from bird-life or seemingly from nowhere at all, which provided opportunities for clear thoughts and solutions to troubling personal and design problems. The same was true when I walked the hills of Wisconsin. Such sounds accompanied us on our walks along the jagged, rock-strewn slopes of the MacDowell Mountains at Taliesin West or over the evergreen, rolling, tree-clad hills of Taliesin in Wisconsin. I continue always to draw inspiration in the form of music from the landscape in which I find myself, as I'm sure do countless others. The call of the cranes on the Illinois River can still beckon, and remind me there is more to landscape than merely "seeing."

After a stint with my own modest practice in Scottsdale, I returned to Taliesin West and learned anew what the wonderful space provided by the place meant to me. Here was a complex of interconnected buildings that were so closely related to the desert through broad terraces, screens of glass, and open courts that one had no feeling of confinement. The campus spread out just enough so that walking was required, and walking for enjoyment was also ours for only a modest effort. Trails in the desert were inviting and the walks were inspiring.[3]

From my own experience at Taliesin, I acquired a feeling for concepts such as "landscape as architecture" and "buildings as extensions of landscape." In any design, starting always with a plan superimposed upon a site survey, it became natural to consider a

The centerpiece of the 825-acre Desert Highlands resort in Scottsdale, Arizona, is the golf course. To conserve water and to make use of indigenous plants, the course is set in the natural desert and boulder terrain, with areas of grass kept to a minimum. Undated photograph by Anthony Puttnam. Courtesy of the Frank Lloyd Wright Foundation.

Landscape as an extension of architecture at La Paloma, a resort and retirement community in Tucson, Arizona. Photograph by George F. Thompson, 1987.

building and its surroundings as one. Building walls extended outward from an enclosed space to wrap around shrubs, trees, or, in some cases, rock outcroppings. Walls merged into the ground. It was important to balance building masses with each other and with natural forms, but achieving "perfect symmetry" was left only for the arrangement of minor spaces. This approach to design had the effect of making the resulting architecture less formal, more relaxed, and more in harmony with nature. Plans of the buildings called for landscaping, and presentation drawings always indicated trees, terraces, shrubs, pools, flowers, and other amenities that integrated an enclosed space with the outdoors.

I have been fortunate to have worked out this idea on many rewarding projects. Near Taliesin West, for example, in a completely different type of desert, I helped to plan a large, 825-acre residential development. The site was a unique desert garden, a fragile environment filled with granite boulders and yucca, saguaro, and palo verde atop fine granite sand. The centerpiece of the development was, not surprisingly, a golf course, but one planned to make use of indigenous plants and the natural terrain. This design resulted in a course that requires about seventy percent of the water needed to maintain a facility of the same size elsewhere. The building sites were confined to specific areas divided into lots, waterways were respected, native plants were protected, and only a limited number of exotic (nonindigenous) plantings were permitted and those only in restricted and wall-enclosed patios on the lots. In the more sensitive areas, dwelling units were clustered, outcroppings were left in open spaces, and parking was kept to a minimum or placed underground. Road-widths were kept narrow with boulders, and native plants were left in the shoulders where possible. Building heights were limited and building envelopes were arranged to provide unobstructed views from each lot. Building on slopes of fifteen percent or more was generally discouraged or disallowed.

Landscapes natural, native, existing, and landscapes human-made. Landscapes are to be cherished, preserved, conserved, enhanced, and enjoyed. They are essential components of life, but too often we treat the land as a commodity to be used, abused, exploited, and consumed. We should always see ourselves as stewards of the land, and understand that as caretakers we are free to take from it what we may need as long as we give something back in return.

Landscape *is* one with the environment. If this recognition and concern prevail, then the design, management, and planning of landscapes will continue to serve us and all of the earth's plants and creatures well.

Gregory Conniff

# Landscape Is a
# Point of View

GREGORY CONNIFF was born in 1944 in Jersey City, New Jersey, and grew up in Montclair, New Jersey. He received a B.A. in political science from Columbia College, Columbia University, and completed an LL.B. at the University of Virginia School of Law. He practiced law until 1978 when he devoted his life full-time to photography and writing. He has been awarded National Endowment for the Arts Fellowships in 1981 and 1993 as well as a John Simon Guggenheim Memorial Foundation Fellowship in 1989 for his work with the American landscape. His photographs have been exhibited widely and are part of numerous collections, including the Museum of Modern Art in New York City, the Corcoran Gallery of Art in Washington, D.C., the Museum of Fine Arts in Boston, the Baltimore Museum of Art, the Center for Creative Photography in Tucson, the High Museum of Art in Atlanta, and the Joseph L. Seagram Collection in New York City. His book *Common Ground* (Yale, 1985) serves as the first of a projected four volumes of photography to be published under the title *An American Field Guide*. Mr. Conniff is a consulting editor to the *Creating the North American Landscape* series (Johns Hopkins University Press), and he resides and works in Madison, Wisconsin.

LANDSCAPE is one source of our humanness. Despite television, culture still has its deepest roots in geography; place is still a shaper of the soul. The visual character of the places where we spend our lives gives us the patterns by which we see.

Landscape is a way of investigating and interpreting these sources of ourselves. Inevitably, though, the paths we choose to approach it—words, pictures, music, dance, gardens, sports—lead us only to points of view which are full of vision, but short of whole sight.

Landscape is about something outside of us without which we would be lost in space.

Sometimes when I juxtapose points of view about landscape and place in which there is deep feeling for the world, the *fact* of creation bursts through the *forms* laid upon it. When that sudden thing happens I can feel the mystery that inhabits much of what I think I know.

Recognizing this mystery makes me feel less easily at home in familiar surroundings, but the new light breaking through from another's viewpoint gives me both the comfort of not being alone and an odd delight in wondering how I got to wherever I am.

For some of us, the big question is, "Why are we here?" I have never gotten past thinking about what "here" is.

**Photographs by Gregory Conniff**

*We had constructed a perfect place. And it was art,*
*it was a vision embodied, and sacred, so it seemed, for a while.*

—WILLIAM KITTREDGE

Oneonta, New York, 1982

*The landscape comes at us from every direction.*
*It comes at us in every way.*

—DENIS WOOD

Youngstown, Ohio: an abandoned steel mill in moonlight, 1989

Iowa County, Wisconsin, 1990

*Trees exist outside of argument.*

—KENNETH LASH

Lafayette County, Mississippi, 1992

Lafayette County, Mississippi: along the banks of the Tallahatchie River, 1992

*We had reinvented our landscape according to the most
persuasive ideal given to us by our culture, and it had gone alien on us.*

—WILLIAM KITTREDGE

Youngstown, Ohio, 1982

Youngstown, Ohio, 1982

*For, while all landscapes are real, some landscapes are imagined.*
*If necessity demands them, they'll be found.*

—THOMAS RABBITT

San Francisco, California, 1978

Yosemite National Park, California, 1981

*Let me add one thing: About nature in the rawest,*
*about living in that landscape, I know nothing.*
*Nothing at all. Few of us even dream about it anymore.*

—KENNETH LASH

Oneonta, New York, 1987

**George F. Thompson**

# Acknowledgments

*I bowed again, deeply, toward the north,*
*and turned south to retrace my steps*
*over the dark cobbles to the home*
*where I was staying. I was full*
*of appreciation for what I had seen.*

—BARRY LOPEZ

A BOOK as difficult to create and direct as *Landscape in America* involves a complete cast of supporting characters on stage and off. I wish to acknowledge the help of all those who participated in the making of this book, directly and indirectly, and to make clear that any errors contained within the book are unintended.

Every project has its heroes and heroines, and so it is an honor to recognize their noteworthy contributions:

Tom Hunt, the brilliant ecologist-turned-geographer, was with me when the idea and plan for the book came to me. We were working a long day on his ambitious mine reclamation project for a taconite tailings basin at the Jackson County Iron Company mine site near Black River Falls, Wisconsin (now shut down). The day was full of intense heat and sweat and (we didn't know it at the time) dioxin. With a few hours of light left in the day—and those who know that country understand what good light that can be—we decided to reward ourselves by taking the long way home to Madison via a series of dirt roads through state forests. We sighted a handsome porcupine climbing a tree and many blue herons along the way—and they are inspirations—but it was a combination of Tom's tough questions and the jarring bumps on those state forest roads that provided the initial stimulus for this book. Tom and Nancy, his wife, have continued to support the project in every way imaginable, for which they have my heartfelt thanks.

At a time when the project was still in the formative stages and could have developed in a number of directions, I received a request from Carol Miles, who was working in France as Robert Wilson's assistant on his magnum opus, *The CIVIL warS: a tree is best measured when it is down,* and she was also creating her own main-stage productions, *40 Landscapes* and *21 Landscapes.* Because this body of work—hers and Mr. Wilson's—involved the interpretation of landscape and developed relationships between people and the land, she was searching for a book that would

provide an adequate introduction to a full range of ideas about
the *experience* of landscape, a basis for new knowledge, and a confidence that her own interests in landscape study and her own
background in theater arts and humanities were enough to build
upon. This correspondence reinforced my belief that the essays in
*Landscape in America* should not replicate other collections (both
literary and geographical), but should deal with the *idea* of landscape and the role that personal experience plays in understanding
*landscape* and *place*. This would be a book for the student and the
common reader, and this message was clearly conveyed to the
contributors when they were invited to write an original and previously unpublished essay for this volume.

For counsel during the initial stages of the project's devel-
opment thanks go to Thompson Webb (Director Emeritus, Uni-
versity of Wisconsin Press), Anders Richter (then Editorial
Director, Johns Hopkins University Press), Malcolm MacDonald
(Director, University of Alabama Press), and the following writ-
ers, artists, and scholars: Ansel Adams, Maurice G. Brooks,
Robert Dash, Richard Ford, Anita Harris, Jamake Highwater,
John O. Holzhueter, Sheldon Judson, Annette Kolodny, Arthur
Krim, Peirce Lewis, Norman Maclean (whose letters provided en-
couragement till the very end), Leo Marx, John McPhee, Wright
Morris, Darrel G. Morrison, Chris Ranier, and Robert Wilson.
Bruce Angell, Margot Backas, Joyce Berry, Nancy Essig, J. G.
Goellner, Eric F. Halpern, Ripley Hugo, Peter Kettler, John
McGuigan, Judith Metro, Steve Miller, David R. Moyer, Dee
Mullen, Bob Roberts, William Sisler, Christine R. Szuter, Ruth
Thompson, Bob Trammell, and Paul Zimmer were also consulted
during the making of the book, and they have my thanks for im-
proving the quality of the work in their own unique ways.

Henry Y. K. Tom suggested the initial organization for the
book, and his ideas became the foundation on which the final
sequence of essays is based. I am very grateful to Henry for such
a significant contribution. Support has also come in special doses
from Frank Gohlke and Lucy Flint-Gohlke, Richard and Linda
Holman, Stuart Klipper, Eric and Laurie Paddock, David Schuyler, Frederick R. Steiner, Martha A. Strawn, Kate Trammell, Yi-
Fu Tuan, Charles Walters, and especially Ellen and Jack Cleveland
and my family. Purna Makaram prepared the manuscript and provided a sense of purpose when vision needed renewal. And many
thanks to those who read and improved earlier versions of the
manuscript: Arnold R. Alanen, John Harrington, Evelyn Howell,
and William H. Tishler at the University of Wisconsin-Madison;
James S. Duncan at Syracuse University; Robert Mugerauer at

the University of Texas; Carol P. Mishler at the Center for American Places; and other reviewers who wish to remain anonymous.

My earliest recollection for wanting to learn more about *landscape* is of an experience my brother and I had one summer when we were boys. The family was loaded down in a maroon 1963 Chevrolet Impala, headed from our home in Connecticut for Tennessee and Alabama to visit my mother's family. Interstate 81 had recently opened in Virginia—replacing U.S. 11 as the main highway and creating a literal slice through the Shenandoah Valley that behaved to us much like a ride in an amusement park—and David and I spent hours in the car's back seat interpreting with pad and pen the farm landscapes and crop rotation arrangements we could see plainly. We were enamored with the land, more with how it worked than with the scenery, though admittedly it is hard to separate the two. We were old enough to comprehend color and shadow and scale and a beauty in the land's organization; its purpose and design were transformed with great concentration to drawings on paper, which we proudly presented to our parents in the front seat.

That experience is likely the book's first memory, so it is an ironic coincidence that I acknowledge the environs where the book eventually took root and shape. In 1983 my wife and I moved from Madison, Wisconsin, to the Shenandoah Valley of Virginia, and for five years we were fortunate to have lived in the old (pre-1800) Shenandoah Schoolhouse on Rolling Hills Farm, a few miles southeast of Berryville, Virginia, the quintessential small town. The desk where most of the book's essays were edited overlooked the beautiful Shenandoah River and Blue Ridge Mountains. That view and that home environment brought much peace and calm to an otherwise brutal commuters' schedule, and there is no doubt that *that* landscape is in this book. In that place we were able to live on the fringe of wild nature yet in a cultivated landscape, where literally the songs of owls would put us to sleep each night. Words cannot express how appreciative we are to Emily T. James and Arch Manuel for making their home available to us. We shall never forget them or Rolling Hills Farm.

Gregory Conniff's intellect, photography, insights on landscape and place, and friendship have been instrumental in pulling this book together and in making possible other ventures of the mind and spirit. Arnold R. Alanen's support has been unwavering. Cotton Mather, one of our greatest geographers, has taught thousands of students and citizens worldwide much about landscape, art, people, and life, all of which, I hope, is reflected in this book. Were the United States Japan, Cotton Mather would be a national treasure. And Charles E. Little, one of our finest writers and conservationists, has taught me much about landscape in America and about creating books for the common reader. It is fitting indeed that Charles has written the foreword to this book.

There would be no book, of course, without the contributors. At the time I approached them about writing an essay for this book, I knew only a few of them personally. I was simply a young turk with a book idea. They provided the work asked for, were willing (within reason) to adapt their essays to the needs of the overall work (which is crucial for an edited collection of original essays), and were examples of goodwill in seeing the process through to its happy conclusion without any guarantee of an honorarium or even book publication. To have done so during the greedy 1980s is simply remarkable. The contributors deserve full credit for whatever success and shelf life *Landscape in America* achieves.

There would be no book either had not the University of Texas Press shared the same vision for its publication that I have had since that first day in Wisconsin. Three cheers to all the good people in Austin who have devoted so much skill and enthusiasm to this project.

Finally, there would be nothing without Cynthia, my companion and wife. If ever an edited collection deserved a dedication, then it would be *for Cynthia,* because, as Richard Hugo once wrote, "love is not second best, but all . . ."

*Vaya con dios.*

# Index